the sweet smell of SUCCESS

LIFESUCCESS PUBLISHING, LLC
8900 E Pinnacle Peak Road, Suite D240
Scottsdale, AZ 85255
Telephone: 800.473.7134
Fax: 480.661.1014
E-mail: admin@lifesuccesspublishing.com

ISBN: 978-1-59930-088-7 (hardcover)
          978-1-59930-282-9 (e-book)

Cover : Fiona Dempsey & LifeSuccess Publishing
Layout: Fiona Dempsey & LifeSuccess Publishing

COMPANIES, ORGANIZATIONS,
INSTITUTIONS, AND INDUSTRY PUBLICATIONS:
*Quantity discounts are available on bulk purchases of this book for reselling, educational
purposes, subscription incentives, gifts,*
sponsorship, or fundraising. Special books or book excerpts can also
be created to fit specific needs such as private labeling with your logo
on the cover and a message from a VIP printed inside.
FOR MORE INFORMATION PLEASE CONTACT OUR
SPECIAL SALES DEPARTMENT AT
LIFESUCCESS PUBLISHING.

PRINTED IN CANADA

the sweet smell *of* SUCCESS

HEALTH & WEALTH SECRETS

JAMES "TAD" GEIGER M.D.

BOARD-CERTIFIED ANESTHESIOLOGIST
MASTER'S DEGREE IN BIOLOGY
CLINICALLY CERTIFIED AROMATHERAPIST
CERTIFIED MASSAGE THERAPIST

Dedication

JAMES PETENBRINK GEIGER, MD, FACS
COLONEL, MC, USA, (RET.)

MY FATHER IS A retired army colonel and a retired cardiothoracic surgeon, commonly known as a heart and chest surgeon. He dedicated his life to his patients, his career, and his family. He is not just my hero but also a lifesaving hero of many soldiers and his patients. His life has been a great inspiration for me. He taught me the meaning of the words duty, honor, and country and fostered my love for the art and the science of medicine. He is a great man who has spent his life in service to others. He paid for me to go to college, graduate school, and medical school. I paid him back in dollars, but I will never really be able to repay him for his sacrifice. He taught me so much in this life and set such a great example for me. Although Dad worked very hard all his life, he got little exercise until he retired. In his latter years he played golf twice a week with his best buddy, Dr. Charles Lithgow. Now in his eighties, Dad continues to be a shining example of meaningful aging as someone who has great strength to continue living his dream. Heroes leverage what they have to make a difference.

Dad had his aortic valve replaced and five coronary vessels revascularized in 2006. The first major complication occurred on the day of surgery, when the surgical team could not wean him from the heart-lung bypass machine. I had sat holding my mother's hand throughout the day, but I knew something was terribly wrong when they had not finished in the regular three-to-five-hour time range. The wait stretched to eight hours. The surgeons were having extreme difficulty. Finally, they weaned him from the heart-lung machine, transitioning to maximum intravenous and balloon-pump therapies. Although they gave him a whole range of blood and blood products when he reached ICU, he continued to bleed severely. I watched his vital sign numbers deteriorate. I watched his chest tubes fill the Pleurovac containers with his blood while his team transfused blood that night. I wanted to join in to help them. He was fighting for his life. We were praying and believing.

The staff obtained a new medication, NovoSeven (recombinant human coagulation factor VIIa), which makes blood coagulate, valued at about $10,000 a dose. Sent for my father from the San Francisco VA Hospital, it saved his life that night. He was in a coma for the next three weeks, thrashing around even though restrained to his bed. He was unable to recognize family or friends. The neurologist told us he had had brain damage and a stroke. Dad was in severe heart failure as well. He was on multiple infusions of drugs and developed diabetes, along with numerous types of infections that required atomic-strength antibiotics. Renal failure developed, requiring daily dialysis for weeks.

Finally, at the very end of one of my visits, I saw the first hint of recovery. Dad responded to the nurse telling him to put his leg back on the bed. I was shocked. Later in the week he began to recognize faces and respond more to commands. Unfortunately, he could not be separated from the mechanical ventilator, so he underwent a tracheotomy and eventual weaning of supportive respiratory care. At that point he was able to begin the long process of a series of transfers to specialized neurological and physical rehabilitation centers.

Dad is looking much better these days. He is alert and active, realizing his dream of living at home with his wife, Helen. During all phases of his recovery, I would visit frequently with members of my family—going to hospitals and a series of rehabilitation facilities, and doing aromatherapy massages for him.

I had performed aromatherapy and massage treatments even when he was comatose to heal his bruised skin, help fight infection, and boost his immune system with touch therapy. Touch, and touch with essential oil massage, raises the count of key immune cells that enhance the immune function.

I would do aromatherapy with him for a week here and there, always having to learn the protocol at each new facility in order to receive consent from the staff to use the essential oils. After my visits, I received reports of how much better he looked and felt. Once, I arrived for a visit and found he had had hiccups for a month. Nothing had worked to stop the hiccups. The side effects of the medications given to treat the hiccups had been miserable, so he was just enduring the hiccups. I gave him one aromatherapy treatment, and the hiccups immediately stopped. He did not see the association until it happened again weeks later, and I gave him another treatment. Again, the hiccups immediately went away. It was then he decided that I needed to tell his story about how essential oils had helped him so much.

Another complication set in about the seventh month after surgery —a type of paralysis of the muscles of his lower extremities. This neurological complication of diabetes temporarily paralyzed his legs so he could not walk. It took another three months for the paralysis to reverse and for him to regain his ability to walk. Recently, my father has undergone two more successful surgeries, including an experimental intracardiac periprosthetic aortic valvular stent procedure performed by the dedicated caregivers of the San Francisco VA.

So it is with great honor that I dedicate this book to my father, my hero, Colonel James P. Geiger, MD, USMC (Ret.), as well as to all of the active duty and retired men and women, and their families, who serve in the armed forces of the United States, intervening for freedom. For two decades, I have heard stories of soldiering and provided anesthesia to the members of the greatest generation who have fought in world conflicts. All over the globe they have served in so many different ways, functioning as one body, with the goal to protect and preserve our freedom.

Table of Contents

Foreword

You know, in my 40 years of business, working with countless people, I can tell you Dr. James "Tad" Geiger is, without question, one of the best I have ever worked with as a doctor, a businessman, and as a human being.

After years of firsthand experience as a medical doctor and anesthesiologist, consulting with his own family, friends and patients, Tad has discovered how to answer their many questions with his amazing book, The Sweet Smell of Success: Health and Wealth Secrets. It reveals a very relevant message for everyone, including baby boomers, gurus, mentors, doctors, fitness-conscious individuals, and especially those seeking to regain lost health.

People are ready to experience the exciting discoveries of the 21st Century wellness specialties such as aromatherapy and therapies with medicinal foods like juices. Henry Ford is roughly quoted as saying that he did not have to know everything, just where to find the knowledge he needed. This book is a gold mine and treasure trove of specialized knowledge, a gift from the good doctor to you and I.

People deserve to have these health secrets revealed and the book's message is delivered in straightforward language that is medically referenced, so that laypeople, like you and I, can readily grasp the concepts along with people who work in the medical world.

Anyone who has ever been sick or hospitalized knows how tenuous and precious his or her health can be. Consider the complex events of nausea following a surgical procedure, or the annoying seasickness that commonly ruins a dream cruise vacation. The Sweet Smell of Success reveals how to promote wellness through natural remedies, treating problems like these with essential oil of ginger.

Tad offers a ton of new insights, valuable common-sense logic and imparts in the reader, a sense of well-being. Anyone who wants to lose weight, improve their love life or just feel good overall, will never want to put this book back on the shelf until they have learned the simple, yet fascinating, keys to natural health therapies.

Doctors may not make house calls anymore but if you want a good doctor's advice at your fingertips when you need it, then this book is a keeper and it belongs in your home.

I am really proud to call Tad my friend and business associate. If you ever have an opportunity to work with him, I would recommend you go for it!

Bob Proctor
Featured in the movie *The Secret*
Author of *You Were Born Rich*
and *It's Not About the Money*

Acknowledgements

I'd like to thank my father, who believes in education and mentored me to become a doctor, and my beloved mother, Helen, who cherishes her husband and her children. Thank you to my virtuous wife, Cheryle, for her awareness, knowledge, wisdom, and loving support. My son Kirk patiently taught me how to upload web content, and my son Jason created the designs for oilMD. My daughter, Erin, let me use her laptop when mine was broken, even though she really wanted to play The Sims. I'd also like to thank Bob Proctor for bringing awareness to the table so I could take it away with me, and my patients, who entrust their lives to me as I put them to sleep and awaken them.

Preface

*A wise man should consider that health is the greatest of human blessings,
and learn how by his own thought to derive benefit from his illnesses.*

—Hippocrates (460–377 BCE)

BOOKS ON WELLNESS AND AROMATHERAPY have been written from many points of view. *The Sweet Smell of Success* takes a very unique approach to both of these topics. As an acute care anesthesiologist, I believe clinical aromatherapy should be integrated with conventional allopathic Western called medicine in the Wellness Revolution of the twenty-first century. Aromatherapy with essential oils is one entity of the vast array of holistic specialties comprising nutritional medicine and complementary alternative medicine. Consider food and essential oils as nutritional medicine. These natural wonders have great potential to enhance and humanize health care when combined with the practice of conventional medicine. Although aromatherapy is not appreciated by many physicians and is often misrepresented to the public, there are tremendous advantages to be gained from its diverse applications. Scientific studies have shown aromatherapy to be effective for a wide variety of common ailments and medical conditions. This information will be presented in *The Sweet Smell of Success*, along with exciting new discoveries, products, techniques, and keys that serve to promote wellness through nature. This "wellness textbook" is an educational and inspirational tool for everyone, including network marketing distributors. I will reveal an abundance of "secret" information pertaining to your health and wealth that will revolutionize your life.

HOW TO USE THIS BOOK

THIS BOOK IS ABOUT wellness and well-being and is meant to serve different groups of people in specialized ways. There is a widening health care information gap between health consumers and care providers. The material presented here bridges the gap between laypeople as health care consumers and medically oriented health care providers, with detailed natural healing information based on medical and scientific knowledge.

First, it is my impression from working with my patients and their families that many people have an interest in using "natural" ways of healing but have doctors who are uninformed, disinterested, or not accepting of alternative medicine. This text contains current and compelling scientific explanations and references. Patients can give this "textbook" to their doctor to provide another medical doctor's viewpoint, a "second opinion," as well as to offer alternatives for nutrition and traditional medical treatment. Second, it is as an educational and motivational tool for various groups of professionals and nonprofessionals in health care and business. Third, since several of the chapters are somewhat technical from a medical and biochemical standpoint, I suggest a layperson use Wikipedia for explanation and clarification of scientific terms and topics, should they care to be a student of this material. Further explanations using streaming video are available on the web at the oilMD wellness network.

THE PREMISE

NATURAL, NUTRITIONAL FOODS, ESSENTIAL oils, and berry fruit juices are key dietary elements that play a significant role in the quest for true physical, emotional, and spiritual wellness. The "healthy energy" found in these superior functional foods is astounding. Incorporating these powerful building block foods into your life will help meet your basic nutritional needs more than abundantly, and when these foods are coordinated with a balanced lifestyle of mentally and physically stimulating exercises, you will attract all the good health that you deserve. This process represents a tremendous shift in thought and action for most people. However, creating better health by supplementation with natural and nutritional functional food products is a worthy goal. As your life improves, you can help others by increasing their awareness of the health and wealth secrets found in the functional food products of the Wellness Revolution.

Awareness and concern for the health of the people of our country and all the nations of the world are increasingly shared by growing numbers of medical and health care workers, professionals, celebrities, and even politicians. The maldistribution of food worldwide perpetuates starvation and obesity epidemics, affecting more adults and children with each passing day. Overweight children today are much more likely to become morbidly obese adults. It is possible that in the future, some obese children will die before their own parents. A generation of premature deaths, whether from obesity or starvation, is a sad and unacceptable result. The obesity and starvation dilemmas of our time will grow to crisis proportions sooner rather than later unless there is intervention. Awareness of these problems is the critical first step to circumvent the predictable progression of illness, disability, and death due to these malnourished states.

Another major concern for our society is aging. Aging increases the need for essential nutritional elements that function as antioxidants, which the body uses as critical building blocks for the formation of free radical scavengers and the energy required for effective metabolism. Over time, our bodies can become progressively deficient in vital ingredients due to poor eating habits unless supplemented with vitamins and minerals. Although many foods are plentiful and cheap, that does not make them healthy. Many people have been seduced into eating the fast and processed foods of our culture. Read, learn, and make a conscious choice to eat food that is naturally good for you.

THE PITCH

DIETARY SUPPLEMENTATION WITH SUPERIOR functional foods, like nature's essential oils and berry fruit juices, will improve your life, and soon you will wonder how you functioned without them. Essential oils are classified as foods by the FDA. The essential oils and juices from plants have amazing properties, such as the reduction of minor aches or major inflammatory pains due to arthritis, and the science to substantiate their benefits. The basic data to prove numerous clinical principles is readily available, and references are included in this book to encourage the further networking of important and substantial research.

Every day entrepreneurs invite you to consume innovative new products of the Wellness Revolution. Companies manufacture life-enhancing products that taste great and are of superior value and quality. Several suggestions for products and business development are included in this book to increase your health and wealth prospects. These new products are convenient and powerful; they can significantly improve your quality of life as well as increase life expectancy.

Medicine is becoming increasingly miniaturized, digitized, and computerized. Gene therapy, microendoscopic robotics, and robotic surgery are vastly different from aromatherapy, and yet they can be combined to enhance the overall benefits of practically any therapy, traditional or modern. Conditions caused by continued poor diet and overall failing of general health increase the urgency to integrate nutritional medicine and complementary alternative medicine (CAM) into acute and chronic care hospitals, as well as the numerous varieties of clinical, therapeutic spa settings and home kitchens.

And God said, 'Behold, I have given you every herb bearing seed, which is upon the face of all the earth, and every tree, in which is the fruit of a tree yielding seed; to you it shall be for meat. And to every beast of the earth, and to every fowl of the air, and to every thing that creepeth upon the earth, wherein there is life, I have given every green herb for meat': and it was so. And God saw every thing that he had made, and, behold, it was very good. And the evening and the morning were the sixth day. (Gen. 1:29–31 KJV)

GOD KNOWS WHAT IS good and ideal. God created the plants, including their fruits, juices, and the essential oils they yield. Concentrated health-oriented natural products of the Wellness Revolution, such as essential oils, wild-crafted and organic foods, and the natural juices from fruits and berries, have been put on earth for us by God, who expects us to use them for our benefit and to promote worldwide wellness. It is time to apply all the good nutritional foods that are available to give us the good health God intends us to have.

—**James "Tad" Geiger, MD**
The oilMD
Promoting Wellness through Nature
www.oilmdwellnessnetwork.com

Introduction

Helping other people make smart economic choices, create a business that they can operate from home, spend more time with their families, and build a stream of income at the same time—and helping so many different people do this—offers its own rewards, far above and beyond the monetary rewards.

—**Paul Zane Pilzer, author of** *The New Wellness Revolution*

TO VARYING DEGREES THE entire world is experiencing a revolution in the fields of wellness and well-being. The increasing awareness of the great need of our time to achieve and maintain one's own state of health and longevity is a driving force behind the Wellness Revolution. Fortunes are being made in the food and medicine industries as well as network marketing businesses, through the distribution of wellness products, wellness knowledge, and wellness services. *The Sweet Smell of Success* reveals health and wealth secrets as seen through the eyes of a physician, offering insight and avenues by which individuals can make well-informed decisions as to how they can best tap into the money to be made through participation in this revolution of wellness, while at the same time attaining health and longevity.

The organized use of specialized knowledge is the fourth step toward riches in the book Think and Grow Rich by Napoleon Hill. Henry Ford once said that he did not need to know everything, just where he could get the information he needed when he needed it. Today, knowledge is important, but the distribution of intellectual services and information marketing really predominates when it comes to selling products. Distributors who sell products directly to client consumers must educate the clients about their products and services. Marketing information is a highlight of business. *The Sweet Smell of Success* is an informational network marketing training tool.

THERE ARE OVER 150 million Internet users in the United States alone, all potential online shoppers. One advantage for direct sales distributors in terms of physical and intellectual products over traditional retail is the ability to adapt rapidly with new wellness products. Meanwhile, both large chain stores and small niche retail businesses operate on the Internet as retailers with more and more effective shopping carts. Highly specialized corporations like Coremetrics provide extensive and effective data management to maximize profit for online goods and services to Internet-based retailers.

According to Mark Brohan of the magazine Internet Retailer, the top "Internet-only" merchants had combined sales figures of over $25 billion in 2005. He has analyzed the data of the progressively increasing online sales figures year after year for more than a decade. Sales grew to more than $136 billion in 2006. That is tremendous growth over the previous year and was propelled primarily by smaller niche retailers. It is imperative to acquire knowledge of clients' needs in order to provide superior service as well as sell intellectual products. This client-knowledge database is a major determinant of the growth rate for online retailers and direct distributors alike. The sales of primary and third-party network marketing informational tools add value for more sales potential to distributorships and their clients. Direct selling distributors can develop multiple sources of income (MSIs) through relationships established with their clients and the clients of their clients.

DISTRIBUTE WELLNESS

THE GROWING MULTITUDE OF wellness specialists fulfilling the needs of the Wellness Revolution, such as personal trainers, instructors, coaches, and mentors working in spas, health clubs, resorts, and other businesses associated with the complementary fields of alternative health care, will benefit by building network businesses. Health and fitness-oriented natural products made from certified organic/wild-crafted functional foods such as essential oils, juices from fruits and berries, fortified meal replacement diet shakes, healthy energy drinks, food bars, skin care products, and the associated services are a significant portion of the market of this new revolution in wellness.

CHAPTER *one*

The Art of Aromatherapy

"This book is not about a fad or a trend—it's about a new and infinite need infusing itself into the way we eat, exercise, sleep, work, save, age, and almost every other aspect of our lives."

—Paul Zane Pilzer

CHAPTER

THE ART OF AROMATHERAPY

HAVE YOU EVER TAKEN a moment to reflect on what the sweet smell of success means to you? How many times have you associated a particular scent with a happy memory or an invigorating experience? While some scents can take you back to a time recalling youthful events, others can actually restore and heal your body, mind, and spirit.

There is duality in life. The art of aromatherapy is a combination of yin and yang. The yin of the art of aromatherapy is feminine, natural, intuitive, gracious, and entreating. The yang aspect is very medical, scientific, and data-oriented. The totality of the care and the cure gained from this experience in wellness is referred to as the art of aromatherapy.

The art of aromatherapy is a holistic treatment using the essence of a plant's essential oils to alleviate common symptoms such as pain, tension, and fatigue, as well as to care for the skin and invigorate the whole body. Oils can be added to a bath, massaged directly into the skin, diffused to scent a room, or directly inhaled. Aromatherapy with essential oils is fashionable and profitable.

Essential oils stimulate your sense of smell wonderfully and powerfully. An odor can have a tremendous impact on feelings. Certain scents evoke a deep sense of inner peace and well-being. Modern researchers believe that smells enter through the membranes lining the nose, along fingerlike projections. The aromatic vapors of scents are absorbed into the bloodstream, lymphatic system, and along nervous pathways to sections of the brain that control moods, memories, and emotions. Essential oils can affect your mood positively, decreasing stress and promoting a wonderful state of relaxation and enhanced awareness. Oils can be utilized during educational testing to activate recall and stimulate memory.

HISTORICAL AROMATHERAPY

THE ANCIENT MEDICAL HISTORY of essential oils was confirmed when Egyptian medicinal scrolls dating back to 1500 BCE were uncovered in the tombs of Egyptian royalty. In 1817, an archaeologist discovered one of the most vital, the Ebers Papyrus medical scroll, tucked between the legs of a mummy in the Egyptian city of Thebes. This 870-foot long scroll describes over eight hundred remedies for diseases, including remedies using many essential oils that have powerful medicinal properties.

Of course, the Egyptians didn't have controlled scientific conditions to test essential oils like we have today. Rather, they uncovered and passed along their secrets and traditions of their healing power learned through trial and error. The Ebers Papyrus medical scroll reveals that Egyptian healers had a remarkably high success rate, treating as many as eighty-one diseases using oils of frankincense, cinnamon, myrrh, rosemary, galbanum, hyssop, cassia, and spikenard often mixed with honey.

Bezaleel, a wise-hearted man of Old Testament times, had the biblically ordained job of "the perfumer" working the "art of the apothecary" in the sanctuary. Based on instructions given by Moses and written in the book of Exodus, Bezaleel formulated the special blend of oils for the holy anointing oil used by the Levites. Biblically, the art of the apothecary had physical and spiritual implications, using plants to create holy anointing oils, healing ointments, and perfumes for their effectual "aromas." In the New Testament, descriptive phrases define the spiritual aspects of the sweet smell of success as a savor, aroma, and fragrance of life.

And walk in love, as Christ also hath loved us, and hath given himself
*for us an offering and a sacrifice to God for a **sweet smelling savour.***
Eph 5:2 KJV

For we are to God the aroma of Christ among those who
are being saved and those who are perishing. To the one we are
*the smell of death; to the other, **the fragrance of life.***
2 Cor 2:15–16 NIV

FOR THOUSANDS OF YEARS, metaphysical healers in cultures around the world have relied on these essential oils to alleviate innumerable ailments and acute and chronic pain, to heal infection, and to improve digestion. All of these same essential oils and many more are just as powerful today, if not more so due to specialized knowledge and extraction techniques. Despite a rich history of medicinal use that is older than any other alternative therapy—even herbs—compiled resources of scientific information on essential oils have been somewhat limited in availability until now. It is also somewhat difficult to locate a specialist in the use of essential oils: a Certified Clinical Aromatherapy Practitioner (CCAP). The fact that there are so few CCAPs inspired me to share the art and science "how-to's" of selecting and using therapeutic quality essential oils to relieve symptoms of common complaints such as arthritis and insomnia.

As the essence and soul of plants, essential oils of medicinal plants have been shown in dozens of small clinical studies to contain concentrated healing power that is natural and safe. The oils are extracted from various parts of trees, grasses, herbs, and spices using the flower, bark, fruit, seed, and leaf. Modern extraction and distillation processes yield essential oils of higher potency than the oils used centuries ago. These modern essential oils are referred to as "therapeutic-grade oils."

Essential oils have also found their way into our marketplace. Take a trip down your favorite department store aisle or surf the Internet. You'll see a wide variety of aromatherapy products in every shape and color ranging from push-button electric plug diffusers and dish soaps to the latest trend of oil-filled glass vase diffusers. The small wooden sticks sprouting from the top of the diffusers spread scent throughout the room.

So what is your definition of the sweet smell of success? A new car? Dining at a different restaurant every night? The smell of a gourmet dinner wafting in your direction as the waiter nears your table? Even fast-food chains have latched onto the idea of aromatherapy: Burger King referenced the power of the sense of smell in a sales slogan.

Let's take the example of a new car. The moment you slide behind the wheel, you are overcome with the almost addictive aroma of leather and plastic. You inhale deeply, filling your senses, which elicit your feeling of accomplishment. I congratulate you on your new car, but unfortunately, that "new-car smell" is potentially harmful to your health.

ENVIRONMENTAL AWARENESS

VOLATILE ORGANIC COMPOUNDS (VOCS) are emitted from the adhesives, sealers, and plastics used in manufacturing your home and vehicle. Styrenes, benzenes, and formaldehyde are just a few of the VOCs found in that new-car smell. VOC concentrations can give off vapors reaching unhealthy levels in a closed environment heated by the sun. In the United States, new car manufacturers are allowed 128 times the VOCs that are allowed in Australia.

The vaporized chemical compounds such as benzene, a known carcinogen found in gasoline, and formaldehyde, a tissue preservative used by pathologists, can cause symptoms such as eye, throat, and nose irritation; headaches; nausea and vomiting; and dizziness. Fortunately, these high concentrations of VOCs dissipate a few months after the car is manufactured.

For me, the sweet smell of success isn't at the hospital either. In the operating room, where unpleasant odors prevail, hospital employees sometimes deodorize with peppermint oil diluted in alcohol. Often there is no written policy or procedure for use of "peppermint spirit," too much oil is often used, causing excessive vapors that burn our eyes. Tearing vision is difficult to fix when you are "scrubbed in" and have to maintain a sterile environment. Instead, I prefer to apply one of my own essential oils, such as ginger, to my disposable face mask to help overshadow the foul odors and calm my stomach.

Aromatherapy is one of the fastest-growing fields in alternative medicine and is quickly working its way into the mainstream. It is commonly used in hospitals and clinics for various applications such as pain relief and for side effects of nausea from chemotherapy, rehabilitation of cardiac patients, and relief of anxiety and pain for women laboring at childbirth. You may be wondering, "If essential oils are so valuable and effective, why isn't everyone using them to stay healthy and energetic?" The answer is simple. With the beginning of modern medicine in the twentieth century, essential oils, like herbs, have been pushed aside for synthetic wonder drugs.

MEDICAL AWARENESS

THERE IS NO DOUBT that modern medical science has given us some incredible lifesaving medicines. That is one reason I became a doctor. However, our reliance on synthetic drugs is a double-edged sword: It's made us healthier, but at the same time, some are suffering from heart attacks and strokes that often result from side effects of synthetic drugs, adverse interactions, and errors in drug administration.

Ironically, many forward-thinking doctors of today are looking back to a simpler and safer time of healing. As you read this, countless scientific labs across the globe are investigating the remarkable science of aromatherapy and the healing properties of essential oils that have existed for centuries. These essential oils include the ones used in ancient Egypt as well as many newly developed oils to fulfill the ever-increasing demand of the individual consumer and industrial giants. There is documentation of oils as successful remedies for many common ailments including pain, host infections of all kinds, bronchitis, and digestive problems. There are very many articles to choose from when researching. Here are several examples of essential oil studies.

- Scientists reporting on the power of peppermint oil for irritable bowel syndrome (IBS) analyzed patients with symptoms for four weeks and discovered that peppermint oil reduces abdominal pain, bloating, constipation, and digestive distress. Enteric-coated capsules also worked well in 75% of pediatric patients with IBS (Kline 2001).

- As published in the journal Medical Hypotheses, an open trial that followed 56 patients revealed that ginger powder was found to contain micronutrients that reduced pain and swelling in patients with rheumatoid arthritis, osteoarthritis, and muscular discomfort (Srivasta 1992).

- In a double blind placebo controlled human study, elderly patients with acute knee pain benefited from three weeks of aroma-massage applications of a combination of oils of ginger and orange (Yip 2009).

- The Journal of Antimicrobial Chemotherapy published a study in which the essential oils of cinnamon and lemon were among fourteen tested for bacteria and virus-fighting ability. The study concluded that all fourteen of these oils, when vaporized, were effective against respiratory pathogens such as influenza (Inouye 2001).

PLANT INFLUENCES

WHEN ESSENTIAL OILS ARE used properly, they are safe, effective, free of side effects, and most of all, very enjoyable. Oils can also be readily integrated into allopathic medical specialties as well as other types of wellness practices. Essential oils operate within body chemistry guidelines. The natural oils from plants act as messengers providing various phytomolecules that naturally influence the organs systems of the body along hormonal and neurological pathways. It's phenomenal the way that body hormones rise and fall in response to the time of the day or night. Plants also respond to cycles of light and dark. The circadian rhythms of the body clock and its chemistry follow physical laws and can be altered by a great many factors, not just the jet lag experienced during long-distance travel across multiple time zones. All of the bodily processes and our decision-making processes are influenced by smells and oils from plants in a multiplicity of obvious and subtle manners. Our reactions to smells occur innately with or without our awareness.

As I mentioned earlier, aromatherapy is also working its way into the mainstream of cultural events. Think you can smell only with your nose? Think again. Now you can visualize the scent of human pheromones as shown at an MIT art show, The Fear of Smell—The Smell of Fear, in the works of the artist of odor, Sissel Tolaas. She consulted with manufacturer International Flavors and Fragrances to microencapsulate scents into the paints she uses in her artwork.

APHRODISIACS AND ENDORPHINS

NEW ENDORPHIN AND APHRODISIAC products claim to encourage intimacy and stimulate sexual desire. These products are manufactured with delivery systems that use the sense of smell to increase the effectiveness the body's natural endorphin and aphrodisiacs hormones. The vomeronasal organ (VNO) is the smell receptor organ of the five senses that is involved in chemical communication between human beings. Synthetic chemical triggers that mimic human pheromones, such as perfume from spray bottles, can be spritzed onto the body for other people to pick up the scent. Essential oils can be applied directly to skin and absorbed. Male and female essential oil-impregnated nontransdermal skin patches worn on the arm can be sniffed to stimulate low libido. Pheromone-like scents stimulate the erotic centers in the brain. When the VNO detects pheromones and certain phytomolecules in essential oils, it sends a message, perhaps sexual, to the brain.

The effect evoked by a scent passing into the brain is a primitive and stimulating process. When an invigorating scent traversing the hypothalamus causes release of noradrenaline, a primal response is felt. An energizing scent passing into the thalamus causes a euphoric response following the release of encephalins into the bloodstream. A provocative scent flowing along pathways to the pituitary gland causes release of endorphins, which act as an aphrodisiac on the sex glands. Stimulation by scents in the hypothalamus in the midbrain causes release of serotonin and a sedative response. These instinctual responses represent survival, emotional, sexual, motivational, and memory stimulation resulting from conscious and unconscious perception of scents that directly influence our primitive thoughts and actions. Certainly the most important sex organ is the brain. Guiding thoughts and scents together along the path to pleasure and intimacy is needful for humans of all ages. Check out my Romantic Encounters product, blended with specific essential oils that are endorphin and aphrodisiac-activating, as discussed in chapter 9.

COMMERCIALIZED AROMATHERAPY

As consumers, we are witnessing our sensibility to scents and smells being taken to a new synthetic level. Large corporations make substantial profits selling the sweet synthetic smell of success in household "aromatherapy" products. These items range from synthetically scented laundry soaps to spray room fresheners. There are enough of these products in the marketplace to make you literally nauseated and headachy, as you may have noticed when walking down certain aisles of your neighborhood supermarket.

Essential oils and other functional fragrances can now be stabilized in cyclodextrins—complex molecules that allow a controlled release in many environments, including the supermarket. Cyclodextrins are utilized as carriers for natural colors, flavors, vitamins; solubilizers of lipids; stabilizers of oil in water emulsions; and aroma modifiers in a variety of processed foods. The food industry widely uses irradiation and chlorine solutions to sanitize and prolong product shelf life of fresh-cut fruits and vegetables, a growing segment of the marketplace. Concerns about the potential formation of carcinogens and ineffective antibacterial properties from usage of chlorine have prompted laboratory researchers to find alternative resources to use as preservatives. The use of cyclodextrins as carriers for phytomolecules with high antioxidant-carrying capacity and antimicrobial properties—such as essential oils—in fresh-cut products is extremely promising.

FUTURISTIC AROMATHERAPY

- The growth of different microorganisms responsible for spoilage of fruit and vegetables can be diminished using essential oils linked to cyclodextrins. Essential oils are antimicrobial in general, and rosemary, oregano, coriander, thyme, sage, and the phytomolecules cinnamaldehyde and eugenol from cinnamon essential oil, are suitable alternatives to chlorine and irradiation for preservation of perishables.

- Commercial aroma-dispensing systems are utilized to provide "signature aromatherapy scents" for corporations, hotels chains, and department stores. These scents are dispensed using the buildings' ventilations systems and with smaller units located near elevators and in lobbies. The scent of lavender and rosemary diffused into social areas calms and soothes customers. Oil of orange dispersed in waiting rooms of dental offices reduces patients' anxiety and improves their mood (Lehrner, 2005). Oil of lemon diffused in banks keeps the tellers alert.

- Movie theaters in Japan have diffused specialized scents precisely timed with the action and music for any given scene in a movie. Also in Japan, mobile phone users will be among the first to send each other aromatherapy-scented email attachments, and watch music and video clips enhanced by smell on their phones. For the time being, people can use their mobile phone or wireless connection to send one of two hundred fragrance recipes to an aromatherapy-generating device via infrared or to a home gateway unit.

- Computers outfitted with peripheral applications such as Universal Serial Bus ports, can utilize scent-releasing devices that trigger release of scents, while you browse certain websites. (Subscribe to real, interactive Smell-O–Vision Internet television at www.scenttv.tv.) In public settings such as airports, robotic detectors can analyze the air for dangerous scents and can sound an alarm for potential threats.

ALL THESE FUTURISTIC AROMATHERAPY inventions are insignificant compared to these seven spectacular natural wonders:

- To love
- To laugh
- To see
- To touch
- To hear
- To taste
- To smell

ENTREPRENEURS ARE REALIZING THEIR intention to utilize the sense of smell and essential oils in order to create an abundance of trademarked and patented products. The imaginative commercial and therapeutic uses of the phytomolecular properties of plants for business and medicine benefits consumers seeking products and alternative remedies of health care. The concepts presented in this book are more complex than just aromatherapy or even the practice of medicine. The necessities and possibilities for these concepts are seemingly endless. Integrating wellness techniques such as aromatherapy as a form of dietary supplementation taken in conjunction with other nutritional medicinal food products is a powerful method for successfully gaining or regaining health. Consciously combining holistic wellness and well-being practices creatively with certain wealth-building activities can maximize your health and your wealth benefits simultaneously.

CHAPTER

Worthy Ideals

"Success is the progressive realization of a worthy ideal".

—Earl Nightingale, author of
The Strangest Secret for Succeeding in the World Today

CHAPTER

WORTHY IDEALS

EARL NIGHTINGALE'S DEFINITION OF success is the best. Nightingale pioneered the art and science of success principles and created the motivational speaker recording industry. Putting his definition of success into practical application takes shape as you answer questions about living passionately. For instance, what are you passionate about? Are you doing what you really want to be doing with your life? The key to successfully doing what you passionately want to be doing requires an in-depth understanding of your purpose, your vision, and your goals. Find your "ideal passion" to fall in love with. Expand your sweet smell of success passionately by working persistently toward the progressive realization of your worthy ideal.

THE ART AND SCIENCE OF SUCCESS

LEARNING THE ART AND SCIENCE of success without stress is an adventure worth pursuing. Your vision of what you aspire to be in this life is your blueprint for success. Initiate your spirit of progress and put the statement of your life's mission in writing. Personalize your unique blueprint for success. The process of discovering your purpose requires searching your heart to determine what you love and what matters most to you. The application and fulfillment of this self-awareness delivers profound meaning to your life.

Following the blueprint of your vision will help you advance with focus, clarity, and verve. Vision reflects what you naturally love to do best: those talents, skills, and gifts that you in particular have to offer the world. Once you align your life with your purpose and vision, you will be energized with an abundance of passion, power, and possibilities. Being led by your purpose to greater strategic visions through the realization of progressively more worthy goals leads ultimately back to the fulfillment of purpose. Your life will overflow with excitement and burst in surprising directions.

GRATITUDE ROCKS

THERE IS A LAW of gratitude, and if you are to get the results you seek, it is absolutely necessary that you should observe this law. The law of gratitude is the natural principle that action and reaction are always equal and in opposite directions. The grateful outreaching of your mind in thankful praise to the Supreme Power is a liberation or expenditure of force; it cannot fail to reach that to which it is addressed. And, as a result, God responds with an instantaneous movement towards you.

—**Wallace Wattles,** *The Science of Getting Rich*

GRATEFULNESS EMPOWERS GOAL SETTING. The process of goal setting allows you to make formal plans for your future. To best achieve the life of your dreams, concentrate your efforts on heartfelt and imaginative plans. Pursuing goals generated from a grateful heart is the most effective way to successfully implement purpose and vision in your life. Focus your mental energy and organize your resources and activities. Clearly defined goals are a measuring tape of your achievements. Achieving your goals enables you to realize your inner greatness and rise to higher levels of competence. See the fruit of living your life with an attitude of gratitude. Be great and grateful. The many positive results you collect along the way will add up to the successful realization of your worthy ideal. Gratitude attracts results and that is why gratitude rocks. Learn to sign "Thank you from the bottom of my heart" to express your gratitude silently to soldiers, teachers, and anyone else who deserves heartfelt thanks.

HEIGHTENED BOOMER AWARENESS

AS A BABY BOOMER, my purpose, vision, and goals are manifested through my desire to be healthy, wealthy, and wise in order to help others. Being a wise boomer means having a heightened awareness of the new Wellness Revolution. Feed on personal growth material for your mind-body-spirit and develop your assets for yourself and your family. Through the creative efforts of many participants in the Wellness Revolution, many people may live a long life filled with progressive realizations of worthy ideals that are greater than their ordinary endeavors or goals. "Progressive" refers to increasing intensity. Analyze your creative ideas and see if they are worthy of your endorphin-generating passions and love. Why do you think this process is referred to as "doing one's passion?"

I have asked myself, as an anesthesiologist, why I should get involved with the subjects of aromatherapy, nutritional therapies, and network marketing, especially in such an enthusiastic and dedicated way. I've created an image for myself, the oilMD; developed my own product line of essential oils; written this book; and appeared on stage and screen. I choose the motto of the oilMD—"promoting wellness through nature"—because all the processes of nature are successful. Nature's plans for success are seen in every living creature and creatively crafted plant. My goal is to inform various specialties, organizations, and communities of the opportunities to respond to the health and wealth calling of the Wellness Revolution. My vision is to offer solutions to problems rather than simply pointing them out. I have chosen to start this process by offering the oilMD essential oils product line, including oil of ginger to prevent and treat the bothersome problem of postoperative nausea and vomiting that is a possible complication of anesthesia.

PRACTICE THE ARTS

MY SPHERE OF INFLUENCE and interest has led me to be a proponent of natural, plant-based health care products, such as those derived from juices, and of aromatherapy with essential oils for use in health care facilities of all sorts and personally as preventative medicine. Aromatherapy is more than just scented candles and potpourri. It is more than just good smells or bad smells associated with good or bad memories. It is certainly more than the commercialism involved with air fresheners, dish soap, or other fragrant cleaning supplies for use at home or in the office. Essential oils contain the chemical and nutritional building blocks to correct, improve, and sustain health, thereby enhancing longevity. Learning how to practice the art and science of aromatherapy for the benefit of yourself and others, as well as selling essential oils and juices from your own distributorship business, will serve both health and wealth purposes.

POWER TO LIVE YOUR DREAM

THE WEALTH ASPECT OF purpose, vision, and goals involves allocating assets and creating multiple sources of income in order to realize your dreams of a prosperous lifestyle. For myself, those dreams include paying forward the good I have experienced in the form of oilMD aromatherapy wellness products, this educational book, and philanthropic gestures toward the veterans of the United States Armed Forces, to whom much is owed.

Every Tuesday is aromatherapy day at the Fort Myle VA nursing facility in San Francisco. Massage therapists are certified with a license to touch, and touch therapy with essential oils brings about tremendous positive changes in the body. Touch during aromatherapy massage stimulates the immune system to produce a rise in the CD8 and CD16 cell lines, which are peripheral blood lymphocytes, in response to essential oils of lavender, cypress, and sweet marjoram (Kuriyama, 2005). That is the sweet smell of success for someone who is immune-depressed, which includes almost everybody, because our immune systems decline in function as we age.

HEALTH IS YOUR GREATEST ASSET

FOR SOME, YOUR OWN sweet smell of success may involve acquiring knowledge-inspired willpower to gain control over your health. Many of today's chronic health concerns are the result of poor diet, which over time leads to increased body weight. Not having good health can bankrupt you financially, emotionally, and spiritually. Health and longevity are directly related to quality of life as you age. Having the financial means and health to maintain and enjoy your preferred lifestyle as you age is imperative. Health is your greatest wealth asset.

To this end, do you have a plan for retirement that includes not living on a fixed minimum income? Having to be dependent on anybody or anything is not a good position be in, especially if that means ringing a call bell to have an employee paid by Medicare change your diaper at age sixty-nine. A vast number of Americans and citizens around the world will come face to face with this serious and very expensive dependency on caregivers if the call to the Wellness Revolution is not heeded. Private, in-home health care currently costs about $25 per hour. That quickly adds up to more than $200,000 per year for full-time care. A fixed minimum income is not nearly enough to cover this type of cost.

Another crisis facing the world's population is the increasing number of people getting fatter. Far too many of the obese and morbidly obese suffer from symptoms of coexisting medical diseases and the side effects of prescribed medications coupled with "super size" induced malnutrition. There are no drive-through breakthroughs to success in this area of life or any other.

BIG KIDS

THE AMERICAN ACADEMY OF Pediatrics has urged physicians to monitor blood pressure beginning at age three and cholesterol beginning at age eight if there is a family history, because one-third of all kids born in 2000 are expected to become diabetic. High blood pressure incidence has tripled in kids over the past decade, and more than 10% of kids have cholesterol levels greater than 200mg/dl. More than one million teens are at risk for heart disease and type 2 diabetes because of their weight. Kids who love the smell of fast food and prefer to eat it instead of tripling their intake of fresh fruits and vegetables (as recommended in the 2008 updated Federal Dietary Guidelines) are most definitely at risk.

BIGGER ADULTS

THE DISEASES ASSOCIATED WITH obesity are serious and life-threatening. The risks for obese patients who need surgery are monumental. I would also like to note the threat to the caregivers, who risk disability from back injury while caring for obese people. I often have to manage patients on hospital gurneys or beds for transport onto and off the operating room table. I have had to rotate patients weighing from two hundred to five hundred pounds onto the abdomen when the surgeon needed access to the back,

I am all too familiar with this subject because for over twenty years, I have performed acute care anesthesia for patients who needed elective and emergency surgery. I feel compelled to express my views regarding this monumental health care crisis in the hope of creating much-needed change.

Anesthesia management of the airway and ventilation for obese patients is very challenging. Metabolic syndrome, diabetes, infections, amputations, blood clots, strokes, heart attacks, and cancer are a few progressively worsening complications of obesity. These are gruesome and unnecessary ways to be sick and disabled. Take a hard look at these medical problems, and you will realize that the majority of these negative health events are preventable. The following abstract from the article by James O'Keefe, MD, *"Dietary strategies for improving post-prandial glucose, lipids, inflammation, and cardiovascular health," published in the Journal of America College of Cardiology, summarizes important state-of-the-art health measures everybody should master* (O'Keefe, 2008.)

The highly processed, calorie-dense, nutrient-depleted diet favored in the current American culture frequently leads to exaggerated supraphysiological post-prandial (after eating) spikes in blood glucose and lipids. This state, called post-prandial dysmetabolism, induces immediate oxidant stress, which increases in direct proportion to the increases in glucose and triglycerides after a meal. The transient increase in free radicals acutely triggers atherogenic changes including inflammation, endothelial dysfunction, hypercoagulability, and sympathetic hyperactivity. Post-prandial dysmetabolism is an independent predictor of future cardiovascular events even in nondiabetic individuals. Improvements in diet exert profound and immediate favorable changes in the post-prandial dysmetabolism. Specifically, a diet high in minimally processed, high-fiber, plant-based foods such as vegetables and fruits, whole grains, legumes, and nuts will markedly blunt the post-meal increase in glucose, triglycerides, and inflammation. Additionally, lean protein, vinegar, fish oil, tea, cinnamon, calorie restriction, weight loss, exercise, and low-dose to moderate-dose alcohol each positively impact post-prandial dysmetabolism. Experimental and epidemiological studies indicate that eating patterns, such as the traditional Mediterranean or Okinawan diets, that incorporate these types of foods and beverages reduce inflammation and cardiovascular risk. This anti-inflammatory diet should be considered for the primary and secondary prevention of coronary artery disease and diabetes.

THE OWNER'S MANUAL FOR IDEAL HEALTH

NEW AND EXCITING TRENDS in the functional foods industry will be a big help to the two-thirds of type 2 diabetics who are overweight, the 46% who are obese, the 55% with high cholesterol, and the 37% with high blood pressure. Grocery purchases are now as much driven by the risk of future health problems as they are by weight management. Half of all households have someone suffering from or at risk for high blood pressure, high cholesterol, and diabetes. Prevention of heart disease is a major aspect of consumer motivation. At least some consumers have used foods that help prevent obesity, high blood pressure, high cholesterol, and diabetes.

Over the past decade, there has been a 30% increase in adults diagnosed with hypertension. That is roughly 65 million people. For those individuals, the sweet smell of success is the New York Times best-seller You: The Owner's Manual, written by Mehmet Oz, MD, and Michael Roizen, MD, American doctors specializing in health, wellness, and pre-emptive medicine. Get it. Read it. Do it. Practice what they teach and actively work toward your worthy ideal of improved health and wellness.

AN IDEAL LIFE IS A WORK IN PROGRESS

HIPPOCRATES, THE FATHER OF medicine, stated his version of an ideal day when he made the first integrative medicine oath in the fourth century BC. He said, "The way to health is to have an aromatic bath and scented massage every day." That statement expresses a simple start to the goal of living healthily, one day at a time. Discover more of the special things that keep you thrilled with your passion. Thoughtfully consider your ideal morning, your ideal day, and worthy ideals for your life. Decide to define your purpose in life, your vision for your life, and your goals in life. Develop your ideal lifestyle. Envision yourself successful in specific areas of life, marriage, family, health, business, career, service, and giving.

WORTHY CHARITIES

LARGE CONTRIBUTIONS MADE BY the great philanthropists, celebrities, and inventors of our times create valuable assets to be utilized in this new revolution of wellness. These generous men and women practice highly intelligent giving and networking, using technology and vision to better humankind. The billions of dollars donated to The Bill and Melinda Gates Foundation by the iconic investor, Warren Buffett, are making an extremely significant and positive impact on world health. The Gates Foundation is a transparent $100 billion charity; it has provided vaccines all over the world and funded malaria prevention programs in Africa. For more information and to donate, go to http://www.gatesfoundation.org/default.htm.

Helping Hands helps people in Africa dealing with AIDS and hunger. Iman and David Bowie are the founders of Keeping a Child Alive, which provides medications, support, and orphan care in Africa. Inner-city schools across America benefit from Health Corps, a foundation patterned after the Peace Corps that educates youth in school seminars to increase awareness of the need for exercise and proper diet. Health Corps (www.healthcorps.org) empowers children to make healthy choices, practice mental resilience, and exude self-esteem.

Shelter is a basic human need. Deserving families can have decent places to call home thanks to Habitat for Humanity, founded in 1976 by Millard and Linda Fuller. Habitat for Humanity (www.habitat.org) is a nonprofit, Christian housing ministry and a worldwide, grassroots movement. There are more than 2,100 active affiliates in all 50 states and 100 countries. It gives families in need shelter, self-respect, and the hope of a better life.

"Winning the fight for charities" is the slogan for Annual Celebrity Fight Night, which donates to such outstanding causes as the National Parkinson Foundation Center of Excellence and the Muhammad Ali Parkinson Center at Barrow Neurological Institute. These centers provide diagnostic and treatment services, research, and education to support groups. The Melonhead Foundation supports the needs of children with cancer at Camp Wannahealyah in Arizona, giving kids with cancer and their families access to natural dietary substances, such as mangosteen juice, and integrative healing techniques, to achieve peace, harmony, and balance through focus on body, mind, and spirit.

RADIATE SUCCESS

FLOWERS RADIATE BEAUTY AND fragrance. Every body exudes its own aroma. Humans give off scents called pheromones. Humans also exude and radiate energy that permeates the atmosphere around them and reflexively returns to them. That radiating energy is charged with the "I can" or the "I can't" attitude of success or failure. Feeling beautiful on the outside and being beautiful on the inside are critical to radiating your success. The process of determining your purpose, vision, and goals empowers you to be successful.

The sweet smell of success is your decision to determine the direction you choose to go, regardless of your present results. Reading the following chapters will lead you mentally beyond your present results to the new health and wealth secrets of ideal scents, ideal anesthetics, ideal products, ideal businesses, and the oilMD prescription for success. We all achieve different results because we manifest our successes based on how we use our thoughts, resources, creativity, and time. You are potentially greater than any given situation or condition. Study to increase your awareness and work persistently in the applications of your gifts and talents so that you can achieve you own sweet smell of success and worthy ideals.

Worldwide Wellness:
A Doctor's Perspective

The art of healing comes from nature and not from the physician.
Therefore, the physician must start from nature with an open mind.

—Paracelsus

three
CHAPTER

WORLDWIDE WELLNESS: A DOCTOR'S PERSPECTIVE

OBESITY AND STARVATION ARE phenomenal worldwide health care problems, growing more in intensity and proportion over the last several decades. Global awareness of this food crisis and the urgent need for healing is also growing. Both the health care and "sick care" industries hold possible solutions but are also the problem, because both are intimately interwoven with global businesses and politics. Childhood and adult-onset obesity and their associated illnesses are preventable. The future ability of the health care system in the United States to cope with the obesity epidemic is questionable, especially in the light of current governmental management of disability, Social Security, and Medicare. Hopefully, the positive contributions exemplified by the top ten trends in health care will combine with the powerful resources of the Wellness Revolution to provide improved quality of health worldwide.

TOP TEN TRENDS IN HEALTH CARE

1. Health freedom laws

2. Consumer-driven health care

3. Poorly controlled costs of Western medicine

4. Rise of biotechnology, nutriogenomics, and nutraceuticals

5. Internet as health account and information resource

6. Large and small businesses opt out of health insurance

7. Dissatisfaction with federal government and socialized medical systems

8. Doctors integrate complementary medicine into their medical practices

9. High-deductible health insurance and health savings accounts

10. Complementary medicine becomes the prominent U.S. health care system

PERSONAL HEALTH RECORDS

AS A PRIVATE CITIZEN, employee, or owner/operator of a large organization, you might consider the 24/7 online availability of personal health records (PHRs) a welcomed solution to the considerable health care data challenges faced today. This vendor service is offered as a practical and convenient method of managing your own health care history and current point-of-service providers (e.g., X-rays, labs and pharmacies). There are numerous topics to understand and consider prior to posting your records on a PHR vendor's "cloud server."

First and foremost, not all online vendors of PHR services operate within the health care system and are therefore not covered under the federal Health

Insurance Portability and Accountability Act (HIPAA). Although a PHR privacy policy may suggest that the vendor is HIPAA compliant, it can still operate outside of HIPAA. A vendor that is not covered under HIPAA lacks basic procedural protection and may become subject to subpoenas. Additionally, the non-HIPAA PHR vendor is not required to notify the individual of the subpoena issued to the vendor. Significant patient-physician privilege matters could also be jeopardized. The PHR privacy policy of any company may become subject to change over time as areas such as marketing, corrections, security, linkage, depository, and consents for disclosure develop. These newly developing business products are making history with our medical histories by creating methods to manage health care data as well as the potential to generate income for these companies.

The Microsoft product HealthVault is one of several marketable online personal medical history database storage programs (http://www.healthvault.com/). Both Jim Clark, the inventor of Netscape and creator of Healtheon and WebMD, and Steve Case of AOL fame and developer of the health and wellness company Revolution Healthline, have major enterprises that upgrade methods of managing personal health care data online (http://www.revolutionhealth.com/).

WebMD leads the industry with over 40 million visitors (http://www.webmd.com/). Revolution Healthline recently acquired Health Talk to cover the chronic illnesses database, placing them in second place, with 12 million annual visitors. On these sites, you can personalize "care pages" by creating your own private social network health blog to connect to other families during illness and recovery.

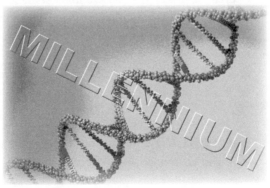

GOOGLE'S SPECIALTY IS DATA and information management. Google has built massive "cloud" servers to coordinate health care data in creative fashions. Many people and organizations seeking answers to personal, business, and scientific health-related questions use Google's search engine. A secure, customized Google health account will allow individuals to decide which providers have access to view or input health data. This open source of data management will develop into a true system that organizes health data for which no system currently exists. Early adopters will be the first to benefit from being able to access their personal health care data from any location with Internet access at any time.

Google has also invested in the concept of combining your medical history with your genetic code online, creatively working with Genentech plus 23andMe to merge the Internet, big business, and biotech. Individuals can link their medical history to personalized genome services to unlock DNA secrets regarding ethnological origin and possible predispositions to genetic diseases. Imagine, as a private consumer of genetic services, having significant single nucleotide polymorphism sections of your DNA sequenced and placed online. Navigenics and 23andMe provide economical DNA analysis for about $1,000. A simple buccal smear (oral mucosal cell swab) or saliva test could lead to medical advice and referral for future genetic products and services. (https://www.23andme.com/)

Consider, however, that the medical and legal communities have not caught up with these new scientific developments. Personal genetic information might be presented by these companies to the individual either as educational or medically purposeful. This is why some state regulatory agencies have taken issue with the "educational" services provided and given notice that licensed doctors are required on staff in order to qualify for permits, issued by regulatory agencies that allow these companies to offer DNA related services. The California Department of Health has licenced both Navigenics and 23andMe for direct-to-consumer testing. At this early stage of development, perhaps a second opinion with a genetic counselor to fully understand the implications and realize the benefits of these types of genetic services is advisable.

Andy Grove of IBM success has a very forward-thinking concept, suggesting that our government manage preventative and catastrophic care while allowing the rest of the medical insurance industry to manage the sick care needs of the American people. Paul Allen has created the Allen Institute for Brain Science to map the mouse brain genome, which has great prospects for medical applications in humans. Craig Venter mapped the human genome and is working on mapping the genome of the life forms found in the worlds' oceans, with the hope of finding cancer cures (Haefner, 2003; Costantino, 2004). All of these people are working toward a goal—better health for humankind.

RESOURCES OF THE WELLNESS REVOLUTION

ENTERPRISING GURUS OF THE Wellness Revolution are creating healthy, fitness-oriented programs and innovative functional food products that consumers can implement. These vast resources can reliably and safely help humanity control body weight and reverse the unhealthy signs and symptoms of obesity and aging by providing the proper balance of nutrition, coupled with imaginative exercise activities like sports fitness. Superior medicinal foods, such as essential oils and juices from plants, are products that have extremely promising potential when harnessed and marketed with programs designed to provide systematic health and wellness benefits for all age groups.

Dietary products and supplements developed from the plants of various food groups can potentially have significant positive impacts on the world's nutrition and health care problems. Turning our thinking and practice to nutritional supplementation could impact both health and wealth individually, locally, and globally. The sale and marketing of information in the form of intellectual knowledge and functional food products in the form of "food as medicine" is destined to become a significant portion of the one-trillion-dollar wellness industry. Since many oils from plants and juices from fruits originate in underdeveloped nations, their production can result in sustainable businesses practices that are a driving force in those economies. Provision for the continued sustainable production of these precious resources must be ensured. The açaí berry and rosewood oil come from the Amazon. Governments worldwide, such as Australia, Canada, and the United States, actively assist farmers of various third world countries to develop an international market for the plants and goods produced on their farms. Goods from crops such as distilled essential oils, concentrates, and standardized extracts of fruits, berries, and herbs can be processed into cash-yielding products for export.

TAXPAYER DOLLARS WORKING GLOBALLY

THE UNITED STATES HAS given foreign aid to sustain essential oil production in part of Africa. In a May 2007 major policy speech on foreign aid, President George W. Bush mentioned essential oils and their importance: http://www.whitehouse.gov/news/releases/2007/05/20070531-9.html

Now 14 additional nations are eligible to negotiate compacts with the Millennium Challenge Corporation, headed by Ambassador Danilovich. Let me give you an example of how this program can make a difference. In Madagascar the leaders of this island nation set a goal in their compact to improve agricultural production. In other words, we work with a nation, they have set the goal; we support their goal. They want their farmers to be able to compete in the global marketplace. We agreed to help by investing in agricultural business centers that work with local farmers. In one village, this initiative helped a group of farmers who were surviving by collecting firewood and producing charcoal. That's how these folks were trying to get ahead. They'd find firewood and make charcoal out of it, and hope they could find a market. It's a tough way to make a living in a modern world.

THE BUSINESS CENTER THAT the compact established helped the farmers work together to identify a new product, a natural oil used in skincare products. I probably could use some of that myself. The center helped these farmers develop a business plan. They acquired financing to set up a distilling plant. They built relationships with buyers in their nation's capital. Before America and Madagascar signed our compact, a typical farmer in this village could earn about $5 a week selling charcoal. After two months of bringing the new product to the market, the livelihood of these farmers increased. One farmer was able to raise his income enough to save about $500, money he plans to use for a child's education.

In Madagascar, a program identified geraniums as a high value-added market, formed a cooperative, doubled production capacity by training farmers, assisted the cooperative in accessing credit and negotiated a contract with a buyer, who is using the geraniums to produce essential oils for sale to the European market. When asked if the farmers enjoyed the smell of geraniums, the head of the cooperative replied, 'We like the smell of money better.' The farmers' income had increased by two-thirds thanks to MCC assistance.

PLANT GENETICS

GLOBALLY, THERE IS A huge plant genetics research industry. The industry spends billions and billions of dollars to fabricate medically oriented pharmaceuticals and phytonutraceuticals either genetically or synthetically, or to process them from plants and bacteria. It configures these creations into genetically modified foods and health care products. The quality and quantity of essential oils produced by plants can be altered genetically. Sugars from plants can be altered as well by efficient transformation of glucose and other natural sugars into hydroxymethylfurfural, a molecule that can easily be manipulated into a variety of chemicals, including plastics.

Gregory Mendel, the monk who discovered dominant and recessive traits of plants and for whom Mendelian genetics is named, would be amazed at the discoveries of our times. Genetically altered plant DNA is created by the usual scientific method, the ever popular trial-and-error method. Experimenting in order to find plants with higher yields of sought-after compounds and traits is risky. Genetically modified organisms (GMOs) are analyzed to discover what intended new end products the resultant plant genome is capable of manufacturing and how much the plants' total DNA was altered during the experiment.

Some people think that the push for certain types of biofuel are well-intentioned but misguided. The rising price of commodities such as corn used for corn ethanol has impacted the world food crisis as well as inflated the price of everything from beef to soft drinks. Biodiesel from other oils—soy, canola, and animal fat—is economically more efficient than petroleum-based diesel fuel, but the downside is that it causes the inflation of agricultural prices called "agflation." Brazil has been successful in the use of sugarcane ethanol because of its warm and rainy climate. Cellulosic ethanol is made in a costly process from the breakdown of cellulose-containing plants. The conversion from biomass-generated fuel in gallons per acre from corn to a new energy crop yielding a new biofuel made from other plants, such as switchgrass or miscanthus, must increase significantly to positively influence the worldwide energy and food crises. Algal biofuels can produce thirty times more energy per acre than alternative biofuels. The biomass needed to convert to algal biofuel is still in the very early stages of practical development. There are significant pros and cons to each of the possible sources of biofuels.

Zinc finger is a genetic engineering technology that uses a naturally occurring plant protein to copy and paste genes, Word-document style, into DNA within a cell nucleus. It can be used to target and regulate genes inside any organism, turning genes on and off or deleting and adding new genes within strands of DNA with greater precision than previously random genetic engineering technology. The European Commission and other regulatory agencies may consider the nature of zinc finger technology different enough to not classify the products it creates as GMO recombinant food, since the zinc finger DNA-altering nuclease does not remain in the plant for more than a few days. However, Friends of the Earth in Europe, Greenpeace International, and other groups advise that zinc finger genetically altered plants deserve GMO labeling and regulation. The DNA of corn, rice, soybeans, rapeseed, and sugarcane are a few of the plants being altered in the laboratory and in the fields.

CROP WATCH

THE EUROPEAN UNION AND South Africa are actively considering changing the current regulations regarding production and labeling of imports of genetically modified crops.

The chemistry of the new genetically modified (GM) plant products may smell and produce similarly, but do they have the same natural God-given reproductive properties and effects intended? Certainly not if the "suicide seeds" they yield are designed not to grow the farmer's next crop. In "The Mutational Consequences of Plant Transformation," published in the Journal of Biomedicine and Biotechnology, describes the creation of unrecognized and unintended genetic changes in the phenotypes of plants and how far-reaching the implications of induced mutations in plants are. Attempting to generate higher-yielding plants is magnified by the risks of current genetic engineering techniques. Latham calls for enhanced regulatory analysis and control of genome-wide mutations before too many plants with complex genetic insertion sites reach the market (Latham, 2006).

Rapeseed, commonly called canola in North America, is the fourth largest GM crop in production in the world after soy, corn, and cotton. Rapeseed oil is increasingly used in the food industry. The rapeseed plant is noted to have exceptionally long seed dormancy. The seeds of some genetically modified crops such as rapeseed appear to remain in the earth for at least a decade. Many volunteer GM rapeseed plants grow with conventional rapeseed after a GM crop. The current problem of total conventional crop contamination causes rising production costs stemming from transgenic GM seeds. The prices of non-GM plants are now significantly higher than GM varieties, and higher raw material costs affect margins in the industry.

On the other hand, blending of the sources of genetically modified plants and techniques to safely generate new products along patentable pathways could create outcomes that have clinical "structure and function" acceptability. Jian Zhao's "Nutraceuticals, Nutritional Therapy, Phytonutrients and Phytotherapy for Improvement of Humans: A Perspective on Plant Biotechnology Application," published in Patents in Biotechnology, analyzes the related epidemiological investigations and clinical studies as well as regulations that have significant implications on our crops (Zhao, 2007).

Genetic engineering has extended into the field of stem cell transplantation, with data suggesting that there is a dose-dependent effect on stem cells by blueberry, green tea, catechins, carnosine, and vitamin D3, alone and in combinations. These phytonutrients synergistically promote proliferation of human bone marrow, implying that these phytonutrients and the nutraceutical products they represent may promote health and healing capability of the human body at the cellular level.

Europe's natural perfumery industry is experiencing incredible regulation-induced turmoil over the use of natural citrus essential oils. Regulatory agencies have proposed rulings based on the unsubstantiated risk assessment of furocoumarin-like substances in citrus essential oils. It is important to have unadulterated plants or products in any way, shape, or form, whether they are foods or perfumes with or without essential oils from citrus. Ensuring proper oversight can rather than over-regulation which suppresses small businesses will ensure safe foods and cosmetics that harness their extremely promising potential when manufactured into products that provide systematic benefits for all age groups. The creation of products for the consumers of the Wellness Revolution can reliably and safely help humanity manage health care issues both globally and locally.

PARADOXICAL PARADIGMS

OUR SENSE OF SMELL is very complex and dependent on a variety of factors, just as the ability of the body to utilize vitamins, minerals, and antioxidants is dependent on each individual's own chemical makeup. Numerous companies now have various methods of measuring total antioxidant capacity for a variety of individual and specific antioxidant agents, such as isoprostanes and vitamins C and E. There are paradigms for taking more than the recommended daily values of supplements, such as taking extra antioxidants for antiaging, based on topical literature. There is no known recommended daily value for supplementation with single entity or broad-spectrum antioxidants for antiaging.

The health paradigm of increasing antioxidant supplementation in order to promote wellness, prevent disease, and enhance antiaging remains controversial because, to date, it is not characterized well (Berger, 2005). There are studies correlating old age and dietary habits in certain populations of the world, but there are no long-term studies on supplementation as we know it. Many studies suggest that supplementation with antioxidants has great benefits; relatively few studies suggest the opposite. The studies suggesting paradoxical effects of antioxidants have not been repeated to clarify the significance of the findings. These paradoxical findings may in part be due to each individual's particular chemical makeup, such as baseline ORAC value resulting from prior experience with vitamins, as well as the quality and quantity of supplement variability.

For example, perhaps the choice of single entity synthetic vitamin E designated as the antioxidant utilized in the materials and methods of the studies caused the negative outcome, rather than having utilized broad-spectrum antioxidants from natural sourced vitamins. There are eight vitamin E substances found with stereoisomer activity: : α-, β-, γ-, and δ-tocopherol; and α-, β-, γ-, and δ-tocotrienol (Chandan, 2006). Evidence supports that members of the vitamin E family are functionally unique in terms of antioxidant capacity, membrane functionality, placental transfer, and cholesterol metabolism, which should caution researchers against empirical claims concluding that vitamin E supplementation may increase "all-cause" mortality.

The 2008 budget for the National Institutes of Health (NIH) is just under $29.5 billion. The National Center for Complementary and Alternative Medicine (NCCAM) is part of the NIH. The budget for NCCAM is about $121.6 million for research studies and other activities. The current studies provide much more data showing that short-term usage of supplements does alter the natural course of many acute and chronic diseases in a positive manner. We can extrapolate from certain studies that much benefit could be gained by the proper dietary intake of functional foods, supplemented with a broad spectrum of vitamins, minerals, and trace elements that generate high antioxidant values.

The effects of using antioxidants concurrent with chemotherapy and radiation are described by various camps as either synergistic or antagonistic to certain cancer therapies (Gordaliza, 2007). Oncologists are concerned because some cancer chemotherapeutic agents they prescribe make free radicals designed to lead to the death of the cancer cell. Free radicals are inactivated by antioxidants, making some forms of chemotherapy less effective.

CHEMOTHERAPEUTIC MEDICATIONS PRODUCING FREE RADICALS

Alkylating and Anthracyclines Medications

cisplatin (Platinol)

carboplatin (Paraplatin)

chlorambucil (Leukeran)

carmustine (BiCNU)

cyclophosphamide (Cytoxan)

busulfan (Myleran)

ifosfamide (Ifex)

doxorubicin (Doxil)

daunorubicin (Cerubidine)

epirubicin (Ellence)

mitomycin (Mutamycin)

bleomycin (Blenoxane)

ONE FACTOR ONCOLOGISTS consider when determining which chemotherapy medications to use to treat a cancer patient is cancer cell type. There is evidence that three specific antioxidants interfere with three specific conventional cancer therapeutics in vivo: flavonoids with tamoxifen, N-acetyl-cysteine with doxorubicin, and beta-carotene with 5-fluorouracil. Paradoxically, antioxidants are prescribed for some patients during cancer treatment to reduce the side effects of chemotherapy. Two prescription antioxidants, mesna (Mesnex) and amifostine (Ethyol), are prescribed to specifically prevent the side effects of the cancer chemo drugs ifosfamide, cyclophosphamide, and cisplatin. The use of these antioxidants does not reduce the effectiveness of cisplatin, cyclophosphamide, or ifosfamide in the treatment of cancer. These two antioxidants are for prescription use only; they have been evaluated in human studies by the Food and Drug Administration (FDA) and are approved for use in this cancer chemotherapy setting. Numerous other studies have shown that patients receive many benefits when treated with certain antioxidants with or without chemotherapy and radiation. Human studies showing the impact of dietary supplements on chemotherapy effectiveness are not required for products marketed as supplements. More research regarding the role of supplements in conventional oncologic treatment is required.

Based on evidence described in "The Biochemical Basis of Antioxidant Therapy in Critical Illness" (Eaton, 2007), diseases such as sepsis and tissue trauma that compromise and unbalance bodily blood chemistry require supplementation with antioxidants, amino acids, and trace elements in order to maintain and enhance the body's defensive networking capacity. In wellness and in certain critical illness, antioxidants are beneficial. We must seek a balance of what's safe and what's effective in evidence-based studies to yield clinical practice.

ENERGY MEDICINE

THERE ARE WAYS OF combining diverse medical specialties with the many different types of care provided by practitioners of energy medicine techniques. Specialized programs in complementary alternative medicine (CAM) are just beginning to be offered as an advanced degree. Qigong breathing exercises are a practice of putative energy medicine (i.e., a type of biofield energy that is not measurable by current scientific methods). Reiki, Johrei, therapeutic touch, and intercessory prayer for emotional and spiritual wellness are considered putative energy medicine practices as well. Veritable energy medicine employs mechanical vibrations, light therapy, and magnetism to generate the effects of wave length and frequency applications. Various therapists, including some acupuncturists, use light therapy to activate the neurological meridians in acupuncture therapy. Graduates of the Fellowship Training Program in Integrative Medicine at the University of Arizona's College of Medicine in Tucson, taught by the wellness visionary Andrew Weil, MD, are experts in the art of integrating CAM practices with allopathic medicine.

Guided imagery can create and shape any intended mind-body connection. Before anesthesia and surgery, essential oil of ginger root can be provided with the guided thought imagery that essential oil of ginger root prevents postoperative nausea. People are looking for something to believe in, and patients want to believe in the caregiver and the care. I literally tell patients that this remedy will help prevent nausea in the recovery room upon awakening. Overall, patients and their families approach nausea as the number one problem to avoid after surgery. Raising awareness worldwide about renovating, rehabilitating, and revitalizing health care is also part of the mission and intended energy of guided imagery.

NATIONAL SENSE OF SMELL DAY

A NOBEL PRIZE WAS given for documentation of the human genotype for sense of smell. There are more genes dedicated to smell than any other of our five senses. Companies and specialists that study the sense of smell have attested to its importance by establishing the National Sense of Smell Day, celebrated on the last Saturday in April. This nationwide museum-based program is sponsored by the Fragrance Foundation Research and Education, a division of the Sense of Smell Institute. For fourteen years the National Sense of Smell Day has entertained and educated children with fun olfactory activities. A recognized authority on smell, Dr. Jay Gottfried has proposed that combining fragrances with sensory stimulus and emotion increases the effectiveness of scents.

Products with fragrances from essential oils, used for appetite modification, can be embedded with education guided toward imaginative sensory stimulus to increase efficacy. Peppermint and grapefruit oils are known to help the brain and stomach communicate the message that you've had enough to eat. In other words, you feel full sooner. The inhalation of vapors and transdermal absorption of the oils prior to meals could help decrease appetite, so you feel full sooner and eat less. Combining these oils with guided imagery can help convince you to eat less, taking in fewer calories and perhaps even eating better foods.

CLINICAL AROMATHERAPY

HAVE YOU EVER USED a medical aromatic plant or essential oil? Many people haven't, but I have used essential oils hundreds of times on my patients in the operating room. Essential oil of ginger root prevents and treats postoperative nausea and vomiting, two of anesthesia's most common unpleasant effects occurring after surgery. Millions of dollars are spent by patients and earned by drug companies annually to treat this expensive and bothersome problem. A recent study stated that the average person about to undergo surgery would spend an extra $100 to prevent getting sick to the stomach after surgery. A remedy of ginger oil given perioperatively costs only a few cents per patient. Very few people know about it or use it in hospitals, although it has been safely used as a cure for many causes of gastrointestinal distress for centuries in many parts of the world.

That is just one example of the usefulness of aromatherapy with therapeutic-grade essential oils in medical practice. There are many examples of how essential oils have been used positively as modern clinical aromatherapy based on scientific discoveries. The use of essential oils in the food, cosmetic, and medical industries is becoming an increasingly fabulous business opportunity in the twenty-first century. There are fabulous psychological benefits of aromatherapy with massage for postpartum women (Imura, 2006). Clinical Aromatherapy, by Jane Buckle, PhD, RN, is an outstanding textbook that describes what essential oils can do for patients in the settings of acute and chronic medical care, and provides remedies for common symptoms and complaints. Buckle also has written a book on aromatherapy for pets.

The phytomolecular chemical structure and properties of many of the aromatic essential oils are like those of the anesthetic gas drugs. Both essential oils and anesthetic drugs are volatile, meaning that they turn into gaseous vapors when exposed to air. Aromatherapy is delivered and absorbed by diffusion of the gaseous vapors into the air and then into the respiratory system, by way of the nose and lungs when inhaled. The anesthetic gas agents, such as the currently popular sevoflurane (Ultane), are long-chain hydrocarbons with known chemical properties. Anesthesiologists put people to sleep using known concentrations of volatile agents that have known possible side effects, such as cardiorespiratory depression and postoperative nausea and vomiting. These anesthetic agents have material safety data sheets (MSDS) just like any other drugs, chemicals, cleaning supplies, or essential oil products. Both essential oils and anesthetic gas agents have enormous potential energy to bring healing to illness and disease.

CROSSOVER PROPERTIES

THE AROMATIC ESSENTIAL OILS distilled from plants have a few qualities similar to anesthesia vapors and are equally complex. These oils have many more phytomolecular chemical components, containing more wonderful properties than anesthesia gases when delivered therapeutically. There are definite caveats as to which oils are better remedies medicinally (i.e., in the treatment of self-limiting ailments and medical conditions). Essential oils are very similar to each other in many regards, but like people, they each have their own strengths and weaknesses, and some will work better for one person than the next.

Essential oils have properties that overlap or cross over one another. When doing a review of body systems for a medical history and physical, doctors determine whether an individual has symptoms in the ear, nose, throat, gastrointestinal tract, cardiac, respiratory, or endocrine systems. Any given essential oil has phytomolecular chemical effects on each of those organ systems, some more pronounced than others. For instance, the alcohol components shoagol and gingerol of essential oil of ginger root are excellent at relieving nausea. Other chemical components found in oil of ginger exert a naturally balanced system of anti-inflammatory and analgesic activity as well. The exquisite and expensive oil of rose has many amazing applications in perfumery, cosmetics, and clinical settings. Plus, it is noted to have anticonflict properties. Perhaps that is the origin of the gifting of roses to loved ones on special occasions.

INGESTING ESSENTIAL OILS

MOUTHWASHES ARE AN example of the safety of oral ingestion of a small percentage of essential oils and their phytomolecular chemical components. Dental literature on mouthwashes used in studies to prevent gingivitis, periodontitis, bad breath, and plaque formation states that mouthwashes are formulated with essential oils having various percentages of the ingredients menthol, eucalyptol, methyl saliclyate, and thymol. Oral rinsing twice daily with mouthwash gives 24-hour protection, killing the various bacteria known to cause plaque, gingivitis, and periodontitis (Fine, 2007). The mechanism of gargling allows for ingestion, resulting from some swallowing and oral mucosal absorption of mouthwash and the phytomolecules of the essential oils. Gargling with essential oil is good oral hygiene (Munoz, 2001).

The prevalence of inflammatory periodontitis is associated with low systemic serum antioxidant concentrations (Chappel, 2007). Periodontitis causes oxidative stress orally, as measured by lowered serum antioxidant levels in saliva. This relationship is especially important because there is an increased incidence of stroke, type 2 diabetes, and heart disease associated with periodontitis. The common bad bacteria of the mouth are more sensitive to the mouthwashes containing essential oils than the other types of mouthwash (Fine, 2007). Periodontitis is associated with tooth loss, secondary to an abnormal inflammatory immune response to bacteria.

The cooking spices commonly found in kitchens throughout the world are made into wonderful essential oils. Essential oils can be used in cooking recipes. Thyme, rosemary, oregano, basil, cinnamon, and clove have potent flavoring properties. A few drops of essential oil are equivalent to a teaspoon of the oil-depleted dried spice. Essential oils of peppermint and fennel are traditionally known as carminatives, which help relieve gas in the digestive system.

The process of digestion causes foam and gas formation. That is why many over-the-counter antacids include antifoaming agents. Gastrointestinal studies with essential oils of peppermint and fennel have demonstrated that these oils are good antifoaming agents to treat bloating. Several articles describe peppermint oil applied during colonoscopy, either topically or by injection into the bowel wall, to have shown good results for normalization of colon spasm and relief from gas. A few drops of essential oil ingested orally is apparently not harmful and may be beneficial, because the crossover properties eliminate pathologic bacteria, support organ system responsiveness to local and systemic illnesses, and contribute to the total bodily antioxidant content.

ANTICIPATING WELLNESS

TOWARD THE END OF the twentieth century, an obesity epidemic began. State by state, super-sizing in the fast food industry started to intensely super size people. The percentage of obese and then morbidly obese people has risen across the whole United States to epidemic proportions. Television food advertising increases children's appetites and subsequently food consumption by over 100%. Australia recently reported a five-fold increase in severe food allergies, especially asthma and anaphylaxis related to peanuts, cashews, and a variety of food products. The implications of the food industry's ability and willingness to manage the potential complicating factors of these dietary and obesity-related issues for the future of our health and health care system are staggering.

As an anesthesiologist, I have to take care of many people whose illnesses are in part due to poor diet. There are certain types of foods that can be considered functionally medicinal foods. Essential oils and berry fruit juices are in that category. My job as an anesthesiologist often involves helping patients prepare themselves for surgery so they are in the best possible condition they can be in prior to surgery. Once, I had referred an acquaintance to a surgeon I know for plastic surgery, only to have my acquaintance come back to me and say that we needed to talk and make special arrangements for surgery. She had such significant irritable bowel syndrome that it was difficult for her to leave the house, much less lay on a surgical table for several hours.

After reviewing her medications, allergies, prior anesthesia history, and preexisting medical conditions, I made several recommendations, including drinking the juices of mangosteen and açaí. Within a few days she reported ecstatically that her incessant bowel symptoms had almost completely disappeared. She was scheduled for surgery and anesthesia, which proceeded remarkably smoothly. She also noted that her skin color improved substantially, which she attributed to drinking the juices.

These juices derived from berry fruits and essential oils derived from plants, spices, and herbs are superior in function to regular foods because of their extensive phytomolecular composition. They contain the concentrated plant essences of phytopigments, phytoestrogens, flavenoids, phenols, anthrocyanins, pterostilbenoids, resveratrol, terpenoids, ligands, lignans, amino acids, minerals, fiber, secondary plant metabolites, trace, and ultra trace elements. These phytomolecules inhibit hardening of the arteries and thrombosis; have antibacterial, antiviral, antifungal, antiparasitic, and antimalarial properties; enhance the immune system; promote suppression of cancer cells; and enhance the transdermal absorption of medications. All of these fascinating attributes of plants and more are reviewed in an excellent article published in the Journal of Phytotherapy Research (January 2007): "Pharmaceutical and Therapeutic Potentials of Essential Oils and Their Volatile Constituents: A Review" (Edris, 2007). For the health care minded individuals and medical practitioners who have little knowledge of essential oils, this article is well worth reading in its entirety.

There is much to be considered when we think about the effects caused by the emotionally charged issues of ill health. What you eat today and what you supplement with today will determine your future health. It is a worthy goal to create an enticing health and wellness plan that is educationally based, while directing one's mental habits to influence physical eating habits to be healthier.

There are real and attainable dreams of health to be enjoyed during the future decades of our lives. We can practice a lifestyle in which we consume natural, wild-crafted, and organically sourced foods, plus various berry fruit juices and essential oils. Many of these sorts of products are available from network marketing companies. Supplementing with superior medicinal foods is a form of health insurance and is much more than just aromatherapy. Considering food as medicine is truly a revolution in anticipation of wellness.

four

CHAPTER

Ideal Scents

"It is more important to know what sort of person has a disease than to know what sort of disease a person has."

—Hippocrates

four

CHAPTER 4

IDEAL SCENTS

THE ART AND SCIENCE OF aromatherapy is intriguing. Essential oils from plants are one piece of the puzzle of remedies for the constellation of ailments that affect the human body on a daily and ongoing basis. Humans interact consciously and unconsciously on physical, psychosocial, and spiritual planes that may be positively influenced by the ideal scents of natural essential oils from plants. It is advisable to learn the basics of the art of aromatherapy and become competent in the use of these God-given plant essences. This book will help you understand aromatherapy in light of the art and science of ideal scents of essential oils.

REMEDIES FOR OVER-THE-COUNTER COMPLAINTS

FOR ALMOST EVERY PLANT there is a corresponding essential oil. Some exceptions exist for succulents, cacti and, herbs. Each plant has many properties and different strengths, just as humans do. As our own awareness of our strengths grows, so do our expectations for more specialized results from ourselves. Education in aromatherapy reveals that essential oils from plants have properties that may prevent and treat many over-the-counter complaints, such as indigestion and nausea. The essential oil of ginger works well for both and for its calming and allergy relief properties as well. Either recommendation would be correct.

Here's a good example of using oil of ginger root. My daughter, Erin, got a virus that gave her stomach cramps, shaking, chills, and fever. As she was lying on the floor in front of the fireplace complaining of how cold and in pain she was, I suggested we put 10% oil of ginger on her abdomen and feet. At first she refused since she felt so miserable, but finally she acquiesced. After the initial application, she felt much better for an hour, and then her symptoms gradually returned. Each hour over the next few hours, I reapplied two teaspoons of 10% oil of ginger to her feet and abdomen, which gave her great relief until the effects of the 24-hour virus subsided. Oil of ginger is a good remedy for the various common causes of gastrointestinal distress.

Other oils could also work well on numerous and varied types of self-limiting physical complaints. The key to a successful practice of the art of aromatherapy is to relax and let the essential oils do the "heavy lifting." Many oils have roughly similar properties. The nuances for the use of the most basic essential oils, such as Lavandula angustifolia, are not that critical. Let the oil do the work. Each essential oil is a naturally balanced phytosolution for many common ailments.

Common complaints such as headaches, backaches, bellyaches, allergies, bug bites, minor burns, hot flashes, anxiety, insomnia, arthritis, and nausea are occasionally more than merely bothersome. Drugstore remedies are manufactured in abundance but other, more natural options are available; for example, essential oil of lavender can be applied for bug bites and burns. Oils of ginger and peppermint can be used for migraine headache and upset stomach.

There are many common garden plants and kitchen spices processed into essential oils that make good remedies for common household ailments. Moms should have bottles of the basic essential oils of lavender, ginger, peppermint, tea tree, mandarin, lemon, basil, and chamomile on hand in the kitchen so they can practice the simple uses of oils instead of reaching for pills first. Simple recipes that resemble cooking recipes are commonly available. To obtain practical and simple aromatherapy recipes using essential oils, download my free e-book, 10 Aromatherapy Secrets Revealed, from one of my oilMD wellness network websites, www.10aromatherapysecrets.com.

I work with a nurse who has a very complex medical history. She cannot take even Tylenol for management of the shoulder pain that bothers her all the time, especially at night so that she cannot sleep very well. I suggested a blend of several essential oils, including eucalyptus and peppermint. She found such great relief that she is finally able to sleep throughout the night without waking in pain.

Health coaching and mentoring family, relatives, and friends on the basic uses of essential oils are needful and wonderful skills. They decrease the dependence on manufactured, over-the-counter pharmaceuticals and prescription medications. Overdependence on these synthetic drugs is becoming increasingly evident as they are rendered ineffective due to unpleasant side effects. Essential oils from plants are natural, working with the body's native organ systems, and therefore are not rendered ineffective.

TRADITIONAL ARTS PRACTICE

Prior to the 1900s, the "doctors" onboard whalers and ancient mariner clipper ships included many essential oils like peppermint and spearmint among the ships' medical supplies. The classic book Back to Eden, by Jethro Kloss, has old terms and remedies for common ailments that are often revisited in modern aromatherapy books. Traditional usage of natural essential oil remedies was commonplace and acceptable. The book describes a variety of indispensable traditional practices, such as making a compress or poultice, vapor baths, and massage. Although Back to Eden was written in the 1930s and is out-of-date in many important medical arenas, especially in terms of antibiotic therapy and cancer treatments, one can glean many skill sets by studying the natural and traditional techniques of these old healing arts. The art of enhanced smell awareness coupled with the inner joy and outer benefits provided by oils of plants is worthy of the time and energy spent to gain a new set of skills.

The field of aromatherapy has been developed and championed by many great pioneers. Jean Valnet, MD, wrote The Practice of Aromatherapy. Edited by Robert Tisserand, this book is a compendium of plant medicine describing internal and external use of plant essences, extracts, and tinctures. The abundance of more than thirty years of practice is compiled in case histories, formulas, and prescriptions, and even medicinal wines. Regarding his therapeutic indices Dr. Valnet comments, "Like any form of treatment, aromatherapy does not claim to be effective, by itself, for every ailment, nor for every patient, nor in every circumstance. It must often be used in conjunction with other medications."

BREATHING IS NOT OPTIONAL

THE MEDICAL DIAGNOSIS OF asthma is significant, and yet I find more and more casual references for the use of essential oils as therapy for a condition that can be both debilitating and dangerous. On the other hand, we have grown up using phytotherapeutic remedies for upper respiratory infections such as Vicks VapoRub. The label contains the following description of the actions and concentrations of the phytomolecules of the essential oils used in the formula: 4.8% camphor and 2.6% menthol functioning as a cough suppressant and topical analgesic, plus 1.2% essential oil of eucalyptus as cough suppressant to calm spastic bronchioles and ease breathing. Puffs plus Vicks facial tissue retains this familiar formulation and includes essential oil of German chamomile, Martricaria recutita. The facial tissues contain bisabolol, a sesquiterpene phytomolecular constituent of chamomile, which is known in the cosmetic industry to have skin healing and anti-inflammatory properties. Asthma is a disease characterized by inflammation within the airways. Traditional breathing techniques such as qigong (pronounced chee-gung) are healing. Cultivate the good energy of qigong, which incorporates slow movement and deep breathing with meditation as a form of exercise to increase flexibility and strength and to relieve stress. Let's treat asthma and breathing airways with the respect they deserve.

SLEEP APNEA: "A NOISY AIRWAY IS AN OBSTRUCTED AIRWAY"

MY FATHER TAUGHT ME that phrase. I read an online report about treating sleep apnea syndrome using a didjeridoo. The didjeridoo is a traditional Australian Aborigine musical wind instrument. The conclusion of the study, published in the British Journal of Medicine, concluded that sleep apnea symptoms decrease with progressive use of the didjeridoo (Puhan, 2006). There is less obstructed breathing (i.e., snoring) when sleeping at night.

It is possible that this decrease is a result of the breathing exercise required by playing the instrument, which strengthens the throat muscles. I found it curious that traditionally, the didjeridoo's beeswax mouthpiece is cleaned with two essential oils, lavender and eucalyptus (species not mentioned). It is difficult to design a study in which essential oils are involved. What caused the benefit is not perfectly clear in this study, because the authors do not mention whether essential oils were used by the test or control group to clean the didjeridoo as traditionally recommended.

The results suggest a proof of principle in this work. Plausible mechanisms to explain the reversal of the sleep apnea problem suggest that, if traditional essential oils were used to clean the instrument, the oils may have acted as astringents to decongest the airways, possibly working in conjunction with the "workout" to strengthen the throat muscles. This example of a medical study making the news sounds fun and appears promising. Playing the didjeridoo might even relieve a person of having to wear a sleep apnea CPAP or BIPAP mask at night, or eliminate the need for corrective surgery. You can buy a didjeridoo online if you want one, without going to Australia.

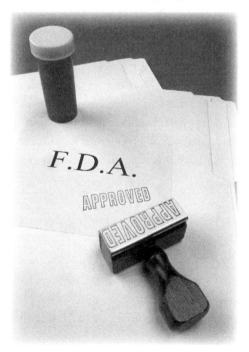

GUIDELINES AND REGULATIONS

THE FEDERAL TRADE COMMISSION (FTC) and Food and Drug Administration (FDA) work together, subdividing oversight of the labeling and advertising of products. The Dietary Supplements Health and Education Act (DSHEA) stipulates that advertising must be truthful, not misleading, and substantiated. The FTC's standards for evaluating product claims are flexible enough to allow consumer access to information about areas of emerging science. This book includes a compilation of new scientific references and third-party literature on the basic science specialities of chemistry, genetics and essential oils. The limited number of human clinical studies referenced suggests that more human research is indicated. The FDA document, an Advertising Guide for Industry provides detailed instructions and recommendations regarding making claims based on consumer testimonials or expert endorsements, as well as claims based on traditional use. A testimonial that states "results may vary" is possibly insufficient.

Traditional claims pertaining to botanical products, for example, which have a longstanding history of use for treatment of symptoms and conditions, may or may not be substantiated by scientific data. Since the FDA has not evaluated supplements, the following DSHEA disclaimer is found frequently on products and websites: "This product is not intended to diagnose, treat, cure, or prevent any disease." This statement is not a release from deceptive advertising or impure products. Traditional uses and testimonies are common place and acceptable. Significant objective scientific data substantiates the clinical use of essential oils but is a global work in progress.

INTERNET NEWS AND PRESS RELEASES

YOU CAN READ NEWS reports on the Internet from across the world for new aromatherapy and essential oil products, plus the most current scientific articles pertaining to essential oils and aromatherapy. Reading and understanding the scientific abstracts found at www.PubMed.gov, HubMed, and Google Scholar for essential oils and their phytomolecular chemical constituents can be challenging because of their intensely scientific nature. Google News Alerts that provide links to anything from head-to-toe aids to beauty remedies and testimonies describing all manner of uses of essential oils make for entertaining reading. Many products containing essential oils are based on the cosmetic arts and traditional practice of aromatherapy, while some articles describe the science of aromatherapy. It is important to find a trusted source of aromatherapy products, preferably containing therapeutic-grade essential oils.

A recent Google News Alert announced that $2.4 billion worth of essential oils are imported annually by the United States. The food chain and cosmetic industry markets many products we use daily that are manufactured using these essential oils as desensitizers, fragrances, and flavorings. Some products use synthetically manufactured oils or the extracted chemical constituents of essential oils. Commonly used oils are peppermint, spearmint, lavender, cinnamon, and eucalyptus. There are, for example, excellent natural toothpastes made with the essential oil myrrh.

For several years, on an almost daily basis, I have been reading press releases to stay informed on the latest developments for all things related to wellness and aromatherapy. Gmail can be customized to deliver Google Alerts for such keywords as "essential oils," "aromatherapy," "medical foods," "alternative medicine," "wellness," "anesthesia," or "oilMD." Make up your own Google News Alerts and subscribe to the Really Simple Syndication (RSS) news feeds on the oilMD wellness network of blogs and streaming videos to stay up-to-date (http://oilmd.wordpress.com/ or http://youtube.com/user/myoilmd).

The newsletter by Andrew Weil, MD, is an excellent example of the assimilation of allopathic, naturopathic, and homeopathic medical practices with personal health care. His Self Healing subscription newsletter has been compiled in book form. There you will find everything, including the latest ideas on the use of nutrition as medicine and essential oils, integrated in an understandable and up-to-date format.

THE SCIENCE OF NATURAL REMEDIES

IN 2005, DR. RICHARD Axel and Dr. Linda Buck were awarded the Nobel Prize in Medicine for discovering and reporting that the human genome is about 3% dedicated to smell. Humans possess over one thousand genes for smell that can identify over ten thousand odors. It would be quite possible to smell all available odors and be able to identify them by the time you die. The anatomy, physiology, and chemistry of smell represent just some of the growing body of knowledge pertaining to the basic sciences of aromatherapy. Cellular and molecular genetics are coming to the forefront of this science as well, just as they are in other fields. It is precisely this increased depth of understanding that caught my interest as a physician and provoked me to start my quest for recognition and utilization of essential oils in acute and chronic care medical and same-day surgical facilities.

NUTRIGENOMICS: PLANT GENETICS AFFECTS EXPRESSION OF HUMAN GENES

NUTRIGENOMICS IS THE STUDY of the molecular relationships between nutrition and genetic response by examining how dietary changes affect human health. Nutrigenomics defines the relationship of specific nutrients and diets to human health. Some medical specialties express growing interest in applications of nutrigenomics on the effect of nutrients on the genome, proteome, and metabolome. Nutrigenomics has been associated with the idea of personalized nutrition based on genotype. There is hope that nutrigenomics will ultimately enable such personalized dietary advice. This science is still in its infancy, but its contribution to public health will become dramatic.

The chemicals made by plants, called phytomolecules, are defined by each plant's genetic coding. Environmental factors such as light, darkness, heat, cold, exposure to toxins, and pathogens may stress and alter a plant during growth. The combination of these influential factors determines not only how a plant smells but what natural chemicals will result from distillation of plant material to yield its' essential oil. Inside the nucleus of human cells, organelles such as mitochondria generate chemical reactions with the phytomolecules of those oils, such as RNA editing, premature stop codon-mediated decay, and protein synthesis.

These phytomolecules defined by each plant's genetic code are key to the function of human physiology at the cellular level, whether ingested as food or enjoyed as aromatherapy. Our human cells are covered with portholes, gateways, and G-protein receptors that function as ionic pumps and regulators of biochemically triggered reactions governed by the phytomolecular ingredients of each plant's essential oil. Our human cellular pumps, when activated by smells and scents, induce secondary metabolic messengers that direct synthesis of specialized proteins in the nucleus of the cell that is defined by human DNA/mRNA. Smells and the essence of a plant's chemistry cause specific proteins to be made that play critical roles in human cellular physiology and health.

Common and exotic plants provide essential oils that are vital health phytosolutions and remedies. For instance, certain oils from plants direct the synthesis of immunoglobulins and other complex proteins. The aromatic vapors of the phytomolecules of ginger root oil, gingerol, and shoagol are absorbed by inhalation through mucous membranes or absorption through the skin to ease nausea. Certain pathways to the synthesis of the products of inflammation are blocked at numerous sites by plants like frankincense and ginger. Plant DNA affects human DNA, transferring the information and the energy of the oils from plants to humans.

Similar examples involving the DNA-determined phytomolecular effects of juices from plants are equally profound. Juices come from sources of berries and fruits that are exceedingly rich in antioxidants such as flavenoids, xanthones, and ligans, which, ideally, are processed in a way that retains potency. The essential juices, like those of the açaí berry and the mangosteen fruit, promote active function in cellular membranes through specialized gateways to the inner workings of the cell. The structure of the xanthones present in the juice of mangosteen, are high-energy double-bonded electron, hexagonal-shaped molecules, that functionally provide the antioxidant activity to energize effective cellular reactions that result in positive changes in body chemistry. Human studies have shown remarkable effects of juice of mangosteen and other fruits, including some of the following benefits:

• Mineral fortifed juices boost and maintain elevated antioxidant values for six hours

• Exert positive effects on T-helper immune cells and CD4/CD8 ratio

• Decrease the inflammatory biomarker C-reactive protein

• Increase interleukin-1a, specific cytokine molecules of the immune system

PHYTOMOLECULES DETERMINED BY PLANT DNA positively influence your health at the cellular level. While talking with the independent contractor I hired to repair my office computer, I learned that he had health issues. His aortic valve had been replaced in his thirties, and he suffered pain and immobility from a type of arthritis called ankylosing spondylitis. He was taking medications for pain control, but his activities of daily living were severely limited. After a trial of juices, he called to place an order for more because he felt so much better that he no longer needed the pain medications. Some weeks later he took his wife and kids out for a weekend to ride their ATVs. At one of our Health and Wealth Seminars, his wife told me, "He is a new man. I got my husband back."

PURITY AND SAFETY

THE KEY WORDS FOR juices and essential oils are purity and safety. We need to be fully informed so that we can truly consent to using self-help remedies. Essential oils are foods that are in an entirely different realm than drugs, yet there are certain goals and standards that must be reached and adhered to if we are to figure out how oils work to heal scientifically. Essential oils should be gas chromatograph-analyzed to ensure they are pure and pesticide-free. Oils are to be used in concentrations safe for particular age groups and for the intended application methods.

Essential oils are classified by the FDA as foods, not prescription medications or drugs. Therefore, aromatherapy clinical trials are not conducted with the kind of complexity as phased 1-2-3 clinical trials for FDA studies of newly proposed pharmaceutical medications. There is great cost to a pharmaceutical company for these FDA clinical medication trials, and yet the benefits to the successful company are potentially astronomical. Multi-billion-dollar medications have been marketed, and multibillion dollar failures have also passed through the system to the consumer and the courts. Clinical practices using medications, oils, juices, or other functional foods should evolve from studies that are evidence-based. It is reasonable not to overregulate to control access to essential oils, but instead to pursue data and studies that can add to our ability to care for people in an integrative fashion.

ESSENTIAL OILS IN ACTION

EARL GREY TEA IS citrus bergamot. This tea is a staple beverage in many countries. Brewed tea yields little oil droplets floating on the surface. These essential oil droplets of citrus bergamot offer a natural antidepressant effect. Patients on medications that are strongly bound to their respective drug receptors may respond differently to essential oils than people who have not taken receptor chemistry altering pharmaceuticals, perhaps with lessened therapeutic results. Evidence-based clinical claims are evaluated on the properties and effects of essential oils that are dictated by each plant's chemistry and person's medical history.

Acknowledging that essential oils are composed of various phytomolecules of numerous concentrations and chemical classifications increases our understanding that the phytomolecules from plants can affect all the organ systems of the body. Each plant's oil has varying percentages of chemical classes such as terpenes, sesquaterpenes, aldehydes, alcohols, ketones, lactones, and coumarins, which are not to be confused with the blood-thinning anticoagulant Coumadin, aka warfarin. There are notable physical effects exerted by even trace and ultra-trace percentages of essential oil phytomolecules. The essence of a plant's actual smell or primary therapeutic value may be exemplified by a tiny molecule that represents a minuscule fraction of the plant's total oil content. Each essential oil has numerous properties that cross over and add synergistic energy to another plant's oil.

A certain company had an employee who was on his feet all day, lifting heavy boxes to prepare them for shipping. He had had prior lumbar spine surgery and ankle surgery as well and used to take prescription pain medications. His back and ankle were becoming more than just aching problems; they were becoming increasingly painful the more he walked and bent over. When I met him and heard of his problems, I suggested he use some blended essential oils of basil, ginger, tea tree, myrrh, and frankincense on these sites repeatedly throughout the day to decrease the pain, inflammation, and swelling. He did so and after a few days no longer experienced the problems.

AWESOME TWOSOME: OILS AND JUICES

ESSENTIAL OILS AND JUICES can treat the signs and symptoms of conditions, such as nausea, anxiety, inflammation, arthritis, and infections caused by virus, bacteria, fungus, or parasites, in combination with other medical treatments. An abundance of laboratory and clinical evidence is available globally that verifies these functional attributes. Many specialties and subspecialties are working on various health care problems, causing intense strain upon the allopathic health care system worldwide that could benefit from the knowledge contained in essential oil and juices studies. Some of the stress on the health care system could be alleviated with elementary dietary changes that provide an abundance of essential amino acids, essential fatty acids, and essential micronutrients such as vitamins, minerals, and the phytomolecules found in essential oils and juices. Juices and oils provide significant amounts of flavenoids, such as the polyphenols that function as antioxidants. The wonderful chemistry of these entities and substrates that supply the functional building blocks and the healing energy sources for the body is awesome.

CURCUMIN (TURMERIC) FAMILY

IN AYURVEDA, GINGER IS portrayed as vishwabhesaj, or "universal medicine." The essential oil of ginger, for example, is a wonderful remedy for headaches and migraines. The Chinese have used it traditionally for male balding and as an aphrodisiac. A recent study describes using the essential oil of ginger as a method for tapering off antidepressant medications. The mechanism of action may be due in part to the serotonin neurotransmitter-receptor strengths of the sesquiterpenes found in oil of ginger. Curcuma longa (turmeric) has many medical indications; being part of the ginger family, its actions include prevention of bone loss and anti-arthritic activity, both preventing and treating rheumatoid arthritis, as reported by the University of Arizona.(http://www.turmeric-curcumin.com/curcumin.html).

My neighbor commented after his knee replacement surgery that he had reached a plateau in his range-of-motion rehabilitation exercises. I suggested that he massage his knee with a blend of essential oils of ginger, rosemary, orange, and grapefruit prior to each workout at the physical therapy center. Within a few visits he pulled me aside to mention that he had a remarkable increase of 20% more range of motion in his knee. His therapist and doctor were impressed by the results, and he was grateful because the swelling and roughness of his scar had subsided as well.

Oil of clove is high in phenolic content, which has antimicrobial, antiemetic (preventing nausea and vomiting), and analgesic properties. Certainly everybody has heard of or even applied clove oil to the gums to obtain relief from a painful tooth. Both turmeric and black pepper inhibits substance P, which is a mediator of pain in the central nervous system. A top-quality Japanese study showed that stroke victims, when exposed to essential oil of pepper by nasal inhalation of the oil's vapors, recovered enough that they could safely swallow liquids and foods without aspirating them into their lungs (Ebihara, 2006). Essential oil of pepper is both anti-inflammatory and analgesic because it is composed of large quantities of high-energy terpenes and sesquiterpenes phytomolecules.

SIGNATURES OF PLANTS

PLANTS ARE UNIQUELY QUALIFIED by their signature shapes to show us how they can help the organs of the human body. Walnuts look like the brain and when shelled intact even have a bridge between the two "cerebral" hemispheres. Walnuts contain neurotransmitters and the omega-3 fatty acids to augment brain function. The root of ginger looks like the intestines and works well on disorders causing gastrointestinal distress. The tomato is divided into chambers like the heart and is low in sodium and high in potassium for integrity of cardiac rhythm. Clusters of grapes are likened to a rolleux (stack of coins) of blood cells facilitating oxygenation with resveratrol.

Eggplant and avocados have phytomolecules targeting the uterus and cervix. Olives are like ovaries, and figs are full of seeds for motility of sperm cells. Celery, rhubarb, and bok choy are rich in minerals and look like long bones. The citrus family, oranges, and grapefruit are likened to breasts and contribute to the health of fat and lymphatic tissues. Carrots sliced in the round could be the eyes, complete with pupil and iris, providing carotene nutrients for vision. The phytomolecules of plants are therapeutic to our organs. Now you can look at a plant differently and consider which organ system it might benefit as a medicinal food.

It is important to know the genus and species of plants as well as the physicality of plants. The various physical properties of plants, such as potencies and actions of essential oils, are determined by where and how the plants are grown. Physicality and species specificity determines the percentages of the phytomolecular constituents present in an essential oil.

For example, the various species of lavender have differing actions. Awareness of this difference is critical when utilizing aromatherapy for the pediatric population. Not just any amount or type of lavender oil may be applied to infants and children. Different lavender species can either act as sedatives or stimulants. It is important to recognize the sensitivity and specificity of babies and children when it comes to aromatherapy remedies. Aster Elliot, author of Raising Children Well with Aromatherapy, offers excellent information with custom essential oil blends for those special little people in our lives.

Wild-crafted oils are perhaps easier to find in some instances than organic essential oils, but all essential oils should be pesticide-free and therapeutic-grade. Finding pesticide free oils from citrus is most difficult, because the processing of citrus oils may not remove the pesticides and pollutants. In a similar vein, plants that produce carrier oils used for cooking, such as olives and grapeseed, may have been sprayed with pesticides or may come from processing facilities that have not tested for pesticides.

Research abstracts suggest that rosemary is great for memory and attention disorders. Lemongrass oil has mixed isoprenoid content so that it works like the same enzyme in statin medications work, suppressing hydroxyl-methylglutaryl co-enzyme-A (HMG-CoA) synthesis to lower cholesterol (Elson, 1989). The same class of isoprenoid compounds found in essential oils mediates an inhibition of the mevalonate synthesis pathway that has other cardiovascular and cancer chemopreventative applications. Geranium oil works as an analgesic, mosquito repellent, and antiviral against the herpes zoster virus. Oils of melaluka and sandalwood are significantly antiviral in vitro in all four stages of herpes virus replication (Koch, 2008).

MOSQUITO PESTS

THE FDA RECENTLY APPROVED oil of lemon eucalyptus as a DEET mosquito repellent equivalent in order to control mosquitoes and, conceivably, the West Nile virus. Essential oils tested against many species of mosquitoes have been found to be effective deterrents to landing and biting on humans and animals. Once stung by a mosquito or other insect, oil of Lavandula angustifolia eases the itch of the bite. There are many commercial avenues to pursue in this discussion of essential oils and synthetic chemical mosquito deterrents found in common over-the-counter and household products. The global impact of illness due to malaria is significant but is less injurious now that mosquito nets have been provided to those at risk. The Global Fund, which received a half-billion dollar grant from the Bill and Melinda Gates Foundation, has undertaken a program distributing pesticide-impregnated mosquito nets in Africa, in conjunction with the Global Alliance for Vaccines and Immunizations program. The Gates Foundation Malaria Forum to control malaria could include programs that create local agricultural production of the essential oil of the lemon eucalyptus with its active ingredient, p-methane-3,8-diol, which wards off the mosquito pest to benefit local health and local market share (Carroll, 2006).

IDEAL SCENTS KEY POINTS

The aromatherapy practice of using essential oils extracted from plants for health issues resonates with the logical rationale for their prowess and beauty as ideal scents. Ideal scents have traditional and scientific benefits that promote and ensure health, such as the following:

- Essential oils are unlike medications and narcotics in particular. The acquired tolerance to narcotic drugs to produce pain relief does not occur with essential oils. Many essential oils have analgesic properties orchestrated through mechanisms such as inhibition of the products of inflammation and blocking of the neuropeptide substance P.

- Essential oils have no glycemic index value since they are volatile aromatic organic chemical compounds. Essential oils are used in foods as flavorings and fragrances in the range of 30 parts per million (ppm), which is exceedingly small at 3 to 5 calories per gram.

- Essential oils are not sugars or fats, as opposed to foods that may have hundreds of calories per ounce and therefore have virtually no caloric value. A typical aromatherapy treatment that uses 5 to 10 drops of essential oil is of virtually no direct caloric consequence. Carrier oil used in an aromatherapy treatment does have minimal caloric value.

- Essential oils are rich in high-energy, double-bonded electron molecules, and as such are exceedingly high in oxygen radical absorbance capacity (ORAC) value to scavenge the free radicals associated with diseases and aging.

AS WE MOVE FORWARD in the twenty-first century, many people of all walks of life are learning about the wonderful art and solid science of aromatherapy. This knowledge has increased clinical usage and marketing of essential oils. Develop your knowledge and practice of the art and science of aromatherapy. Enjoy the benefits of ideal scents everywhere. Home, spa, gym, work, kiosk, place of worship, or businesses such as the hospital, surgery center, chiropractic and dental office, or cosmetology shop are all open sources to explore with ideal scents.

CHAPTER

Medical Aromatherapy
in the 21st Century

"The subject of clinical aromatherapy is vast and will be of interest to nurses and physicians, chiropractors and massage therapists, pharmacists and naturopaths, pharmaceutical companies and herbalists."

—Mehmet Oz, M.D. Cardiac Surgeon author of
You on a Diet and You the Owner's Manual

five

CHAPTER

MEDICAL AROMATHERAPY
IN THE TWENTY-FIRST CENTURY

SMELL IS A LEARNED PROCESS shaped by the associations of thought with language, experiences, neurogenesis, and genetics (Geiger, 2004). Medical aromatherapy with therapeutic-grade essential oils is one element of holistic healing expressed in the practice of integrative medicine. In this context, essential oils are the concentrated distillations of volatile aromatic compounds extracted from plants to yield apothecary-like compounds used to promote health and wellness as part of the vast field of complementary alternative medicine (CAM).

EVIDENCE-BASED AROMATICS

THE WORD ESSENTIAL, WHEN discussing extracted oils from plants, refers to the aromatic, fragrant, adaptogenic, and phytomolecular essence of plants. Embodied in the chemical constituents found in these plant distillates are the energy and informational building blocks that produce complex emotional and intricate physiological effects in humans and animals. The essential oil used in medical aromatherapy in the twenty-first century is pure therapeutic-grade, noted for medicinal properties that do not produce tolerance, have virtually no glycemic index value, and are exceedingly high in ORAC value to scavenge free radicals associated with disease and aging.

THE MOLECULAR BIOLOGY OF DISEASE

OUR BIOLOGICAL UNDERSTANDING OF the intracellular molecular events evoked from clinical applications of essential oils is growing. Essential oil phytomolecules impact intracellular synthesis pathways. The NF-kappa B (NF-KB) transcription factor regulates many genes that permit cells to respond to infection and inflammation. The inflammatory protein NF-KB product expression is inhibited by sesquiterpenes, compounds that are commonly present in essential oils (Tipton, 2006). The dreaded Trypanosoma cruzi of South America that causes Chagas cardiac disease is killed in vitro by the thymols present in essential oil of thyme (Santoro, 2006). Clinically, topically applied essential oil phytomolecules have been used to treat the inflammation and malodorous ulcerated lesions of diabetic gangrene and cancer, while promoting growth of new skin (Sherry, 2003, 2005). Oil of pepper (Piper nigra) enabled stroke patients with swallowing difficulties to swallow and resume eating, thus limiting the mortality and morbidities of aspiration and malnutrition (Ebihara, 2006).

Essential oils act as neurotransmitters exerting end-organ effects, which are becoming clearer over time, narrowing the gap between mind and body. Knowing and applying essential oils clinically is exciting and helpful. The brain responds differently to each class of phytomolecules, such as the phenylpropanoid molecules of ylang ylang, jasmine, vanilla, and the terpenes of the more aromatic essential oils. These positively impact brain chemistry. Chemist and author of Medical Aromatherapy, Kurt Schnaubelt, PhD, is the founder of the Pacific Institute of Aromatherapy. He provides remarkable insight into essential oil research, fabulously innovative products, and superb seminars and tours of the lavender-producing regions of France.

BLOCKING INFLAMMATORY PATHWAYS

"PRESCRIPTIONS" OF ESSENTIAL OILS, herbal medicines, and drugs should be dispensed with knowledge of a person's preexisting medical conditions and evidenced-based clinical information. Essential oils have crossover properties and therefore multiple clinical areas of application and interaction. For instance, oils of ginger, helichrysum, and frankincense are true dual inhibitors of inflammation, blocking enzymatic synthesis of both LOX and COX1-2 pathways from synthesizing proinflammatory mediators like leukotriene B4 and thromboxane. These essential oils are also true inhibitors of oxidation, blocking the pathway to formation of free radical reactive oxidative species, like F2-isoprostanes. Limbrel (flavocoxid), the new nutraceutical indicated for treatment of osteoarthritis, is derived from the bark and roots of specific plants that provide dual anti-inflammatory properties for pain relief.

The potential for complications from the herb-drug interactions between traditional Chinese medicine (TCM) and anesthesia was studied in "Herbal Medicines and Perioperative Care." (Lee, 2006). This study verifies the relative safety of ginger among surgical patients in regard to blood coagulation parameters such as platelet aggregation and international normal ratios, and INR values (Lee, 2006). The overall morbidity due to interactions between TCM prescriptions and anesthesia was negligible. However, a two-week hiatus from all TCM prescriptions and herbals was recommended prior to surgery based on rare but possible minor interactions.

INTRODUCTION TO CANCER

THE CAUSES OF CANCER are multifactorial. Three of the cancer-causing viruses in humans noted by the U.S. Department of Health are hepatitis B, hepatitis C, and human papillomavirus. The mechanism of chronic inflammation leading to cellular hyperproliferation that then leads to replacement of damaged tissue contributes to the development of infection-associated cancers of the colon, stomach, bladder, and liver (Cousins, 2002). The oxidant stresses of inflammation caused by infections that lead to cellular malignant degeneration are responsible for a number of human cancers, not just viral-induced cancers.

Chronic infection leading to chronic inflammation, coupled with inherited defects and acquired cellular defense defects against infection and oxidative stress causes cancer of prostate (Klein, 2006). Lycopene, zinc, and saw palmetto are only isolated supplements of indeterminate effectiveness against prostatic hypertrophy and cancer. On the other hand, broad-spectrum antioxidants of superior potency, like that of pomegranate juice, may well prove the best avenue of prevention and possibly an adjunct to treatment because the deleterious effects of oxidative stress are so pronounced.

CELLULAR DEFENSE MECHANISMS

DNA DAMAGE FROM BOTH endogenous (inside) and exogenous (outside) sources caused by oxidative stresses is implicated in the accumulation of injury to DNA that coexists with the aging process and progresses toward various malignancies. Oxidative stresses are mediated by both reactive oxygen species and reactive nitrogen species that bind to DNA, causing mutational consequences that are transcribed ultimately into the DNA-derived cancer cells. Human cellular defense mechanisms against these processes are numerous but not effective enough, unless provided with significant folic acid and antioxidant-carrying capacity to scavenge the large quantities of ROS and RNS generated by oxidative stresses induced by infection, inflammation, exercise, and high altitude. If not repairable, cellular defenses "enable" the cell to undergo apoptosis, or cell death, if the DNA damage is too severe. Proper nutritional building blocks from functional foods and supplements are required to make adequate repairs of damaged DNA.

Carbon dioxide distilled oil of ginger (Zingiber officinale Roscoe, Zingiberaceae) contains potent phytomolecules, as [6]-gingerol and [6]-paradol, which also have antitumor promotional and antiproliferative effects. Resveratrol (3, 5, 4'-trihydroxy-trans-stilbene), a phytoalexin found in grapes, creates a longevity-inducing metabolic environment of caloric restriction. Resveratrol and epigallocatechin gallate, a major antioxidative green tea polyphenol, exert striking inhibitory effects on diverse cellular events associated with multistage carcinogenesis. In addition, these phytomolecules have the ability to suppress proliferation of human cancer cells via induction of cell death (Surh, 1999).

CHAMPIONS OF THE CAUSE

NICCOLO MACHIAVELLI, 1469–1527, propounded moral leadership and political treatises for the welfare of people. His precepts implied pushing directly against or indirectly toward that which one is opposing in an effort to win. Some accomplishments are attributable to this manner of creation. To increase the results of our efforts to further expand the availability of essential oils into such traditional medical settings as hospitals, surgi-centers and schools, we operate by other principles pertaining to the laws of the universe, in particular the law of attraction. We want to create a system of health that supplies all the best venues and modalities of prevention and remedy, offering the ultimate in quality of health and wellness for all. Essential oils from plants are positioned in the most vital section of our universe.

Providing professional aromatherapy services requires an enlightened approach applying detailed situational awareness. It is mandatory to define the intended program model and position within each chosen medical system, as it pertains to services and departments impacted. The principles of integrative medicine imply a partnership of consent between patient, provider, and institution. Since hospitals require substantial legal documentation, the entrance of essential oils into this rigorous setting of acute medical care requires an understanding of hospital policies and procedures. Specialized committees in health care facilities must be educated about aromatherapy and other complementary modalities, so they can vote to allow their inclusion into clinical practice.

Each hospital committee, including medical staff, pharmacy, formulary, anesthesia, and executive, will absolutely require assurance of adherence to specific policies and procedures and regulatory guidelines as well as to corporate philosophy. Physicians, nurses, and administrators who will help champion the cause by lobbying and making presentations to committees for approval of the proposed services must be found. That includes identifying quality service providers to be on staff, which may necessitate credentialing allied health professionals as independent contractors. Defining the financial ramifications of services, such as forecasted expenses, earnings, billing processes, and potential for obtaining grants and access to gratuities is imperative. The allied health professionals' scope of practice should be defined ("license to touch") within well-thought-out policy and procedures guidelines. Design of informed consent, policy and procedure, and Health Insurance Portability and Accountability Act (HIPAA) documents will require draft review and approval as well.

THE RIGHT QUESTIONS SHOULD be asked and answered, specific to each facility, defining such topics as:

- How will the use of oils or any CAM be documented in the medical records?

- Who can initiate a request for an aromatherapy consultation?

- Can a registered nurse initiate a request for an aromatherapy consultation based on a preexisting diagnosis?

- Does an essential oil belong on a medical or diet sheet of the patient's medical chart?

- Should the medical record progress notes contain an entry regarding aromatherapy consult and diagnosis, and an action plan regarding the prescribed essential oils?

ALL PARTIES NEED TO be aware of the 1994 Chemical Information and Packaging and Control of Substances Hazardous to Health regulations, noting their provisions for the management and handling of essential oils (e.g., "toxic spill"). Material safety data sheets (MSDS) for each essential oil should be on file in the pharmacy formulary. If clinical studies are to be undertaken, the investigational review board (must be consulted and its recommendations adhered to, since Medicare payments and federal funding are intimately interwoven with regulations pertaining to scientific studies.

PROOF OF PRINCIPLE

GINGER IS A FOOD, and as such, has been used in many forms as a traditional remedy. Powdered ginger (i.e., oil-depleted ginger) has been shown to reduce morning sickness in pregnant women and to have varying degrees of success treating postoperative nausea and vomiting (PONV) during laparoscopic gynecological surgical procedures that are high risk for PONV. Obstetrics-gynecology journal articles in the last several years have verified the safety and efficacy of ginger during pregnancy (Smith et al., 2004).

Oil of ginger is a fine example of an essential oil that currently has proof of principle established, and moreover, serves as an example of the successful entry of essential oil of ginger into surgical preop and anesthesia recovery in surgery centers and hospitals to decrease the incidence of PONV. Application of 10% carbon dioxide-distilled essential oil of ginger root to the palms, wrists, soles, ears, and in the oxygen face-mask reduces the ill effects of anesthesia, as well as patient anxiety. The inhalation and dermal application of ginger oil in general anesthesia patients, combined with the use of guided imagery, showed a more than 30% decrease in the incidence of nausea in patients at high risk for nausea during recovery from anesthesia.

Adverse events and side effects can be associated with standard intravenous medications given to prevent and treat nausea and vomiting. All drugs have a known incidence of side effects. The commonly administered antinausea drug ondansetron (Zofran) has a 10% incidence of headaches. The FDA has established a special "black box" alert for the medication droperidol, due to the possibility of significant side effects, such as mild confusion, dysphoria, headache, tics, torticolis, serotonin syndrome, neuroleptic malignant syndrome, alterations in blood pressure, and cardiac rhythm disturbances. Use of oil of ginger routinely with anesthesia would save significant health care dollars and decrease the rate of adverse drug reactions.

Prophylaxis with ginger increases patient satisfaction significantly, is very inexpensive, extremely low risk, and potentially of use in procedural situations that might induce vaso-vagal or gastrointestinal distress such as bowel preparations, endoscopy, and decreasing gag reflex during dental procedures. The mind does control outcomes, so it is very difficult to design and implement a scientific study that controls for the vast effects of the mind on the body. Aromatherapy research is equally challenging to accomplish, because the scents of essential oils are so quickly recognizable. The oil of ginger treatment series presented in chapter 7 shows the proof of principle, plus considerations for control and treatment group parameters on which to base further investigations.

ESSENTIAL OILS ARE GENERALLY REGARDED AS SAFE

THE ESSENTIAL OILS OF spices are used for cooking, just as any other generally regarded as safe (GRAS) essential oil for human consumption. The list of GRAS essential oils is available in Section 21CFR182.20 of the Federal Code of Regulations. A good guideline for cooking is one drop of essential oil for each teaspoon of dry spice in a recipe. The Complete Book of Essential Oils, by Valerie Worwood, has a fine chapter on cooking with essential oils. Labeling for cooking oils is different than aromatherapy. Note that black pepper oil does not contain piperine, so it lacks the "pepper bite." Essential oil of black pepper when diffused has been shown to reverse the paralysis of swallowing defects secondary to stroke. Essential oil of black pepper also blocks substance P, which is a mediator of painful sensations pathways. Oils from herbs such as peppermint and spearmint are very commonly used in the fragrances and flavorings industry.

The fragrances and flavorings industry synthesizes tastes and smells for a worldwide market of products, utilizing essential oils and the phytomolecular chemical constituents of essential oils from plants. Since essential oils are classified by the FDA as foods, many of these oils and forms of them have been incorporated into our food and household product chain extensively for years. Research undertaken by the Research Institute for Fragrance Materials studies and documents the effects of these natural and synthetic additives while investigating how to keep them safe for human consumption.

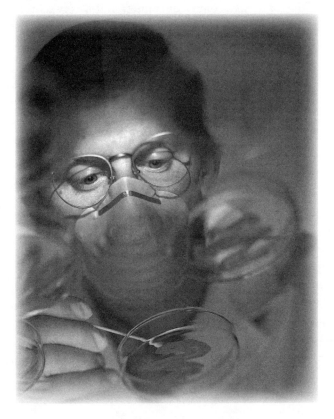

TEA TREE OIL

IN A RECENT CLINICAL research study of drug-resistant infectious diseases, the progressive change in incidence from hospital-acquired methicillin-resistant Staphylococcus aureus (MRSA) to greater than 75% community-acquired MRSA is alarming (Moran, 2006). MRSA is one of the "super bugs" you hear of these days on news reports. The terpinen-4-ol molecule present in tea tree oil kills Staphylococcus better than six known antibiotics, including the top guns vancomycin and methicillin in vitro (Ferrini, 2006). Osteoset, an orthopedic bone cement product, contains tea tree oil and has successfully treated osteomyelitis due to MRSA (Sherry et al., 2001). Tea tree oil kills multidrug-resistant (MDR) melanoma cells in vitro (Calcabrini et al., 2004). These findings suggest that the clinical use, as well as prophylactic applications, of tea tree oil could be considered.

TEA TREE EDITORIAL

THE FOLLOWING EDITORIAL STATEMENT by Robert Tisserand, author of Essential Oil Safety, titled "Neither Lavender Oil nor Tea Tree Oil Can Be Linked to Breast Growth in Young Boys," is quite clear. The report states: Breast growth in pre-pubertal boys is extremely uncommon, yet three cases are reported within a short period of time, and all in the same clinic. Considering that some 200 tons per annum are produced of both lavender and tea tree oil, that most of this goes into personal care products, and that very little of the evidence presented for these three cases is convincing, the press reports of caution are premature. Even if one or more of these cases was linked to product use, any connection with either lavender or tea tree oil is unproven. Other known endocrine-disrupting ingredients in the products could have played a role. Furthermore, we do not know what other factors, such as dietary or environmental, may have played a part.

The in vitro work reported by Henley et al. (2007) does indicate a hormonal effect. However, this cannot be extrapolated to estimate actual human risk, especially without knowing more about the essential oil constituents causing the in vitro effects seen. No connection was established between the in vitro work and the three cases, and the case for tea tree oil having an effect on pre-pubertal gynecomastia is especially weak. Phytoestrogens generally have a very weak hormonal activity, and it is implausible that the amounts of essential oil that enter the body from product use would have a significant effect. Further research will hopefully clarify these issues.

VIBRATIONALIST AND SHAPIST THEORIES

THERE ARE MANY THEORIES of how essential oils actually promote healing in the body. Some theories suggest that the shape of the odorant molecules causes their effects because receptor binding is determined by shape of the hydrocarbon phytomolecular structures. These phytomolecules often have special-interest chemical groups hanging off the sides to identify them and make them each conformationally different. The special-interest groups confer special chemical configurations and the shapes of the implied "shapist" theory. The shapist theory proposes molecular binding in a lock and key form as the odorant literally "plugs into" a receptor and blocks (antagonizes) or stimulates (agonizes) further pathways of chemical reactions.

There is also a "vibrationalist" theory of smell. All molecules vibrate because everything consists of moving atoms. Every essential oil phytomolecule vibrates with atomic energy. Whichever theory applies, shapist or vibrationalist, receptor binding of oil molecules on odorant receptor sites influences chemical chain reactions.

Energy medicine is a fantastically growing new specialty. The vibrationalist theory of molecules determined by the electrical energy of electrons is very attractive. High-energy chemical bonds on hydrocarbon molecules, such as double-bonded terpenes and aromatic sesquaterpenes, are rich in energy comprised of constantly vibrating and vibrant electrons. Essential oils carry "energy" with them as they enter into the body and deliver energy-generating electrons to the major energy pathways in the body. These pathways to intracellular chemical synthesis direct the information and energy from a plant's genome of chlorophyll in chloroplasts and reaches out to human mitochondria and the human genome, making proteins on ribosomes in the nucleus of each human cell. Whether shapist theory or vibrationalist theory, the transfer of energy and information is ultimately expressed through receptor chemistry.

The theories of smell used to explain the transduction of smell information (i.e., how smell is actually moved from the original vapor of a scent into a new and internalized chemical that is passed along nerves as chemical neurotransmitters into the brain). Both shapist and vibrationalist camps still have to present the same data to the brain for interpretation. The scent and the information must cross cell membranes at various stages. The olfactory bulbs of the paired cranial nerves in the brain have two types of receptors, which are well-known to anesthesiologists and scientists: NMDA and GABA.

FROM THEORY TO RELIEF

PAIN IS MEDIATED THROUGH the N-methyl-D asparate (NMDA) receptors. Sedation and anesthesia are mediated through the gamma-aminobutyric acid (GABA) receptors located in the same smell portion of the nose. The benzodiazepines (e.g., midazolam and certain aromatic gases) work through GABA receptors causing sedation and relief of anxiety and amnesia. Patients almost always receive the benzodiazepine drug midazolam intravenously, before entering into any surgery or medical procedure.

The NMDA pain and psychometric receptors are stimulated or blocked by medications such as dextromethorphan and amantadine (Namenda). Essential oils are also suggested to be instrumental in diseases such as dementia and Alzheimer's. Melissa officinalis (lemon balm) and lavender has been described as an effective treatment in the management of severe, agitated dementia (Holmes, 2002; Ballard, 2002).

Certain properties of olfaction make it unique among the five senses: There are several types of odor recognition memory. There is background elimination, which can be a good thing. When you drive past a cow pasture, you would probably prefer the smell a women's perfume, which would hopefully eliminate the background scent. Component separation determines how you can identify and distinguish that any given odor has a higher concentration of one scent over another. Odor separation allows discrimination of scents; you can tell that both turkey and pie are baking at the same time.

Cranial nerve 1, which is embedded in the base of the frontal lobes of the brain, is engulfed in a rich vasculolymphatic plexus, vasculo meaning "vascular," and plexus meaning that they are all intertwined, forming a network of tissues. These highly vascular sites, where lymphatic tissues and nervous tissues all meet, become saturated with the inhaled, vaporized scents of fragrances that are then absorbed into the bloodstream and cross cell membranes to thoroughly engulf the brain in the phytomolecules of inhaled scents.

MESSENGER OILS AND SECONDARY METABOLITES

THE THALAMUS, WHICH SITS In the midst of the brain's limbic system, receives and sends scent-derived neurotransmitter-oriented messages that are initiated by essential oils. These secondary chemical impressions are propagated as a vapor from an oil of a plant. They arrive into the nose and traverse the cribiform plate, converted from a vapor chemical scent into a neurological chemical transmitting informational data. This phytomolecular information rushes into the brain along a series of neuronal pathways, perhaps evoking a memory or releasing peptides into the bloodstream from the hypothalamus. The newly released peptides flow to the reticular formation of the midbrain, which is the "going shopping" part of the human brain. Advertisers want to understand and influence this portion of the brain in order to increase sales of merchandise. This fantastically intricate and integrated nervous system is intimately linked all the way from the olfactory bulbs embedded underneath the temporal lobes of the brain to every cell in your body. The ideal scents of life instigate a multitude of measurable physiological and psychological responses.

Essential oils are known to work within the central nervous system (CNS) to stimulate or relax it via the components of the sympathetic nervous system (SNS) or parasympathetic nervous system (PNS). Consider ylang ylang, the so-called "harmonizer" oil. This oil has curious simultaneous effects of provoking increased mental awareness while enhancing a profound sense of relaxation. Essential oils can be exceptional for obtaining relief during certain high-stress situations, such as taking an exam or performing in a symphony, where beta-blockers such as propranolol were once prescribed.

The glycoproteins (G-proteins) on cell surfaces of mitral cells in the nose that are associated with smell are also found as anatomical structures of the other five senses. Vision has its own unique G-proteins. There is something else unique and wonderful about the olfactory nervous cells that cover the first cranial nerve in the brain: They are potent stem cells. When they are experimentally harvested, cultured, and placed intrathecally (surgically, in the spine), regeneration of the central nervous system begins, partially restoring previously lost sensory and motor ability.

ESSENTIAL OILS AND SLEEP

EVERY BODY CRAVES SLEEP. Sleep rejuvenates the body-mind connection. Sleep has very complex neurological, hormonal, and chemical physiology. The sleep hormone melatonin works on GABA receptors. There are specialists, often pulmonologists, who operate sleep laboratories to determine if insomnia and other sleep disturbances are associated with cessation of breathing during sleep (sleep apnea). Electroencephalogram (EEG) studies have shown that human brain waves are altered by various essential oils in differing patterns during sleep and wake states, as well as when experiencing pain, which can make it impossible to sleep.

National Institutes of Health (NIH) statistics show that 100 million people complain of insomnia, costing the nation $150 billion annually. The combination of direct costs, such as medications, and indirect costs due to accidents and absenteeism make insomnia one of the nation's most costly conditions. It often goes undiagnosed and untreated. Insomnia is an independent risk factor in diabetics and in men aged 48 to 65 with coronary artery disease.

CIRCADIAN RHYTHM SYNCHRONIZATION

MOST HUMAN CLOCK GENES are regulated by the hormone melatonin, produced by the pineal gland in the brain during the night. Melatonin is a natural hormone that regulates the sleep-wake cycle. Melatonin once synthesized is released into the bloodstream and acts on cells through glycoproteins (G-proteins) and later is degraded in the liver along genetically determined cytochrome P450 enzymatic pathways. Certain plants, such as valerian and tomatoes, contain the largest amount of the phytohormone melatonin. Valerian synergizes with anesthesia and should be avoided prior to surgery since it works through the 5-hydroxytryptophan (5-HT) receptor to promote sleep. Currently, the only melatonin drug on the market approved by the FDA for insomnia is ramelteon (Rozerem).

People respond to drugs and chemicals differently at varying times of the day, due to the chemical circadian rhythm of hormonally mediated neuroendocrine responses. Essential oils can be consumed to enhance and synchronize the biorhythm of the body. Brain hormones such as melatonin and serotonin have definite receptor-driven interactions with certain chemical components found in essential oils. Essential oils that are known stimulants of the central nervous system, such as pepper and grapefruit, cause a twofold increase in sympathetic activity and probably should not be used prior to naptime or bedtime. The essential oils that have stimulating properties can be readily used as a pick-me-up in the late afternoon or as a natural exercise or sports performance enhancer.

Certain other oils calm and relax the nervous system. Rose and patchouli oils cause a 30% decrease in sympathetic activity. Rose oil also has anticonflict and antianxiety properties. Sleep chemistry is cyclic and is readily disrupted by events or medical conditions like sleep apnea, which is often associated with obesity. Certain essential oils act as astringents and decongestants that may shrink the mucosal membranes to clear air passages while relaxing the nervous system for a restful sleep.

ESSENTIAL OILS IN THE SLEEP LABORATORY

THERE ARE OLFACTORY AND circadian rhythm experiments done on humans and rats that are somewhat informative, although the folklore of aromatherapy and sleep far exceeds the scientific research. Dr. N. Goel published a concise human study in Chronobiology International stating that essential oil of Lavandula angustifolia increased the percentage of deep and restorative slow-wave sleep in men and women. All subjects reported more morning vigor. Oil of lavender had opposite effects in men and women in terms of how long it took to reach a wakened state after falling asleep.

Different essential oils have different effects on sleep patterns in men, women, and animals. Therefore, choosing a particular essential oil as a sleep aid is difficult. The inhaled essence of essential oil of cedar in humans significantly shortened the daytime napping nonrapid eye movement stage 2 sleep latency. The shortened napping cycle could possibly be due to the stimulation of neural or humoral mechanisms in humans by the cedrol in the essential oil of cedar. The cedar oil had the opposite effect in rats, as noted in the Journal of Psychiatry Clinical Neuroscience (Sano, 1998). Valerian blocks gamma-aminobutyric acid transaminase, thus enhancing GABA subreceptor activity and promoting sleep. Lemon may worsen insomnia, as reported by in an article in Chemical Senses titled "The Sleep-Enhancing Effect of Valerian Inhalation and the Sleep-Shortening Effect of Lemon Inhalation" (Komori et al., 2006).

Essential oils can have specific stimulating or inhibiting effects on the parasympathetic and sympathetic nervous systems of the human body that together form the autonomic nervous system. Essential oil of rose, for example, decreases adrenal cortisol release, which is a sympathetic response to stress, by greater than 30% (Haze, 2002). In other words, you become greatly relaxed because your body is not excited in a sympathetic manner by reactions to worry and fears that may be a significant contribution to the causes of insomnia.

Insomnia is an individual experience just as any remedy or treatment by prescription is an experiment on the individual. Testing different essential oils in different fashions may provide a natural solution to obtain better sleep. At bedtime less essential aroma is better. A strong concentration of any aroma can be stimulating, just as loud music played when attempting to go to sleep can keep you awake. Experiment to find your ideal scent for sleep by using an oil of choice on a cotton ball placed under the pillow, diffused throughout the room, diluted in an atomizer of water "spritzed" as a hydrosol on the body, or massaged on the reflexology points under the big toes.

The following essential oils have been suggested to be safe sleep aids: bergamot, Lavandula angustifolia, Ravensara aromatica, mandarin, neroli, sweet orange, Melissa officinalis, sandalwood, roman chamomile, and valerian.

ESSENTIAL OILS AND APPETITE

THERE ARE SIX BASIC "diet disconnects," or misconceptions due to numerous and often overwhelming dietary practices and information. These disconnects are calories, exercise, breakfast, fats, carbohydrates, and functional foods. Basically, Americans do not eat the right number of calories or participate regularly in exercise. Few start their day with a nutritious breakfast, and most are still consuming unhealthy amounts of trans fats, unaware of which carbohydrates are good for them and which are not. The vast majority do not thoughtfully consume foods designed for heart health. These findings by the International Food Information Council (IFIC) highlight the gaps in dietary knowledge and willpower application. The message expressed by IFIC to Americans is that balance is essential, and gradual improvements in diet and exercise behavior bring positive results.

The neuroendocrine regulatory power on hunger is complex and redundant. The stress hormone cortisol, which influences blood sugar levels, is decreased in saliva by smelling lavender and rosemary oils, while increasing salivary free radical scavenging activity. Some oils may actually stimulate appetite and may increase nighttime eating habits associated with obesity, while other oils, such as grapefruit oil, can hormonally inhibit appetite and make women look seven years younger. The scent of grapefruit elevates plasma glycerol via autonomic neurotransmission causing lipolysis. Scent of lavender has the opposite effect on plasma glycerol.

Oils high in terpenoid compounds help regulate irritating symptoms of neuroendocrine imbalance, which members of modern society are prone to exhibit in the form of restlessness, anxiety, headaches, migraines, circulatory insufficiencies, and temperature sensitivity. This neuroendocrine imbalance can be caused by stress, whether related to lifestyle or oxidatively induced. Rats with high blood pressure and insulin insensitivity that used various blends of essential oils, "Effects of a Novel Formulation of Essential Oil on Glucose-Insulin Metabolism in Diabetic Hypertensive Rats: A Pilot Study," showed that both lower blood pressure and increased insulin sensitivity could be achieved with essential oils (Talpur, 2005). The blend with the best results contained oregano, fenugreek, cumin, and myrtle. Pumpkinseed oil and extra virgin olive oil were used as carrier oils to dilute and deliver the essential oils. Two other blends containing cinnamon, fennel, and ginger were also effective in lowering blood pressure and improving glucose tolerance.

CRITICAL CAVEATS OF ESSENTIAL OILS

GENERALLY REGARDED AS SAFE, (GRAS) ESSENTIAL OILS ARE listed in books as well as online. Essential oils that have significant benefits and are used in products are not on the GRAS list. There are potential toxicology-related issues associated with specific chemical components of specific essential oils. Oils containing more than 5% methylsalicylates, such as wintergreen and birch, should have child-safety caps. There have been records of wrongful ingestion of essential oils, but these are very rare and isolated medical cases. These case reports are much less frequent in comparison to medical drug errors of wrongful drug administration or adverse drug reactions.

Sense of smell can be affected by medications or vitamin deficiency, causing a loss of sense of smell known as anosmia. All classes of medications from A to Z, whether they are antibiotics, anti-inflammatory agents, anti-Parkinsonian drugs, antihistamines, antidepressants, or anticonvulsants (These are just some of the drug families starting with the first letter of the alphabet.) can cause anosmia. It is noteworthy that vitamin A deficiency is a leading cause of loss of sense of smell, though this is reversible with supplementation of vitamin A.

Some oils are light-sensitive and can cause pigmentation of the skin after exposure to the sun. Therefore, certain oils, such as lemon, should not be worn on skin exposed to direct sunlight within a certain time frame, even as long as six to twelve hours. Those oils with high phenol content, such as clove oil, can cause contact dermatitis, sensitivity, or irritation, especially if you work in them constantly. For example, there are a few reports of workers in the essential oils industry, such as perfumers and aromatherapists, who developed contact dermatitis from constant exposure to concentrated tea tree oil. You can perform a personal skin test using the patch test technique, which is helpful to determine if you could have an adverse reaction to any given product or oil. Take a 1% dilution and apply the solution to the skin. Observe over six to twelve hours to evaluate the response.

The industry giants Research Institute of Fragrance Materials and International Fragrance Association work to ensure that the following criteria are met when analyzing materials actually used in the industry: Specimens are submitted with the name and identification number, and must be accompanied by gas-chromatographic analysis as a means of identification. Screening parameters include allergy and phototoxic testing, plus general toxicity by both oral and dermal routes. Dermal testing for irritant and allergy testing of the concentration of the materials is at ten times the maximum-use level. Studies have been undertaken to determine which components of oils can be blended to enhance desensitizing effects of sensitizing components of materials in manufactured products. The results of the screening of these materials are submitted to the International Fragrance Association.

MATERIAL SAFETY DATA SHEETS

ALL ESSENTIAL OILS HAVE a prepared MSDS, which describes chemical toxicity information. The data includes which chemical family a substance is in, when it was certified, revision dates, components involved in it, how to identify it from another hazardous substance, its color, physical form, odor, major health risk, potential health effects, what happens with inhalation in the long term and short term, and ingestion in the long term and short term.

By law, essential oils and essential oil-containing products have MSDS forms. Anesthetics have MSDS forms, as do cleaning products and medical substances. Large binders containing the data of all products used in businesses and medical facilities are kept up-to-date and readily available for immediate access in order to provide hazardous material instructions in the event of spills associated with any given product or substance.

CLINICAL COMPETENCY

A CLINICAL AROMATHERAPIST ACQUIRES competency though a certified course of education and clinical training, namely, experience. Although clinical aromatherapy certification is an unregulated specialty, there are numerous places where you can obtain a good course that leads to certification. Consent from the patient for health care information required under HIPAA is a standard of care. Competent certification should empower the therapist with the education to do the following tasks:

• Perform a complete evaluation on an inpatient or outpatient; take a complete medical history; allergy and sensitivity history, taking note of types of adverse drug reactions, adverse food reactions, including screening for herbals, noting possible interactions with oils and medications.

• Perform a review of the symptoms of the body, everything from the neurological to the gastrointestinal tract; review of medications; checking for coexisting medical conditions such as bleeding, heart failure, dysrhythmias, asthma, cancer, diabetes.

• Detailed consultation that includes an assessment and plan for aromatherapy treatment, defining which essential oils to utilize and how to utilize them safely in that particular setting.

IT IS IMPORTANT TO realize when working in hospitals and other types of medical facilities that there are numerous considerations regarding policy and procedure for the use of essential oils. Departmental oversight by integrative therapies or other departments, perhaps formulary or pharmacy, would be appropriate. There are certain regulations, safety policies, and facility philosophies that must be adhered to.

PHENOMENAL HEALTH CARE
POSSIBILITIES

MANY PEOPLE WORKING IN health care today have the desire and ability to realize the growth and further development of medical aromatherapy in the twenty-first century. This material has the great potential to impact many people as the understanding of and familiarity for the subject develops over time. The research being actively undertaken in this century in the use of essential oils as a branch of integrative medicine is encouraging. Yet as most studies conclude, more study is needed. Increasing awareness of the significant advances and contributions available to expand health care possibilities is phenomenal. Proper treatment regimens that safely use essential oils in conjunction with allopathic medicine are being employed in many institutions that offer aromatherapy services as a complementary method of treatment.

CHAPTER

Ideal Anesthesia

"Fear is largely the cause of failures; it cannot be eliminated by either drugs or by the surgeon's knife. The only remedy known for fear is understanding. When one understands that the universe is filled with the presence of God, there is nothing to fear."

—Raymond Holliwell Author of Working with the Law

CHAPTER *six*

IDEAL ANESTHESIA

PATIENTS KNOW THAT THE day of surgery is filled with many emotions. The anesthesiologist can bring calmness to surgery in several ways that reassure the patient. Anesthesiologists can give sedative medications prior to entering the operating room to allay anxiety, but the discussion just prior to surgery has the biggest impact. An ideal anesthetic can begin during that preoperative discussion, when the patient's heart is won by instilling understanding. Patient education begins with a team-teaching approach during the preoperative admitting process for surgery. Education and preparation continues as part of the informed-consent discussion to determine the type of anesthesia that is required and planned. Discussing the potential risks and benefits of the anesthetic plan prepares the patient and family from an informed-consent standpoint. Also at this time, if indicated, integration of complementary alternative medicine techniques, such as mind-body awareness and the use of essential oils perioperatively, brings a positive focus to the setting. Surgery is always a team effort.

TELEMEDICINE EDUCATION AND ADVERTISING

THE ADVENT OF TELEMEDICINE has improved health care in underserved areas of the world. The American Telemedicine Association defines the use of telemedicine as the exchange of medical information from one site to another via electronic communications to improve patients' health status. Telemedicine was first pioneered and adopted by the Department of Defense for ships at sea and later implemented into the Veterans Affairs system and Indian Health Service.

The digital age has changed medicine radically. Digitized signals can be broadcast live so that physicians can remotely monitor intensive care units in other hospitals, other states, and other countries and treat them as one electronic intensive care unit (eICU). Critical care specialists trained to use computers monitoring vital signs and laboratory values of critically ill patients can make interventions rapidly and remotely.

In the United States, we spend over a trillion dollars on health care annually. Soon it will rival our gross national product. Millions are spent on artfully presented TV ads for prescription medications that also include frightful lists of side effects. The FDA and the Institute for Safe Medication Practices have established a national campaign to eliminate the use of potentially harmful error-prone abbreviations in all forms of medical communication, including written and computer-generated prescriptions, records, labels, packaging, and advertising. The food and drug industries have changed enormously across the approximately 150 years of the history of anesthesia. Medicinal foods were the topic of an article in the Journal of the American Medical Association as far back as 100 years ago. Volatile anesthesia gas agents have been around for over 150 years and have improved greatly.

IN ETHER DAY, JULIE M. Fester narrates the strange tale of America's greatest medical discovery and the men who made it. It is the greatest discovery because William Morton's patent for anesthesia ushered in the commercialization of modern medicine. Celebrated around the world on October 16, "Ether Day" at Massachusetts General Hospital first occurred in 1846. Volatilized anesthetic gas, like ether vapors, smell fruity, pungent and are potentially explosive. Fortunately, the days of ether explosions in the operating room are past. Nitrous oxide gas was discovered in 1772 by Joseph Priestley and is a safer gas. However, the abuse of nitrous oxide by inhalant huffing causes neurological damage to the nervous system.

Great scientists throughout the twentieth century have contributed to the fund of medications and medical hardware necessary to give safe anesthesia. In 1902, Emil Fischer, PhD, was awarded a Nobel Prize in Chemistry for his work on sugars and purine bases (DNA). In 1912, he synthesized barbiturates and phenobarbital. Pentobarbital soon followed and became the first intravenous induction agent of major significance for decades.

In 1929, William Allen published an article about inhalation reflexes in man when using essential oils of wintergreen, clove, orange, rose, lavender, bergamot, eucalyptus, and mustard, plus the chemicals butyric acid, menthol, camphor, xylol, benzol, formalin, ammonia, and chloroform. He measured the respiratory and blood pressure effects in subjects, including his son, some of whom were anosmic (having no sense of smell), sleeping, or anesthetized while under open-cone drop ether anesthesia.

Interestingly, Allen describes an inhibitory respiratory reflex reaction obtained during inhalation of each agent's vapors on unanesthetized and anesthetized subjects that is akin to the olfactory trigeminal reflex known in rabbits. This implies oropharyngeal absorption of the vapors of essential oils and other chemical compounds affecting the chemosensory ability of cranial nerves. The oral-pharyngeal nervous tissue absorption of the vapor of anesthetic agents as well as vapors of essential oils is significant but not well-quantified. Cranial nerves 5, 7, and 9, the trigeminal, facial, and hypoglossal, all have nerve endings intimately related to the tongue, posterior tongue, anterior tongue, back of the throat, and trachea.

It is critical to properly mix and match all medications including those applied externally during an operation. For instance, topical application at the time of surgery of surgical skin soap, like the iodine-containing scrub solution betadene, might be harmful to those who have experienced an adverse reaction to iodine-containing intravenous contrast media. Before iodine was used as surgical skin prep, patients in France stood alongside the operating table prior to surgery and had essential oil of lavender applied with brushes to sterilize the skin. It must have smelled wonderful and apparently it worked adequately.

AROMATIC ANESTHESIA

UNDERSTANDING HOW GENERAL ANESTHETIC drugs work in multifactorial fashions is the lifelong pursuit of Dr. Edmond Eger. In 2006 he completed a landmark study using eight aromatic benzene-like compounds (benzene, fluorobenzene, o-difluorobenzene, p-difluorobenzene, 1,2,4-trifluorobenzene, 1,3,5-trifluorobenzene, pentafluorobenzene, and hexafluorobenzene) and found that these aromatic compounds produce immobility in the face of noxious stimulation by blocking the action of glutamate on the NMDA receptor. The eight conventional anesthetic agents (cyclopropane, desflurane, enflurane, halothane, isoflurane, nitrous oxide, sevoflurane, and xenon), which include those used every day in the operating room to induce anesthesia (sevoflurane, isoflurane, and desflurane), did not block movement in the face of noxious stimulation by that same NMDA receptor. One point of the studies by Allen and Eger, published ninety years apart, is that the phytomolecules from the essential oils from plants are similar to other aromatic compounds that induce various types of anesthesia, possibly through similar mechanisms.

An article in a recent issue of Anesthesiology described a study that utilized lavender oil to calm patients by binding with the sedating GABA receptor, during breast biopsy surgeries. Those who received lavender oil in the oxygen mask as well as intravenous sedation anesthesia were considerably more relaxed during the procedure and expressed greater overall satisfaction than those who did not receive the oil in their anesthesia oxygen mask and received only similar intravenous anesthesia (Wajda, 2005). The combined technique allows patients to answer the hospital's postoperative questionnaire with improved satisfaction, which provides great statistics for hospitals to publicize.

The specialty of anesthesia has benefited from inventors of medical devices and gas agents. Dr. John W. Severinghouse invented and patented blood-gas-analysis electrodes and vital-signs monitors. For decades, Dr. Edmond Eger has tested and authored papers on the latest anesthetic gases derived from ether. This work has greatly enhanced the ability of the daily anesthesiologist to provide safe and successful anesthesia on a routine basis. American pioneers have educated and trained generations of anesthesiologists who provide exceptional measures of comfort and lifesaving skills learned in national training programs. With each passing year it becomes increasingly safer to have surgery, because of the improved skills of anesthesiologists, and because of the surgeons and staff at hospitals and centers that provide these services.

WHAT IS THE IDEAL ANESTHETIC?

WHEN I WAS IN anesthesia residency at Los Angeles-USC Medical Center in 1986, we were asked to consider the characteristics of ideal anesthetic agents, whether gas or intravenous. One of my examiners asked me, if I was stranded on a desert island (this was before Survivor and Lost), which anesthetic would I want to have with me and why? Lidocaine could be considered the most versatile and therefore best suited for survival situations. It is a highly specialized potent and yet safe local anesthetic agent of the amino amide classification. That question ideally had no correct answer since no such scenario exists. Nonetheless, I like the thought process, since it involves creativity; many great inventions have come from such mental exercises. Adapting from known characteristics of anesthetic agents gives us insight to develop properties and to expand the ideal effects of anesthesia, all the way down to receptors at the molecular level.

PREANESTHETIC CONDITIONING

THE IDEAL PREANESTHETIC CONDITION to achieve prior to any given surgery, whether elective, urgent, or emergent, would be that state of the best possible physical and nutritional health. Planning for that surgical event could include having taken supplements or prescriptions to prepare for the stress of anesthesia, surgery, and rehabilitation. A normal red blood count is desirable at the time of surgery, although iron-deficiency anemia is a relatively common preoperative finding. This condition, which can occur in healthy athletes too, is readily correctable with advanced preparation if indicated, but rarely implemented, by giving intravenous iron within limits defined in the article "Treatment of Iron Deficiency Anemia in Orthopedic Surgery with Intravenous Iron" (Theusinger et al., 2007).

Dehydroepiandrostrone (DHEA) is released as a hormonal response to the stress of surgery. Normal bodily production of DHEA decreases progressively with advancing age. Taking 50 to100 milligrams per day for several months prior to elective surgery has been suggested. This drug is not to be confused with DHA, the more desirable component of omega-3. Supplementation with other vitamins, such as C and D3, and minerals, such as calcium and zinc for the antioxidant value, is suggested. Supplementation with L-carnitine, an amine usually derived from meat sources that transport free fatty acids across inner cell mitochondrial membranes for use in adenosine tri-phosphate energy synthesis, has been suggested. Supplementing with two grams twice daily for two weeks prior and two weeks postsurgery helps to increase muscle mass. Entrepreneurs are creating and marketing new complete meal replacement weight-loss programs in the form of smoothies that are fortified with vitamins and minerals such as calcium and trace elements. The many forms of preparation for surgery and anesthesia should be cleared by your own specialist in advance of undergoing any procedure.

Surgeons may suggest or require weight loss prior to surgery, especially for total joint replacement surgery in the obese and morbidly obese patient. Unfortunately, improper loss of weight can lead to significant loss of muscle mass. Fortunately, specialists such as those certified by the American Academy of Physical and Rehabilitation Medicine can be consulted to prepare patients for surgery and recovery afterward. Monitoring your health during weight loss in preparation for surgery is important. For more details, read the excellent new medical textbook edited by Ingrid Kohlstadt, MD, Scientific Evidence for Musculoskeletal, Bariatric, and Sports Nutrition, in particular the chapter coauthored with Vilma Joseph, MD, "Preparing for Orthopedic Surgery." Dr. Kohlstadt's second book, Food and Nutrients in Disease Management, will emphasize whole foods over isolated nutrients.

As discussed earlier, sleep apnea is a preexisting condition often associated with obesity. Obstructive sleep apnea (OSA) is associated with increased perioperative cardiac and respiratory complications. "Identifying patients with OSA is the first step in preventing postoperative complications. Untreated OSA patients are known to have a higher incidence of difficult intubation, postoperative complications, increased intensive care admissions and greater duration of hospital stay," states Dr. Francis Chung, of the University of Toronto, and author of the STOP questionnaire and study, published in the May 2008 issue of Anesthesiology. Polysomnography is the best diagnostic tool for OSA (Chung, 2008). The STOP questionnaire has predictive value for detecting sleep apnea using a combination of questions and parameters, such as high body mass index (BMI), age over 50, large neck circumference, and being male.

THERE ARE FOUR SIMPLE QUESTIONS:

- Do you snore loudly?

- Do you often feel tired, fatigued, or sleepy during daytime?

- Has anyone observed that you stop breathing during sleep?

- Do you have or are you being treated for high blood pressure?

IF A PATIENT ANSWERS yes to two or more of these questions, the patient is considered to be at high risk for OSA. When the risk factors for OSA—male, more than 50 years of age, BMI greater than 35 kg/m2, and neck circumference less than 44 centimeters—were combined with the answers to the STOP questionnaire, the ability to predict OSA was increased significantly. Become aware of your sleep apnea status and make arrangements for treatment as preparation for possible surgery and to prevent the complications of untreated sleep apnea.

BOWEL FLORA

THE SIZE OF A person's abdomen can be influenced by digestive bacteria. Research at the Virginia Commonwealth University suggests that an unfriendly member of the bacteroides family Firmicutes may contribute to obesity. Probiotic formulations of common cell strains, such as Acidophilus plantarum, Bifidobacterium plantarum, and Lactobacillus plantarum, are made into products containing billions of cells to increase friendly bowel flora. There is also a connection between "prebiotics," foods that contain carbohydrate-inulin (a fructan and storage carbohydrate) and that are the food source of the probiotic bacteria. Certain products and food combinations might be necessary, because antibiotics that kill friendly bowel flora are commonly given at surgery as part of the course of prophylaxis to prevent the complication of infection. Probiotics are measured in cell-forming units not milligrams. Most researchers suggest taking 15 billion or more cells per day of multiple strains to aid in the synthesis of vitamins B and K. Because they are a source of fiber, these cell cultures help regulate transit time of colon contents. These cultured cells reduce inflammation while protecting the mucosal lining of the intestines to maximize bowel health.

Preoperatively, patients are directed to follow specialized instructions, such as discontinuing intake of herbal preparations, including traditional Chinese medicine prescriptions, for up to ten days. Prescribed cardiac medications, especially metoprolol, taken with a sip of water the morning of surgery is a recommended method of cardiac prophylaxis. Follow instructions carefully regarding the timing of the last intake of food and drink for the time period specified prior to scheduled surgery and induction of anesthesia.

The Supplement Education Alliance study announced that $24 billion in health care costs could be saved by including consumer consumption of the following supplements: calcium, vitamin D3 for hip fracture prevention, leutin, zeaxanthin for age-related macular degeneration, omega-3 for heart diseases, and folic acid for neural tube defect prevention and to reduce stroke risk by one-fifth. Zeaxanthin is a phytopigment ligand found in varying amounts in some varieties of juices from plants. The future of nutritional preparation for anesthesia to maximize health is improving significantly as the field of nutritional medicine expands. Individuals who properly prepare for surgery will receive the best outcome possible.

IDEAL ANESTHESIA IS SAFE

ANESTHESIA HAS CHANGED RADICALLY in the last twenty years. Guidelines written by concerned anesthesiologists have been practiced, and the results studied and refined. Learning from the errors analyzed in the Closed Claims Project, established by the American Society of Anesthesiologists in 1985, and examination of malpractice claims settled identified patterns of errors and determined which safety improvement activities should be implemented. Since then respiratory-related claims have dropped substantially with the use of medical equipment advances such as pulse oximeters, which measure blood oxygenation.

The new computerized anesthesia machines have built-in ventilators offering different forms of ventilating ability, coupled with real-time pulmonary flow volume loops, capnographs to measure airway carbon dioxide, and quantitative analysis of anesthesia gas, both inhaled and exhaled to guide depth of anesthesia management. These major monitoring improvements work well in conjunction with the new shorter-acting and more receptor-specific intravenous drugs. They can be given through improved intravenous pumps to make them titratable. Specialized laboratory investigations utilize intravenous pumps that are operated based on computer feedback of vital signs and the blood concentrations of the drugs being administered.

Neuroaxial regional anesthesia and peripheral nerve blocks using ultrasound-guided catheter placement for administration of infused local anesthetics that provide improved postoperative pain management are coming to the forefront. Patients can rest assured that further research by anesthesia safety societies is ongoing. Ideally, these newly created inventions are available when and where needed.

TIME IS MONEY IN SURGERY

PERHAPS THE BEST ANESTHETIC is like the easiest cooking technique—just add water and you have instant anesthesia. Well, there is no such thing as instant anesthesia, although some surgeons think there is. The best anesthetic agent would exhibit rapid onset and rapid offset, which shortens the time to get to a surgical plane of anesthesia and then to awaken from it. Therefore, the ideal anesthetic agent would have the perfect solubility (oil doesn't dissolve in water easily), pharmacodynamics (what the drug does to our body), and pharmacokinetics (what the body does to the drug). The rapid onset and offset of anesthesia drug effect makes the turnaround time between surgeries faster and therefore more efficient. Time is money in surgery: money spent and/or money earned.

YOUR RIGHT HAND IS a mirror image of your left hand. Many medications exist as a combination of right and left mirror image molecules. Medications can be manipulated and manufactured to become even safer for clinical applications by removing the right-handed molecule from the mixture, leaving the left-handed molecule to yield new medications. New medical drugs are being fabricated from old medical drugs almost as fast as there are new actions taken to limit or eliminate trans fats from foods. During surgery, anesthesiologists may need to administer a neuromuscular-blocking drug. Atracurium is an example of an older drug in this class that consists of both molecular mirror images that rotate plane-polarized light to the right or left. Atracurium, like some other drugs, has a known incidence of histamine release, which can cause adverse reactions during intravenous injection due to one mirror-image molecule. Removing the offending mirror-image molecules from Atracurium created a new drug called cisatracurium besylate (Nimbex). The new molecule, an enantiomer of Atracurium, has fewer side effects of histamine release.

Levalbuterol (Xopenex) is the left-handed molecule for asthma treatments and is newly created from the older medication albuterol, which has fewer side effects such as of rapid heart rate. Levobupivacaine, (Chirocaine) is the left-handed local anesthetic molecule from bupivacaine, and has fewer cardiotoxic side effects. The newer gastroesophageal reflux (GERD) treatment medication Nexium is an enantiomer of the older drug Prilosec. These drugs act the same, but because they are more "purified," chemically speaking, they do not produce as many side effects. Theoretically, computer-generated drugs could be created that would turn out to be safer and more practical improvements of our already existing choices of medications.

SIMILARITIES OF OILS AND ANESTHETICS

VOLATILE GAS ANESTHETIC DRUGS are diluted prior to administration. Anesthesiologists refill the vaporizers on the anesthesia machine from a large bottle of liquid anesthetic drug. The anesthesia vaporizer mixes the anesthetic drug with oxygen and possibly other gases, such as nitrous oxide, to dilute concentrations of a 1% to 10% range, depending on the specific anesthetic gas used. Throughout the course of an operation, varying concentrations of anesthetic gas is administered through a breathing device into the lungs. Essential oils are diluted before application onto the skin, usually in a concentration of a 1% to 10% range. Most essential oils are also long-chain aromatic hydrocarbons that, like anesthetic molecules, have dynamic cell membrane receptor activity similar to anesthesia gases.

Vaporized chemicals, whether anesthetics or essential oils, pass into the organs of the body after being absorbed as chemicals into the vascular system. Transdermal absorption of oils generates blood levels and plasma levels of phytomolecules that then flow throughout the body, some functioning as neurotransmitters in the brain. Brain tissue is rich in NMDA receptors. The phytomolecules of the essential oils act as a second messenger of scent information, binding to the olfactory G-protein embedded in the membrane of the cell wall. The activated olfactory G-protein receptor then stimulates the molecular cascade of chemical reactions inside the cell, starting with cyclic adenosine monophosphate and cal modulin. All these metabolic pathways bring the odorant and its information into the cell so that proteins can be synthesized. Aromatic and anesthetic gases cause similar receptor events on cell membranes.

Many physiologic responses are specifically receptor-controlled. General anesthesia often involves using intravenously administered neuromuscular blockers, invoking a reversible skeletal muscle paralysis mediated through muscarinic and nicotinic receptors. Certain essential oils act upon these identical receptors as well as calcium and histamine receptors. An individual can have down-regulated receptors or up-regulated receptors, meaning they have stronger or weaker receptor responsiveness. People who have suffered paralysis due to stroke, polio, or a burn injury have significant alterations in the receptors on their muscles and may respond in an exaggerated fashion to the drug succinylcholine, which is used for tracheal intubation during induction of anesthesia. People with heart failure have altered cardiac beta-receptors and respond differently to catecholamines when they are used to stimulate the weak heart.

IDEAL ANESTHETIC MEDICATIONS

IDEALLY, ANESTHETIC MEDICATIONS SHOULD have only positive effects. There would be no unpleasant side effects or potential for complications due to adverse drug interactions or allergic reactions. Safe to use by relatively untrained caregivers, they could be used in areas of the world where anesthesia caregivers are in short supply. No special delivery system, special handling, or special disposal should be required. The ideal anesthetic drug should be safe for patients with compromised organs function, even overt multiple organ failure. The ideal anesthetic drug should also be safe for any age group. No nausea would be associated with such ideal anesthesia agents, as it is now in rather large, expensive, and annoying proportions across the whole anesthetic industry. It would be a very pleasant anesthetic from which to recover.

In the meantime, the best new drug on the anesthesia horizon is a selective relaxant binding agent, a cylodextrin carbohydrate. Called "the reviver," Sugammadex, manufactured by Organon, looks like an eight-armed octopus. Sugammadex is computer designed to rapidly reverse the intended deep neuromuscular blockade of rocuronium bromide (Zemuron). The

Europeans have approved Sugammadex as the first selective relaxant binding medication. Meanwhile the FDA has found certain hypersensitivity or allergic reaction side effects which may preclude the approval of sugammadex in the USA. Apparently even anesthesia drugs that are computer designed have no guarantee of achieving ideal medication status because of the risk of adverse reactions.

PK-MAC MINIMALLY INVASIVE ANESTHESIA

AN IDEAL ANESTHETIC WOULD have no need of an anesthesia machine or anesthesia vaporizer. Propofol-ketamine monitored anesthesia care (PK-MAC) is currently used in some offices and surgery centers by plastic surgeons and the military. This technique of so-called "balanced anesthesia" does not require the use of volatile anesthetic gas. Barry L. Friedberg, MD, author of the book Anesthesia in Cosmetic Surgery and the article "Minimally Invasive Ancsthesia (MIA) for Minimally Invasive Surgery," received a U.S. congressional award for his development of the specialized PK-MAC trauma technique used in the war zones of Afghanistan and Iraq. Currently, Dr Friedberg lectures worldwide on the PK-MAC modality of anesthesia for office-based cosmetic surgery.

This technique uses a combination of the intravenous medications propofol and ketamine, and local anesthetics for anesthesia. No anesthesia vaporizer is required, just basic vital signs monitors and a bispectral index monitor (BIS) to monitor brain waves that correspond to depth of anesthesia. The BIS monitor analyzes brain waves and compresses the encephalographic representation to determine the level of consciousness or unconsciousness, depicted by a number. The displayed numbers range from about 40 to 60, depending on the brand of monitor, when the surgical plane of anesthesia is reached. This monitoring technique is the key to knowing the depth of anesthesia, which is a measure of the synergistic effects of the anesthesia medications on the nervous system and EEG waves in particular. Once the patient is rendered unconscious, the procedure continues with administration of local anesthesia and more intravenous medications as required.

This method is very satisfactory method for undergoing some types of surgery. Perhaps it is the closest thing to an ideal anesthetic from my viewpoint, since I am a big proponent of nausea-free anesthesia. Of course, from my standpoint, an ideal anesthetic incorporates the antinausea properties of the essential oil ginger root, Z. officinale, as well.

MODULATORS OF IMMUNITY

ANESTHESIOLOGISTS ROUTINELY GIVE ANTIBIOTICS prophylactically before surgery, if indicated. Antibiotics are given intravenously for many operations, preferably within one hour of surgical incision. Hospitals are "graded" on the performance of these statistics, and the results are posted on the Internet. The practice of the proper timing of intravenous administration of preoperative antibiotics is designed to achieve skin tissue levels of antibiotic prior to surgical incision of the skin in order to prevent postoperative infections and maximize outcomes.

Each anesthetic gas agent has properties besides putting a person to sleep on a surgical plane of anesthesia. Many drugs cause the immune system to be stronger or weaker. Drugs are modulators of the immune system. Anesthetics and antibiotics have immunomodulatory properties, as do such foods as the essential oils and berry fruit juices. Immunomodulatory drugs may negatively influence the defensive mechanism by either stimulating the inflammatory response or inhibiting the anti-inflammatory response. Anesthesia gases including nitrous oxide and some intravenous agents (except muscle relaxants) decrease white blood cell chemotaxis (chemical-directed cell movement) and polymorphonuclear phagocytosis (white cells that eat bad cells). That means they lessen the ability of certain cells of the immune system to combat infection. Certain classes of antibiotics decrease immune system function. These macrolide antibiotics have immunomodulatory and anti-inflammatory effects: erythromycin, azithromycin, clarithromycin, dirithromycin, roxithromycin, and tetracycline.

Inflammation is a syndrome that can be modulated by diet and is brought on by illnesses such as infection, obesity, autoimmune disorders, and cancer. The phytomolecules found in essential oils, berry fruit juices, and the essential sugars positively affect bodily systems, reducing inflammation and enhancing immune system strength through the delivery of antioxidants, flavones, xanthones, ligands, and glycoproteins. The topic of inflammation is so critical to our understanding and application of good health that I recommend the book The Inflammation Syndrome, by Jack Challem, rather than attempting to go into the great detail it deserves. Read the book and get the information to convince yourself that it is worth the effort to change your dietary habits to one consistent with an anti-inflammatory diet regimen.

MONITOR WITH VIGILANCE

THE MOTTO OF ANESTHESIA practice is vigilance. Anesthesiologists and critical care doctors use the "rule of trends" in acute care medicine settings to assess and measure response to treatment. Illness can be measured suddenly in seconds or over decades, as in persistently poor diet leading to malnutrition and obesity. The trend is not your friend when it comes to obesity in the United States. In the last thirty years, in every state, the percentage of the population defined as overweight to morbidly obese has increased. That time span correlates directly with the massive rise and commercialization of the fast food industry.

Every few minutes during an operation, the vital signs of heart rate and rhythm, blood pressure, respiration, temperature, oxygenation, ventilations parameters, and more are noted and charted. When making adjustments to anesthetic doses, we retake the vitals to obtain a measure of the effect of the drugs given. There are sometimes up to a dozen or more drugs given over the course of an entire surgery. We are still awaiting the arrival of the "ideal" monitor for depth of anesthesia. Monitoring of vital signs is crucial.

"The best person to monitor your health is you," says Michael F. Roizen, MD, the newly designated chief wellness officer of the Cleveland Clinic and author of Real Age: Are You as Young as You Can Be? He advises finding a doctor who is trustworthy and likable. The material presented in his book is insightful and worth mastering. Actually working toward developing increased personal wellness and well-being is extremely beneficial. When adjusting your own physiology in terms of weight loss, it is important to monitor yourself closely, perhaps even working closely with your doctor, especially if you are taking prescription medications.

Hopefully, you will need to use less medication as you eat and exercise properly and lose weight. Drinking berry fruit juices and using essential oils as part of your diet plan will alter and perhaps reset your bodily systems. You may need to have your vital signs and laboratory values monitored frequently by your health care provider. Insulin-dependent diabetics should monitor their blood sugar level at regular intervals throughout the day. Take proper care of yourself and get the appropriate support you may need.

SURGERY ON THE MIND-BODY CONNECTION

IDEAL ANESTHESIA PREPARES PATIENTS to be in the best possible shape prior to surgery by integrating allopathic medicine with complementary alternative medicine practices. For those going "under anesthesia and under the knife," I recommend the book Prepare for Surgery, Heal Faster, by Peggy Huddleston. It is a guide to mind-body techniques. If you must have surgery or decide to have elective surgery, you should be prepared as best you can physically as well as mentally and spiritually. You will feel calmer before surgery, have less pain after surgery, and recover faster with no complications.

AWARENESS AND ANESTHESIA

TO ARRIVE AT THE ideal anesthetic, we need to understand more about how anesthesia works and how people consent to have anesthesia. Some types of surgical procedures can and should be accomplished using a technique called conscious sedation, with monitored anesthesia care. Some awareness is intended and expected during conscious sedation, so patients need to be educated and consent to undergo that type of surgery and anesthesia if indicated. In my experience, many people do not understand the difference between conscious sedation and general anesthesia when it is explained before surgery, nor do they remember the discussion after surgery. Awareness while under the influence of general anesthesia is very rare. It is a potential complication of general anesthesia.

The awareness during general anesthesia portrayed in the Hollywood thriller Awake reveals a frightening medical issue. In reality, this unintended situation could be due to numerous types of problems resulting from mechanical failure or human error. It is challenging to accurately analyze questionnaire and interview data in order to differentiate unconscious memory formation, dreaming, and drug-induced hallucinations from actual inappropriate awareness under general anesthesia. Studies determining the statistical incidence of these events vary significantly. The posttraumatic stress syndrome (PTSS) that may develop as a result of a medical sentinel event such as awareness under general anesthesia requires specialized intervention. Anyone experiencing an awareness event can obtain help from special interest groups that can provide support, such as the Anesthesia Awareness Campaign founded by Carol Weihrer, and obtain appropriate referral to qualified mental health care professionals.

Theories of anesthesia have been changing over the years to adapt to new molecular knowledge and understanding, but there is still a gap, especially relating to anesthetizing the conscious mind and the unconscious mind. The conscious and unconscious minds have properties yet to be revealed. Various kinds of learning and memory occur while under general anesthesia. Until there are pure anesthetic agents whose effective depths can be measured faithfully with monitors better than bispectral analysis, in order to guarantee that each and every anesthetized patient does not experience unintended awareness during surgery, there is no ideal agent or monitor or mechanical fail-safe. Increasing patients' overall educational awareness about the events surrounding surgery pertaining to anesthesia improves patient satisfaction and surgical outcomes. Providing the satisfactory service of patient safety and comfort is the goal of every anesthesiologist.

NANO-HEALING

THE NANOTECHNOLOGY INDUSTRY IS growing, creating such subparticle industries as robonanotech, genonanotech, and glyconanotech. One day, your genetically determined molecular fingerprint will determine which of the latest anesthesia drugs will make your anesthetic more precise and therefore better tolerated. In the future, a patient's point-of-service preoperative laboratory work will precisely define clinically useful data to be used by the surgeon and anesthesiologist to determine the best care possible. This information could suggest the best medications that will correspond with a patient's preexisting medical conditions, based on genetic profile and acquired changes such as trace mineral deficiencies, antioxidant carrying capacity, and status of various cancer biomarkers. Consumers will use these specialized services first, and then insurers will adopt and "cover" them when they have been proven to save money and improve clinical outcomes.

FUTURE DRUGS

IDEAL ANESTHETIC AGENTS WILL be developed for many different classes of drugs, increasing the certainty of true anesthesia effect without adverse drug reactions. A defined dosage of anesthesia will yield a definite depth of anesthesia. For more details on the future of anesthesia, I recommend reading Beverly Orser's article in Scientific American (2007), "Lifting the Fog Around Anesthesia." It will increase your awareness and appreciation for the detailed work being done to develop cleaner anesthesia agents. Better drugs need to be developed that will invoke the full range of anesthesia, from sedation to unconsciousness to the surgical plane of anesthesia. Drugs that provoke selective time-oriented amnesia and hypnosis, coupled with lack of painful surgical sensation brought on by complete sensory analgesia, will be developed. Anesthetic medications influence many specialized aspects of physiology.

Melatonin, a hormone that has antibiotic properties, is produced nocturnally by the pineal gland, independently of sleep. Melatonin has powerful GABAa receptor effects that potentiate both intravenous and gaseous anesthetic drugs (Naguib, 2007). This activity is shown using flumazenil, a selective ligand that antagonizes benzodiazepines at the GABAa receptor. Because it is anxiolytic (decreases anxiety), melatonin could be utilized as a preoperative medication without altering motor skills or causing the "hangover" that currently employed benzodiazepine medications such as midazolam cause. Benzodiazepines have varied time effects on memory. In general, midazolam is known to cause primarily retrograde amnesia, whereas lorazepam also causes antegrade amnesia.

Melatonin synthesis begins with L-tryptophan and progresses via cyclic AMP and norepinephrine to serotonin. Melatonin and serotonin production are inversely regulated between light and dark cycles. Serotonin rate limits the production of melatonin, and serotonin production is blocked by certain 5-hydroxytryptophan (5-HT) antinausea drugs, such as Zofran, given during surgery to prevent postoperative nausea. Managing specialized receptors with drug therapy is a growing trend in treating nausea. A new choice of drug that has just been brought to market is the drug aprepitant (Emend), a brand new class of neurokinin NK1 receptor antagonist. Taken orally before surgery, it lasts up to 48 hours after surgery to prevent nausea.

IDEAL THERAPEUTICS

MEDICATIONS THAT PRODUCE ANALGESIA-induced pain-free states of anesthesia and immobility of skeletal muscles have very different and very specialized receptor profiles. Besides regulating circadian rhythm, which anesthesia and surgery disrupt, melatonin physiologically also regulates the reproductive axis and has antibiotic, anticonvulsant, anti-inflammatory, analgesic, and antioxidant effects while maintaining mitochondrial function in the face of oxidative stress (Tekas, 2007). Melatonin promotes the release of B-endorphins, resulting in analgesia.

Currently, the only melatonin drug on the market approved by the FDA for insomnia is ramelteon (Rozerem). Perhaps other melatonin-related medications can be designed that utilize similar mechanisms of melatonin for premedication, to induce anesthesia, and to help children with autism sleep better. Addiction medicine and psychotherapy will benefit from advances of newly developed anesthetic agents since similar receptor profiles are applicable. Drugs that are efficiently metabolized, readily reversible, and personalized, and that nanoanesthetize, will create the ideal anesthetic.

CHAPTER

seven

Ginger and Anesthesia

*"Unless one is aware of a research methodology's potential weaknesses,
scientific activity can become a mechanical ritual."*

—*Ted J. Kaptchuk*

CHAPTER

GINGER AND ANESTHESIA

SMELL IS A LEARNED PROCESS shaped by genetics (Buck et al., 1992), experiences such as language (Stevenson and Boakes, 2003), music, and other five senses-mediated cues. The medical science of nausea is complexly interwoven with coexisting disease states. Safe practical choices in essential oil therapy can be extrapolated from evidenced-based clinical references that may be integrated into the medical management of various conditions. Specifically, the transdermal application and nasal inhalation of vapors of 10% CO_2 extracted essential oil of ginger Zingiber officinale can be a safe and effective addition to the medical management for the prevention and treatment of complications of nausea and vomiting associated with general anesthesia. This clinical and scientifically oriented chapter is based on my article published in the International Journal of Aromatherapy.

NOBEL FOR SMELL

THE 2004 NOBEL PRIZE in Physiology or Medicine was awarded to Richard Axel and Linda Buck for their discoveries of odorant receptors and the organization of the olfaction system. Previously, numerous similar theories for odorant detection systems and mechanisms of actions of anesthesia had been proposed. These theories are the spectral recognition of vibrational molecules (Turin, 1996), metalloprotein "shuttlecock" mechanism (Wang et al, 2003), mnemonic perception (Stevenson and Boakes, 2003), agonist-antagonist receptor binding (Firestein, 2004), cell membrane molecular configuration stress (Cantor, 2001), and cyclic nucleotide ligand-gated ion channels (Yamakura et al., 2004). Our understanding of the odorant detection system is evolving; the mechanism of action of the chemical constituents of scents at the cellular level involves significant intracellular protein synthesis from DNA and messenger RNA genetic data.

STRESSED MOLECULAR MEMBRANES

THE UPTAKE AND DISTRIBUTION mechanism of anesthetics is known (Eger, 1998). The previously accepted theory ascribed to the action of anesthetics, namely "molecular membrane stress" applied to the bi-lipid layer of cell membranes (Ueda, 2001), could conceivably be applied to explain some of the actions of essential oils at the cellular membrane level. A predominantly accepted theory for the contiguous mechanisms of consciousness and anesthesia results from the weak quantum interactions of van der Waals and London forces acting in hydrophobic pockets of proteins that link synaptically integrated dendrites of brains cells. Many essential oils and many anesthetic molecules are aliphatic hydrocarbon chains (Hameroff, 2006). Some essential oils are rich in molecules that are steroidal in structure.

The natural plasticity of the bi-lipid layers of cell walls and organelles of various body tissues is due in part to the orientation of the hydrophilic and hydrophobic lipid layers. The cell membranes have abundant embedded essential sugar-coated glycoprotein receptors for cell-to-cell immunity communication and gated ligand ionic channels thought to be acted upon by the various volatile chemicals of the anesthetic gas agents.

PHYTOMOLECULAR TRANSMISSION

THE PHYTOMOLECULES OF THE vapors from the nasal, oropharyngeal mucosal, and respiratory absorption of essential oils vapors, as well as the transdermal and intestinally absorbed phytomolecules, act directly as chemical messengers on cell membranes and other intracellular components. The gingerol in Z. officinale is thought to have a stimulating cardiotonic effect on cardiac muscle, mediated by ionic calcium channels via ATPase (Kobayashi et al., 1987). Many essential oils have calcium channel effects.

The second messenger neurotransmitter, cyclic adenosine monophosphate (c-AMP), working with olfactory G-protein and ionic calcium, modulates an excitatory synapse at the olfactory bulb of the first cranial nerve, mediating gamma aminobutryic acid (GABA) and N-methyl-D-aspartate (NMDA) receptors (Chen et al, 2000). These secondary messenger effects are prime examples of neurotransmitter physiology. A single amino acid molecule, histidine, mediates the GABAa subunit binding of benzodiazepine agonist binding. A single scent molecule can be recognized as bitter or sweet, depending on which way the molecule rotates plane-polarized light. The phytomolecules of essential oils that function as the scent or odor of plant or animal pheromones binds to the odorant receptor sites through G-proteins on the cell membrane.

GABA is a receptor system that functions as the gateway to the human brain for awareness, sedation, and anesthesia. NMDA is a receptor system for pain and anesthesia mediated by the NMDA antagonist aromatic gases and nitrous oxide. Huffing abuse of nitrous oxide results in a myeloneuropathy associated with the diagnostic symptoms of sensory loss and paresthesias. Laboratory data show greatly increased homocysteine levels. Administration of vitamin B12 corrects the condition if nitrous oxide is discontinued. Clinically, these side effects of nitrous oxide are limited, because anesthesia often concomitantly utilizes GABAa agonists (i.e., benzodiazepines such as etomidate and midazolam). Management of agitation in severe dementia is an example of NMDA (Note the similarity with the name of the new class of drug therapy, Namenda, indicated for Alzheimer's disease.) receptor-mediated disease affected positively by essential oils, especially Melissa officinalis (lemon balm).

PHARMACOKINETICS: WHAT THE BODY DOES TO THE CHEMISTRY

AFTER AN ESSENTIAL OIL is applied to the skin, a blood level is achieved by transdermal absorption through venous capillaries and arterioles.

The following example is given for Lavandula angustifolia. A 2.0% dilution of L. angustifolia oil applied to the abdomen of a volunteer showed that approximately 10% of the lavender oil was absorbed into the general blood circulation. Plasma levels peaked 20 minutes after application, as circulation via capillaries to tissue continued. After 90 minutes, both phytomolecules of linalool and linalyl acetate had dropped almost to zero, illustrating almost complete metabolism (Jäger, 1992). Supposed renal and hepatic mechanisms account for the metabolism of the majority of an average essential oil treatment dose.

Similar kinetics applies to transnasal inhalational absorption. There is potentially even more rapid absorption across the highly vascular cribiform plate in the nose, which is a direct transdural pathway to the brain. This complex cellular vasculolymphatic plexus, associated with abundant glomerulo-mitral apparatus of the olfactory bulb, crosses the blood brain barrier to perfuse brain tissue. This profound anatomical configuration allows for instantaneous vapor transmutation of the chemical data contained in a scent into neurotransmitter data. The scent is communicated instantly along neurological pathways to major centers of the brain.

The kinetic action of an anesthetic agent is similar in that the volatilized gas is absorbed across the basement membranes of the lungs and potentially nasopharyngeally as well. The anesthetic chemicals cross into the bloodstream and rapidly circulate to vascular-rich organs first, such as brain, liver, lungs, heart, kidney, and muscles. Then, by mass action, as concentration effect increases over time, less vascular-rich organs, such as bowels, epidermis, bones, and fat, gain tissue-anesthetic content.

AROMA PATHWAYS

AROMATHERAPY WITH ESSENTIAL OILS is somewhat similar to general anesthesia in that volatile anesthetic vapor is delivered diluted in the carrier gases oxygen and/or nitrous oxide via a breathing circuit. In the field of oil therapy, 100% pure volatile essential oils from select plant parts are diluted with various carrier oils for delivery by numerous methods in concentrations, usually ranging from 1% to 10%. The concentration chosen depends on the clinical circumstances, which is similar to administration of anesthesia vapor. The uptake and distribution of the phytomolecules of essential oils are transmitted via chemical messengers directly into the brain and brain stem via complex neuronal and circulatory pathways when inhaled.

The first cranial nerves are paired. These olfactory nerves are embedded bilaterally into the base of the frontal lobes of the brain. There appears to be right nasal to right hemisphere dominance of unfamiliar odor recognition. Familiar odors are recognized symmetrically when language is involved (Savic and Berglund, 2000). The sensory cells for odors have receptor binding sites that have unique properties for odorant chemical recognition and information mediation. In the olfactory bulb, olfactory receptor cells recognize, convert, and transmit chemical odorant-generated information into chemical messengers across glomerulo-mitral pathways by G-protein activation. These chemical messages are transmitted as chemical data along aroma-mediated pathways to various areas of the brain, such as the amygdala, hippocampus, and thalamus. The stress of surgery activates the amygdala, and learning occurs during general anesthesia (Gidron et al., 2002; Andrade, 1995).

THE SCIENCE OF NAUSEA

THE CRANIAL NERVES (CN) of the oropharynx—facial, CN7; glossopharyngeal, CN9; and vagus, CN10, located at the base of the tongue and back of the throat—have taste receptors that transmit chemically translated data to the medulla in the brain stem. Located next to the medulla is the chemotactic trigger zone, which mediates nausea and vomiting. These receptors for nausea and vomiting respond to vagal and sympathetic afferents, as well as blood-borne toxins. The most commonly used volatile anesthetic, sevoflurane, is ether based. Ether is known as a highly emetic anesthetic vapor agent. Intravenous medications work on specific pathways and receptors for nausea prevention and treatment. Various classes of intravenous medications administered as combination therapy are established as the foundation of effective multimodal therapy for prevention and treatment of nausea and vomiting of various origins (Scuderi et al., 2000). Some causes of nausea and vomiting respond better to different drug choices to manage specific nausea receptors (Bone et al., 1990). Escalating multiple drug therapy for the management of nausea is generally accepted as effective, evidence-based, best practice with known failure rates of nausea prevention (Habib and Gan, 2002; Apfel et al., 2004).

COMMON FORMULATIONS OF GINGER OIL ZINGIBER OFFICINALE

- The powdered root of ginger is as effective as metoclopramide (Reglan) in the prevention of nausea in certain settings (Ernst and Pittler, 2000).

- Ginger juice produces antimotion-sickness action and has antihistaminic effects (Qian and Liu, 1992).

- Ginger syrup decreased duration and severity of nausea in pregnancy (Keating and Chez, 2002).

- Powered ginger root was shown to be as effective as Vitamin B6 in reducing the symptoms of nausea, vomiting, and dry retching of pregnancy. No teratogenic effects (birth defects) associated with use of ginger were evident (Portnoi, et al., 2003; Smith and Crowther, 2004).

- Powered ginger root has shown negative results for effective prevention of nausea in one setting after laparoscopic surgery (Eberhart et al., 2003).

THERE APPEARS TO BE a difference between the potency of ginger preparations and the degree of the effects they mediate when comparing the various preparations administered orally, such as ginger juice, ginger powdered root, and syrup of ginger. To date, no other studies have examined the efficacy of ginger oil Z. officinale when administered as combined inhalational and transdermal therapies, with and without, with or without guided imagery, for the prevention of nausea and vomiting in conjunction with surgery and general anesthesia.

RECEPTOR CHEMISTRY APPLICATIONS

RECEPTOR CHEMISTRY IS A challenging field of study, because every system has system-specific receptor sites serving as information conversion stations. The well-known muscarinic receptors are mediated by acetylcholine. The chemoreceptor trigger zone has receptor sites for benzodiazepines, histamine, and dopamine. D3 dopaminergic receptors are blocked by dopamine antagonists. The therapeutic successes of the expensive intravenous medications, the 5-HT3 serotonin receptor antagonists, work slowly but degrade quickly, having half-lives on the order of two to three hours. This peripherally acting class works indirectly via the vagus nerve to block receptor sites to circulating serotonin at end-organs.

APPLICATIONS FOR GINGER OIL ZINGIBER OFFICINALE

- Ginger exhibits 5-HT3 receptor antagonism that effectively antagonizes serotonin at 5-HT3 receptors. This effect is mediated by galanolactone, a diterpenoid isolated from ginger (Huang et al., 1991).

- Ginger oil appears to mediate its warming effects by decreasing body serotonin (Huang et al., 1990).

- The capsaicin-like effect of (6)-shogaol is possibly the analgesic substance found in ginger inhibiting the release of the neuropeptide, substance P (Onogi et al., 1992).

- Ginger oil is thought to be analgesic as well as anxiolytic (Vishwakarma et al., 2002).

- Ginger powder taken orally decreased osteoarthritis symptomatology (Altman and Marcussen, 2001).

- The gingerols are found in CO2 extracted essential oil of ginger. The shogaols and [6]-, [8]-, and [10]-gingerols, isolated from the methanolic extract of Z. officinale rhizome, exhibit antiemetic principles. (Kawai et al., 1994).

APREPITANT (EMEND), A NEUROKININ (NK1) receptor antagonist, is a new antiemetic agent that works by blocking substance P receptors. It is indicated for nausea related to anesthesia and chemotherapy. Aprepitant is more effective when combined with a 5-HT3 class of medication and a steroid. This NK1 receptor and substance P antagonist offers potential anxiolytic and antidepressant modulation as well (Dando and Perry, 2004).

SIDE EFFECT PROFILES OF ANTINAUSEA MEDICATIONS

THERE ARE RARE BUT potentially serious adverse drug reactions attributed to the various classes of antinausea medications. These adverse drug reactions range from mild confusion, dysphoria, headache, phlebitis, tics, torticolis, serotonin syndrome, neuroleptic malignant syndrome, and alpha blockade alterations in blood pressure to potential life-threatening cardiac rhythm disturbances. Droperidol is the subject of a black box warning by the FDA (Habib and Gan, 2003). This controversial warning describes the rational for patients to have a normal Q-T interval documented by ECG prior to intravenous administration of droperidol. The risk of the malignant ventricular dysrhythmias, called torsades de pointes, associated with droperidol is also known to occur with several of the new selective blocking agents of the serotonin 5-HT3 receptor antagonists. Perhaps ginger oil Z.

officinale could be considered an alternative for droperidol, even though one investigation failed to show antinausea benefit when droperidol was compared with powdered ginger root (Visalyuputra et al., 1998).

Ginger is a food product that is both safe and nontoxic, although sensitization could pose a potential problem. IgE allergy and food spice allergy had negative prick-test results for sensitization to ginger (Moneret-Vautrin et al., 2002). Mild gastrointestinal burning and sedation appear to be the only side effects of several grams orally ingested per day (Sripramote and Lekhyanada, 2003). The essential oil of ginger Z. officinale can be safely and directly administered to the emetic centers of the brain in the chemoreceptor trigger zone via the olfactory pathways as aromatic vapors and via skin absorption, transdermally. The nasal route of administration is utilized successfully for many FDA-approved medications, especially those related to the treatment of allergic and vasomotor rhinitis.

Ginger oil Z. officinale had been thought to adversely affect platelet aggregation. Newer studies show that eating large doses of ginger powder or raw ginger root does change thromboxane concentration, which is reversible (Guh et al., 1995), but does not adversely affect the clotting ability of platelets as measured with clinical laboratory data (Lamb, 1994; Jannsen et al., 1996). Some preanesthetic check lists, name "ginger" as a potential source of herbal-drug interactions, possibly associated with bleeding (Hodges and Kam, 2002). This consideration possibly should be modified to include safe applications for the use of ginger.

MEDICAL MANAGEMENT OF POSTOPERATIVE NAUSEA AND VOMITING

INFORMED CONSENT SHOULD BE obtained for the provision of a general anesthetic prior to surgery. A specific consent for the use of complementary alternative medicine (CAM) also should be obtained. The use of essential oil of ginger Z. officinale perioperatively, in conjunction with positive suggestions that applications of ginger oil could assist in the prevention of postoperative nausea and vomiting, should be discussed. Adding ginger oil Z. officinale to the physician or nursing management of nausea can significantly impact the patients of any given facilities' daily casework. The essential oil of ginger, in a 10% solution of carrier oil such as jojoba oil, can be applied to ears, wrists, palms, and in children, the feet. Taking deep inhalations from the cupped palms over the nose and mouth during the preoperative time period immediately prior to surgery and during anesthesia evaluation, with the suggestion for the patient to smell oil ad lib prior to induction of general anesthesia, is convenient. Continuing the application of oil perioperatively and in the recovery room is even more effective.

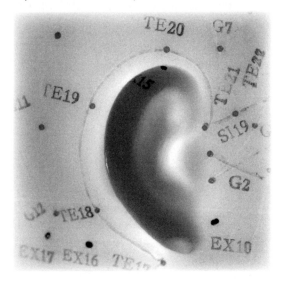

THE ROLL-ON METHOD can be used to apply 10% ginger oil Z. officinale to the ears and volar aspects of palms and wrists at the P6 Nei-Kuan acupressure points (Wang and Kain, 2002). Apply enough volume of oil to cover approximately a 4 cm2 area, using slight pressure at the P6 sites bilaterally. Another interesting option for PONV management utilizes a transcutaneous electrical nerve stimulator (TENS) unit, which delivers stimulation through gel electrodes oriented along the wrist at the P6 site. Electrical stimulation of P6 during anesthesia may reduce PONV by about 15% (Arnberger et al., 2007).

Clinical experience over four years with over 1000 patients at high risk for nausea, using ginger oil in combination with and without intravenous multimodal therapy when indicated to prevent nausea, has been very successful. The surgeries chosen have been open gynecological surgeries, upper and lower abdominal laparoscopic procedures, and operations requiring high-dose intravenous narcotic management of major postsurgical pain, as seen in spine fusion or total joint replacement. Patients were excluded if there was lack of time, interest, known ginger sensitivity, or surgical or personnel considerations. Possible congenital, acquired, or iatrogenic coagulation disorders, including patients requiring preoperative thromboembolic prophylaxis, were also excluded on a case-by-case basis. Patients can be prescribed multimodal antiemetic medication regimens, including various combinations of the following intravenous drugs: the selective blocking agent of the serotonin 5-HT3 receptor class, H1 and H2 blockers, metoclopramide, or dexamethazone, should they have breakthrough nausea.

CLINICAL IMPRESSIONS

PREVENTION OF POSTOP NAUSEA for nausea patients at high risk, using prophylactic multimodal intravenous medication therapy plus oil of ginger Z. Officinale, can be effective over 80% of the time, as measured by no complaint of nausea when questioned during the postanesthesia care unit (PACU) recovery period. In a similar group of patients prophylactically treated with multimodal intravenous therapy without ginger oil, one can expect almost no difference in the incidence of nausea/no nausea nor in PACU outcome, which is approximately 50/50. A previous multimodal antiemetic study indicated that choice of intravenous medication prophylaxis offered little impact on clinical outcome or in patient satisfaction (Darkow et al., 2001).

There have been no ill effects, such as dermal or gastric burning or sensitization, reported in any patients utilizing this application of ginger, when administered prior to the induction of general anesthesia. In this situation, in which sometimes as many as five to fifteen different medicines are given intravenously during the course of the anesthetic and surgery, no known adverse drug interactions, reactions, or bleeding due to oil of ginger Z. officinale are seen to occur.

LIMITATIONS AND CONSIDERATIONS FOR FUTURE INVESTIGATIONS

THE FOLLOWING DISCUSSION ENUMERATES the problems with these types of clinical experiences. Risk factors mentioned in studies that influence a meaningful clinical investigation included control for multiple variables such as age, gender, and nonsmoking history (Apfel and Roewer, 2003). More challenging control group considerations possibly could include nasal dominance, blood pressure, dependent or nondependent learned states, alternations in sense of smell due to medications and coexisting disease states, and prior ginger experience. Standardized extracts of phytopharmaceutical preparations are available and have been utilized for specific investigations of the various effects of the chemical constituents of ginger (Bonati, 1991).

These more challenging and perhaps unquantifiable control variables are potentially significant and relatively difficult to manage for most investigational purposes. A review of the clinical investigation intended should be presented to the investigational review board to ensure procedural protocols and respect for the patient's Health Insurance Portability and Accountability Act (HIPAA) privacy regulations. These considerations should be a primary concern in the care provided by aromatherapy practitioners (Miles and Tan, 2003).

Increasing numbers of adults are using Complementary Alternative Medicine (CAM) to improve their health. Some patients and surgeries may not be suited to receive essential oils. Ginger is considered a CAM therapy for migraine headaches (Mustafa and Srivastava, 1990). Perhaps the serotonin-mediated vasodilating properties of ginger are propagated via nasal inhalation. Cutaneous application of ginger oil, perioperatively, might contribute in the maintenance of critical body temperature during surgery. Other properties of the various chemical constituents of ginger are recognized, such as the antitumor promoting effects of [6]-gingerol and [6]-paradol, and the antimicrobial effects of monoterpenes 1,8-cineole, beta-pinene and alpha-terpineol found in ginger oil (Surh et al., 1999; Martins et al.., 2001).

CLINICAL INVESTIGATIONS

A REFERENCED LETTER PORTRAYS a general anesthesia study approved by the Ethics Research Committee, utilizing sweet orange essential oil. Children assessed themselves as more relaxed and cooperative at induction of anesthesia for dental surgery. Four drops of sweet orange essential oil were applied into a filter of the anesthesia circuit. This application was utilized to promote acceptance of the sevoflurane vapor gas mask induction of anesthesia and then removed for surgery to proceed in sixty children (Mehta, 1998). Several advantages were noted, and sweet orange essential oil was concluded to be safe and was recommended for continued use.

Different essential oils have been used to evaluate the prevention and treatment of nausea, such as the essential oil of peppermint (Anderson and Gross, 2004). Medical literature shows evidence pertaining to the effective use of essential oil of peppermint therapy in this field of postoperative nausea and vomiting (Tate, 1997). Peppermint has possible toxicity issues involving a disease known as G6PD deficiency (Olowe et al., 1980). No other phytopharmaceutical preparations have data in the medical literature that pertains to safety and efficacy in association with general anesthesia to the same extent as the studies with the various preparations of ginger oil Z. officinale.

Integrating prophylactic intravenous multimodal therapy with the essential oil of ginger Z. officinale therapy in acute care and ambulatory settings to prevent anesthesia-related potential complications of PONV significantly increases successful outcomes resulting in increased patient satisfaction. This clinical experience has methodological weaknesses. It is presented as having generated meaningful proof of principle data indicating a 10% solution CO_2 extracted oil of ginger Z. officinale to be a safe and effective choice for the prevention of PONV.

INCREASED PATIENT SATISFACTION

THE RESULTING CLINICAL IMPRESSION implies increased patient satisfaction and outcomes, and warrants further evaluation as well as consideration for change in the anesthetic perioperative assessment and management of PONV. These findings are similar to a previous study demonstrating the need for less intravenous antinausea medication during the recovery period in those patients who received ginger powder Z. officinale (Philips et al., 1993). Reducing the incidence of nausea by approximately 30%, if reproducible, is noteworthy. Perhaps other patients having fewer risk factors for nausea would benefit from application of ginger oil alone. Ginger oil effectively treats the three major components of nausea related to surgical interventions: general anesthetic agents, narcotics, and motion sickness.

These improved results over previous clinical investigations using powered ginger root taken as an oral premedication (Eberhart et al., 2003; Morin et al., 2004) are possibly due to the following combined effects: Therapeutic success may be attributed to the learned smell associated with ginger aromatherapy, utilizing the mind-body suggestion and guided imagery perioperatively; the increased potency of the essential oil of ginger Z. officinale as compared to other preparations as well as the method of application; the combined nasal and transdermal administration of the essential oil of ginger.

CHAPTER

Ideal Business

"Success, in any particular business, depends for one thing upon your possessing in a well-developed state the faculties required in that business."

—*Wallace D. Wattles Author of The Science of Getting Rich*

eight

CHAPTER

IDEAL BUSINESS

THE WELLNESS REVOLUTION IS rich in ideal remedies and ideal business opportunities. In ideal businesses, distributorships can be set up in special ways to provide multiple streams of income that continue through the years so that you can supplement your health and well-being. Having your health as well as the satisfaction of time, money, and the freedom to enjoy them is a viable goal. Establishing your independence from the government for Social Security or the stock market to maintain your mutual funds and retirement plan are also viable goals. These goals of financial independence could start with a decision to build a network marketing business now.

IDEAL "GREENHOUSE EARTH" BUSINESSES

RECEIVING EXTRA DIRECT DEPOSITS into your bank account is wonderful. You can "wake up with a smile," as Sir Richard Branson, creator of the Virgin brand, says he does. Sir Richard has created, among his many accomplishments, the suborbital passenger spaceship Virgin Galactica and the Virgin Earth Challenge, which offers a $25 million prize to the creative genius who helps our "Earth greenhouse" by designing a device to remove carbon from the atmosphere. Perhaps that person will invent a "scrubber" device that properly scavenges and scrubs the waste anesthetic gases from anesthesia machines around the world currently vented outside every operating room to the roof of hospitals and surgery centers. Waste anesthesia vapors are halogenated hydrocarbon gases that deplete the ozone.

That would give everybody, including former vice president, venture capitalist, presenter in the documentary film An Inconvenient Truth, and Nobel Peace Prize winner Al Gore, some much-needed help in the campaign to save the earth. The work of the Alliance for Climate Protection and Al Gore's visionary crusade for a global climate protection treaty was presented in Bali in 2008, and is intended to be brought into effect by 2010. Virtual networking "telepresence" videoconferencing will play a big role in reducing the greenhouse gas emissions causing global warming by decreasing the need for business travel. The sweet smell of that success will be a cleaner environment to live in and fresher air to breathe. For more information, visit http://www.climateprotect.org/.

We have a purpose. We are many. For this
purpose we will rise, and we will act.

—Al Gore

IMPRESSION OF INCREASE

FOR SEVERAL CENTURIES, AMERICAN philanthropists have abounded in good works, starting schools, hospitals, and businesses. Henry Ford, Napoleon Hill, and Eleanor Roosevelt among others, enabled cultural changes by their directed and undirected awards given for meritorious ideas and works. Philanthropy and community service are essential activities to complement one's personal life and integrate into one's business practice.

We have many current examples of successful givers paying their wealth forward to designated causes. Philanthropic causes that donors have chosen to support are documented to yield significant impacts on the basic wellness and well-being of the world's population, which is likely to persist for generations to come. You, too, could become a great philanthropist and help the helpless, like Warren Buffet, Bill Gates, Melinda Gates, Oprah Winfrey, and many others.

It is frequently stated that modern business cannot be conducted
on the line of the Sermon on the Mount. I can only say that a business
conducted on any other basis will never be permanently successful.

—Lord Leverhulme

"PERMANENTLY" IS A LONG time for a business to last, especially since many businesses fail early. All giving equals receiving. Therefore, in order for your business to become permanent, giving superior service will ensure that your client knows they have received maximum value for their purchase.

There are seven basic and admirable strategic policies of business ethics: recognizable trust, team-oriented and open-minded leadership, honoring commitments, respect and courtesy for all, documentation and accountability, hands-on accounting, and philanthropic community involvement. The lasting impression derived from the delivery of good service is increased good will between both businesses.

ALL THE GOOD THAT YOU DESERVE: NETWORK MARKETING

ARE YOU A PERSON who can develop relationships galore? Are you a dreamer with creative ideas, skills, and talents to be reckoned with? There are many potential multiple sources of income (MSI). The ideal business for you may be your current W-2 job, but not if you are an informed risk-taker with purpose, vision, and defined goals. My purpose in this chapter is to compare and contrast key elements of starting your own business from scratch, such as I did with oilMD, versus becoming a distributor of a product line that has a known track record, great potential, and superb support structure. This is the ideal network marketing business. Don't miss the next big thing by being fearful and unwilling to take quantified risks. Make the quantum jump, take that leap of faith, and then grow your wings and fly into your own new business. Do it informed.

You can get a spot in a network marketing company by enrolling with a sponsor, kick-starting a second career as a health and wealth mentor while you work at your own pace using other people's money. The network marketing company pays the expenses to operate the business, such as research and development, payroll, fulfillment center, websites, the physical plant, manufacturing, employees, and much more. Your investment is in time and tools. Information costs but it more than pays for itself.

> *When you choose a direct selling company, you're not simple affiliating with a supplier—you're selecting a partner for your business.*
> —**Paul Pilzer, author of *The New Wellness Revolution***

YOUR HOME-BASED BUSINESS

IF THIS SOUNDS ATTRACTIVE to you, then you can enroll with some of the friendly people of multilevel marketing (MLM). Find a business with a payment plan that is rich and fair, with no breakage and good compression. Find a business with no complicated bookkeeping or paperwork. Start operating your own home-based business. Get business cards and get psyched when you pick a personalized universal resource locator (URL) for your business using the basic website that the network marketing company provides you as part of your enrollment. Use a business credit card and business checking account to document expenses so the tax benefits are both legal and significant.

There is a small investment for minimal product line inventory, marketing tools, and personal growth study materials. There are no employees until you realize you need a personal assistant. Start building your team. Make a commitment and do the things required to be successful. Enrolling several qualified people per week per year to develop a substantial business is a realistic goal.

Very early on, your sales goal will be to cover the cost of your own household's dietary and supplement requirements. Realize that goal and build from there. A home-based business operates without deliveries to make unless you want to, because your distributors and consumers have their products shipped to them automatically each month. That way, there is no stress to anyone—just consumption.

BE YOUR OWN BOSS

AS THE DISTRIBUTOR FOR a large company, you do the marketing and enroll new partners in your own business as well as take orders. Certain other requirements for success involve participating in company meetings and conference calls. Practice a low-pressure, calm lifestyle free from management of extensive product inventory, overhead, and costly investments in a physical plant. A practical and immediate business opportunity would be to enroll in a network marketing company that provides templates of websites customizable for their products for a fraction of the cost and effort. Then advise your clients to purchase the products online. Get new contacts using advanced services provided by autoresponder resources to purchase qualified leads, that drive new customers to your own website for a cost-effective, web-based sales and marketing experience.

DISTRIBUTE THE AWESOME TWOSOME: HEALTH AND WEALTH

THE NEW PRODUCTS OF the Wellness Revolution bring new paradigms of health benefits. Up-sell around town to the places where you normally shop and use services, such as the gym, hardware store, hair and nail salon, dental and doctors offices. These businesses could be actively consuming and selling essential oils, juices, and other "green" wellness products to their clients, developing more lines of revenue. Offer an educational in-service to the owner, office manager, and staff, teaching how the products offer a strong wellness platform that they can promote with confidence. Present third-party literature as well as emerging scientific reference articles and abstracts. Enroll the employees in the office's new business model, creating a novel form of profit sharing for the employees so they can be motivated to promote the sales program and enjoy their new revenue stream. Enroll qualified and quality people hungry to benefit from the health and wealth products sold by your own home-based distributorship. You can help keep the baby boomers youthful and in the green.

Be a super prospector for new enrollees to get a fast start on a flowing stream of income. Rejection is part of prospecting, so accept it graciously and keep moving forward. Join a team and follow the team plan. Read and distribute specialized magazines, such as Your Business at Home and Success from Home, from the publisher of Success Magazine, which are available at major bookstores. Meet people and build relationships. Distribute the awesome twosome: health and wealth.

Nice Girls Do Get the Sale, by Elinor Stutz, is highly profitable reading. Her book about relationship building teaches how to gets results with remarkably detailed and inspirational material. It provides a clear path to success in any network marketing business. Her career could be described as the model for relationship selling. Her technique is to overdeliver information at a fair price, and her book is loaded with Nice Girl Sales Tips, such as look forward to each day, share the passion with your prospects, let others help you, hold a helping hand out to those one step behind you, spread the joy of philanthropic activities, and become known as the expert. She is a wonderful storyteller. Catch her fire!

THE BEST COMMUNICATOR WINS

STORYTELLING IS A MARVELOUS skill to develop. You can build relationships by telling your story with sincere, heartfelt passion and eye contact. Applying the techniques of "permission marketing" will grow your business. Using this technique, you ask for permission to tell your story. People love to hear a good story and will permit a complete business presentation to follow one. Practice to do both well, because it is never certain which parts of your story or presentation will convince a prospect to enroll. People will appreciate that extra effort to be complete. Gerry Robert, speaker and author of *The Millionaire Mindset* and *A Tale of Two Websites*, tells his success story, vividly revealing how personal tribulation led to tremendous personal growth and net worth through the development of successful business strategies and relationships.

There are many good books and tools of the success industry. *Closers Get Paid*, by Mark Wilson, is one example of a resource that teaches techniques for closing any deal. There are audio tools that you can use, turning your car into a mobile success university as you transform hundreds of commuting hours into an inspirational education. Invest in yourself by taking a private morning hour to get oriented, educated, and fired up for a day of prospecting for clients.

Persistence is the sustained effort necessary to induce faith.
—Napoleon Hill

IN THIS IDEAL BUSINESS, you are not absolutely required to become a product expert, but it's been proven that education in network marketing skills and a home-business mindset are essential for success in this industry. If you don't like multilevel marketing, you can change your thinking until you do like it. You can get a new education and develop new skills. Hang out with the movers and shakers at the meetings. Network with other dreamers. Join Loral Langemeier's Big Table group and experience the thrill of getting an education in wealth cycle investing. Langemeier's book, *The Millionaire Maker*, tells a series of engaging stories about individual financial challenges and wins. It is the real deal. Build new relationships with those who have similar dreams for time and money freedom. Be prepared to accept rejection from your warm market of family and friends along the way without discouragement and keep on keeping on. You can think and grow rich by acting in a certain way.

CURRENT AND FUTURE ELEMENTS OF BUSINESS NETWORKING

- Enroll with a business model that is proven successful.

- Utilize corporate support.

- Develop empowered network marketing skills.

- Get mentored and coached for personal growth.

- Educate yourself with promotional materials by notable experts in their field.

- Read books, journals, and business magazines.

- Do business presentations and attend training calls.

- Get a personalized URL template and hosted website.

- Distribute video-embedded website and email content.

- Use telepresence videoconferencing and webinars.

- Manage a database of market leads with web autoresponders.

- Network in communities, forums, and blogs.

- Distribute third-party tools, such as CDs, DVDs, magazines, brochures.

- Utilize professional product fulfillment.

- Merge web 2.0 technology with service-oriented architecture.

INVEST IN THE TOOLS

DR. ANIL K. AGARWAHL, author of *Extreme Dental Practice Makeover* and developer of WIN Practice Performance Dental Seminars, is a stellar example of an entrepreneur creating an ideal business. The methods and materials Dr. Agarwahl describes are stellar in design and practice. All business operations should operate within universal guidelines, benefiting from applying the principles of the Law of Compensation and the Golden Rules of Business. The spiritual and financial laws of the universe pertaining to creation of wealth are explained eloquently by Karen Russo in her book, *The Money Keys*. Russo's book and course materials are important investments in your growth toward achieving freedom and financial power.

By using your own mental faculties and the tools of your trade, you can create successful enterprises for multiple sources of income. People with creative ideas and ingenuity build the new commercial phases of the web and beyond. Patricia Drain, author of *Seven Secrets for Building a Business That Has Value*, teaches how to work on your business instead of working in your business. You can learn how to get paid twice from the income the business earns and ultimately enjoy the income from the sale of the business because you developed an exit strategy. The Wellness Revolution is looking for innovative men and women to use their creative mental faculties to do well.

CREATIVE MENTAL FACILITIES

TAKE A QUANTUM LEAP into new possibilities. Envision yourself making enough money to require that you have a professionally written job description as president of your business. This justifies the salary you pay yourself for providing significant amounts of service in the form of education and direct management of your business. It will take more than extra measures of brain power and willpower to create your own business from scratch. It takes investment cash to cover all the consultations and independent services that must be contracted to be a legal start-up.

Exercise the due diligence required to make an informed decision before starting any business, because any given company, franchise, or business opportunity might be on shaky ground financially or morally. Every venture and enterprise entails risk, but if the proposed company and the products check out and your team is solid, your dreams can come to pass.

The law of attraction responds to your paradigm not your intellect.

—Bob Proctor

Your risk-taking paradigms determine what you get out of life. Invest in yourself by joining the Science of Getting Rich Club (SGRC) so you can learn how to identify and eliminate viral paradigms and realize your creative possibilities. Learn how and why risk-takers make things happen. Read the SGR advertisement found in the back of this book and consider how much this seminar will cost you if you do not take it. You can enroll for SGR using the oilMD affiliate program by going to www.SGROILMD.com. Once enrolled, you will receive an affiliate URL, which you can redirect using your own personalized SGR URL. You can purchase your own name and any other URL that you create at Go Daddy or Network Solutions and redirect it to your SGR affiliate URL, network marketing website or blog. Your enrollment buys you the seminar and the right to sell it for $500 profit. Each subsequent sale generates $250. You will be happy and grateful you took The Science of Getting Rich Seminar, presented by teachers Bob Proctor, Jack Canfield, and the Rev. Michel Beckwith, and based on the book by Wallace D. Wattles. Become associated with people for whom wealth is a predictable result.

Fall back on the contemplation of your vision, and increase your purpose and faith. And by all means, in times of doubt and indecision, cultivate gratitude.

—Wallace Wattles

INCORPORATION, PRIVATE LABELING, AND TRADEMARKS

HIRE SPECIALIZED LEGAL COUNSEL to assist you in creating a professional corporation (PC) or limited liability corporation (LLC), which are often based on professional credentials (e.g., MD, or intended tax status). It is important to get legal advice if you intend to sell your own or another company's products. You may need specialty insurance coverage plans for businesses of the Wellness Revolution. You should procure product liability and business liability insurance through an insurance broker.

Private labeling and trademarks are considerable expenses for each and every product and mark. At the U.S. Patent and Trademark Office website, you can easily do a name search to get your creative juices started. A lawyer specializing in trademarks could be essential for easing the implementation of worldwide trademarks. I recommend the service noted in the ad in the back of this book. You will receive numerous mailings after you apply for a trademark. Your lawyer should complete all registrations.

Running your own business operations alone is not ideal. It is much better to build a team of professionals. Hire independent contractors, such as Your Entity Solutions (Y.E.S.), for their expertise and specialized services in entity formation, keeping tax implications in mind. Independent contractors can provide the services necessary to fulfill certain jobs such as minutes, accounting, legal consultations, web design, and product fulfillment. Check online business bureaus for affiliations and ask for recommendations.

SUCCESS IS IN THE MARGINS

HOW BIG OR HOW small are the margins for the products of your start-up business? Estimate production costs (which might include private labeling), sales and marketing costs, and other costs to determine the total business budget. Create a complete business profile and plan. Public relations and a media package are integral to the business marketing plan. Include advertising in that budget. An advertising budget promotes creativity by enabling the formulation of ideas that will work within a framework promoting the bottom line (i.e., improved margin and more profits). The corporation will save money by finding "e-ways" to do business. Create new income streams by turning by-products of your business into new sources of revenue. Learn how to maintain all intellectual property rights and copyrights for brochures and sales and marketing materials. Turn your written works into specialized e-books, profitable by-products of your own intellectual property that you self-publish and sell online. (www.youpublish.com)

THERE ARE REGULATIONS AND policies that govern the structure and function of your ideal business. When you file for LLC or PC status, or for a URL, choose the name carefully. Think globally and think universally. Determine ownership, funding, and loan payback responsibilities. Open secure online bank accounts, credit cards, and merchant accounts. Some network marketing companies are multinational. Dream of a plan that directs payments to your bank accounts 24/7 from all business sales made through affiliates, distributorships, and retail sales as MSIs from all over the world. Advertise on the web with tools from a multiplicity of avenues, including streaming videos.

MAKING THE WEB WORK

HIRE PROFESSIONALS TO DESIGN your website for the look, feel, and function that will entice your demographic to shop online. Search engine optimization (SEO) and shopping cart content are best written in conjunction with an SEO copywriter. Website materials for refund policies and frequently asked questions (FAQs) should be legally reviewed by professional copywriting services. Hire professional designers to create all materials and graphics. Set up your own blogs on various sites and fill them with specialized front page content for Google's blog search engine. Consider enlisting a product fulfillment business with call centers that provide 24/7 live service representatives from other time zones around the world. Setting up merchant accounts to process credit cards and a fulfillment center to expedite shipping, receiving, and returns of goods is costly but essential. Locate a contracted and SSL-secure host server for website content and shopping cart.

To build your database, your e-commerce websites should include a special content management system (CMS) that provides the framework on which to build add-ons for playing videos and downloading free content such as an e-book, MP3 file, or newsletter to those who register. You can also become your own YouTube by showing streaming video clip content on your website. Broadcast your own intellectual property on the web to computers and televisions, using subscription-on-demand and pay-per-view services. You can also embed yourself in your business emails by creating a personalized audio-video content message. Enroll through my affiliation with Virtual Media Direct found at www.GeigerVideo.com, which provides eye-catching web-based tools for your business as well as another potential MSI for you. Redirect your contacts from your personalized URL to the company video presentation and collect prospect data to receive a series of autoresponder-generated emails. VMDirect enables your business, whether large or small, to broadcast on the web, communicating by using your intellectual property as webinars and teleseminars in combined audio-video broadcasts. The media suite also includes blogging and podcasting abilities as well as autoformatting for all types of uploaded and broadcast media services.

You can get really creative and make a series of videos to introduce and promote a lead capture page. The oilMD www.10aromatherapysecrets.com lead capture page is set up with specialized script to allow the addition of names and email addresses in exchange for the oilMD's ebook. This process builds a business database that can managed with an autoresponder like AWEBBER to send out informative newsletters and teleconferencing call alerts. These new methods of social marketing and techniques for product launch use the web for increased leverage, which enables the inspired, globally minded businessperson to build a database of potential customers who will receive personalized opt-in autoresponder email advertisements. Make the web work for your businesses.

STREAMING VIDEO COMMERCIALIZED

WATCHING GOOGLE WATCHING US is fun and profitable, especially if you are into the new and rapidly advancing future of online streaming video. YouTube is a very popular place to upload videos. Every day, more video is placed on YouTube than there are searches on the Google search engine. Google's free tool, YouTube Insight, is akin to Google Analytics, the paid advertiser metric service. YouTube Insight enables users, partners, and advertisers that have YouTube accounts to view detailed metrics about the videos they upload and how viewers came to view a specific video. Uploaders can view data defining the viewing habits of the public in terms of geographic region, how long it takes for a video to become popular, and what happens to video views as popularity peaks. This service provides insight into viewing trends for enhanced target market acquisition. Evaluating video metrics will become increasingly crucial to monitor the effectiveness of digital video ads on socially and mobile-targeted networks.

Use social and viral network marketing to reach the ever-increasing millions of people on social websites such as MySpace, iGoogle, Tagworld, Friendster, Facebook, and the counterpart for boomers called TeeBeeDee, which stands for "to be determined," found at www.TBD.com. Numerous media players can be customized with embedded advertisements promoting your own network marketing products. Try XLrevsharemedia.com for starters. You can get banner ads from the Better Business Bureau for your website, which will give your shopping cart more credibility. Enlist all the ingredients necessary to validate and promote any type of businesses on the web, especially wellness products and services like those of holistic spas.

OPEN A MED-SPA OR HEALING ARTS CENTER

CONSUMERS CRAVE CREATIVE SPA services. Consider opening a wellness or healing arts center or medical spa that offer the new laser skin therapies. Sell privately labeled skin-care products with essential oils or offer such unique services as aromatherapy massage in an upscale environment. Since med-spas are vehicles for medical procedures, they must be directed by a licensed physician. A med-spa must have properly licensed and certified personnel for each procedure to be an ideal business. The degree of supervision by nurses, physician assistants, or cosmetologists is a critical element. All procedures should be preceded by informed consent, meaning the consumer is told what they really need to know about the risks of any given technique or procedure. Trust those who demonstrate caution and competence when selling services and obtaining consent.

Ask about complications and who is available to handle them. Ask if there is a plan for the physician to transport to a hospital and admit a client/patient who experiences a serious complication. Observe the facility and verify that it is clean. Note the style of advertising done by the medical spa. Evaluate the ad campaign to see if the expectations presented are reasonable, or if the claims made are high pressure and unrealistic. Check for recommendations pertaining to any given spa services and the physician in charge. Spa services can be life-changing events, either positive or negative.

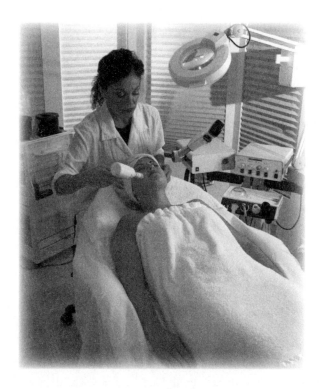

SKIN CARE IS BIG BUSINESS

SPAS TAKE THEIR SKIN services very seriously. Skin is the body's largest organ. Skin that is very dry can benefit from certain foods taken internally and specific types of supplements, lotions, and oils applied externally. Skin becomes thinner, less elastic, and drier with age. Aging also decreases production of natural oils of the skin. You can protect skin from within with dietary intake of foods rich in antioxidants, such as fruits, vegetables, beans, whole grains, and especially foods that contain certain types of healthy fat, such as monounsaturated fat from olive oil. It also helps to increase your intake of omega-3s from salmon, walnuts, and white and green teas. Eliminating polyunsaturated vegetable oil and partially hydrogenated oils from the diet is a good dietary strategy for healthy skin. Find skin care products that are organic juice solutions to complement your inner beauty.

HEALING PHYTOMOLECULES

THE PHYTOMOLECULES IN MEDICINAL plants protect and heal skin. Oils from plants can reduce the undesirable effects of aging and the harmful effects of the sun, as well as reduce swelling and redness caused by inflammation. Jojoba oil, from a desert shrub, is 50% of the jojoba seed by weight. Jojoba oil consists of esters, a nongreasy, waxy substance that is not readily absorbed by the skin. The oil is a straight chain ester made up of 35 to 46 carbons. Each molecule consists of a fatty acid and a fatty alcohol joined by an ester bond. Jojoba oil has significant anti-inflammatory properties and forms a smoothing, healing coating on the skin. It is a natural preservative and can be blended in conjunction with essential oils as a versatile carrier oil for dry skin, normal skin, oily skin, and mature skin.

The term "vulnerary" refers to healing or treating wounds with a preparation, plant, or drug used to cure them. It comes from the Greek word vulnus, meaning "wound."

Tamanu (Calophyllum inophyllum) oil, another fine example of carrier oil, is great for burns, and radiation burns in particular. It contains terpenes, sterols, and vitamin F from fatty acids, plus the flavonoid coumarinic derivatives. Interestingly, tamanu is a member of the mangostin family (like the mangosteen fruit), which is rich in xanthones and also has strong anti-inflammatory properties. Skin acts as a reservoir for the chemicals and phytomolecules of all skin-care products and treatments, which allows for prolonged local and possibly systemic effects from gradual reabsorption of those chemicals and phytomolecules. Therefore, choose carefully which ingredients you place on the skin.

BOTANICAL HOLISTIC SKIN CARE

LEARN TO LOVE YOUR skin with essential oils. It is wonderful to mix a rich, long-lasting base note essential oil, a middle note essential oil, and an effervescent top note essential oil with jojoba in order to create the best blend for your skin type. Certain essential oils with specific properties work better than others for each of the four skin types. They can be applied mixed with moisturizer or as a compress. Use therapeutic-grade essential oils diluted with jojoba or rose hip seed oil that has been analyzed to ensure purity. Awaken your skin to botanical holistic healing.

Mature and dry skin types associated with aging and arid climate commonly benefit from revitalizing essential oil remedies. A mixture of ylang ylang, Lavandula angustifolia, and patchouli or vanilla oils in a 4% solution with jojoba oil is a wonderful dry skin therapy. Oily skin may benefit from astringent oils such as tea tree, geranium, and German chamomile. Sensitive skin types may benefit from lavender, rose, and neroli. Products and recipes are abundant but be certain to "patch test" each product or blend you create on the skin somewhere besides the face.

Skin is inhabited by two bacterial groups, resident and transient. Some skin-cleansing products contain essential oils that have been shown to decrease but not totally remove both groups of skin bacteria. Doctors, nurses, food handlers, and people who provide spa treatments must wash their hands between contacts to prevent transfer of pathologic skin-contaminating bacteria. Freshen up with essential oils on the hands while traveling. Hand washing with skin-cleansing products containing essential oils is effective and refreshing.

SPA FOR THE SENSES, SOUL, AND SPIRIT

THERE ARE MORE THAN ten thousand spas in the United States, plus thousands more worldwide. It would take a life time to visit even the most enticing of spas. Consider the endless possibilities of day spas, retreat spas, resort spas, spas with thermal/mineral springs, or medical spas. Each spa has its own exotic personality exemplified by holistic wellness, intuitive healing, culinary creativity, seasonal recreation, cultural bounty, and ecogeographic magnificence. Service-oriented excellence is expected by all those who seek satisfaction for their senses, soul, and spirit. Getting acquainted with all the spas and their services could be a delightful pursuit of therapeutic tranquility! One place to begin harmonizing your body and soul is the Sacred Soul Spa. (www.sacredsoulspa.com)

Spa luxuries and indulgences are available on any continent. Your five senses and spiritual awareness can be stimulated and magnified with the ideal scents of essential oils, the vibrations of Tibetan bowls, and the energized light that comes through an eastern window. Visualize yourself shrouded in the spa secrets of China, embedded in the Costa Rican jungle canopy, or sensing the powerful vortex energy generated by the red rocks of Sedona at the Sedona Spa in Arizona.

The original Canyon Ranch in Tucson, Arizona, which opened in 1979, is the epitome of the spa industry's sweet smell of success, having branched out to SpaClubs in Las Vegas and Florida, and on the Queen Mary II. Canyon Ranch living communities are selling well in Tucson, Miami Beach, and Chicago. Spa Magazine, featuring spas from all over the world, is an excellent place to research Canyon Ranch or plan your dream destination for a blissful spa experience. (www.spamagazine.com)

The previously mentioned examples of possible business opportunities of the wellness industry and network marketing are business models. They require something special of the owner to become successful, not to mention a great deal of work. Remember, you can own and operate a network marketing business that distributes wellness products that are being sold appropriately in spas and many other business settings. Make an appointment with the office manager or owner to tell your success story and get the sale. Enrolling spas, chiropractic offices, and massage clinics is a fabulous way to improve business for all parties. These businesses are happy marketplaces. Have a social networking party, invite contacts, and celebrate the new business venture together.

Success in health and wealth follows happiness. Jack Canfield, highlighted in *The Secret* and author of *The Success Principles,* is one of America's preeminent success coaches who co-authors the phenomenally sensational *Chicken Soup for the Soul* series with his partner, another great philanthropist, Mark Victor Hansen. One of their latest books, *Chicken Soup for the Network Marketer's Soul,* is a truly inspirational read. This book unveils the greatest network marketing stories ever told. Together, these wonderful cocreators have produced a great many written publications and seminars that have motivated and changed people's lives worldwide. Their worthy ideal goal is to publish the first billion coauthored books of a series. The sweet smell of that success is the change in people's soul life when they make a choice to grow.

Change is inevitable. Personal growth is a choice.
—**Bob Proctor**

LIVES GOVERNED BY LAWS
IN THE AGE OF GRACE

BOB PROCTOR'S LIFELONG PURSUIT to apply success principles is transmuted into his seminars, coaching programs, and public-speaking presentations, because as Wallace D. Wattles has noted, There is a thinking stuff from which all things are made, and in which, in its original state, permeates, penetrates, and fills the interspaces of the universe. A thought in this substance produces the thing that is imagined by the thought. A person can form things in their thought, and by impressing their thoughts upon formless substance, can cause the thing one thinks about to be created.

Above all, it's important to realize that we have to place business in its proper perspective. That's why I enjoy books like *Business for the Glory of God: The Bible's Teaching on the Moral Goodness of Business*, by Wayne Grudem. He specifically states in the chapter titled "Money": "In fact money is fundamentally good because it is a human invention that sets us apart from the animal kingdom and enables us to subdue the earth by producing from the earthgoods and services that bring benefit to others."

CERTAINLY THE RICHEST MAN of all time, King Solomon, knew that. In *The Richest Man Who Ever Lived: King Solomon's Secret to Success, Wealth and Happiness*, author Steven K. Scott writes, "Being prudent is a choice you must make every day. Being prudent is a decision that needs to be made every time you face an important decision in any area of life. Whether you are facing a business decision, a financial decision, or a personal decision, choose first to look well into the matter. If you make that choice and apply the appropriate steps of action you will find wise decisions being made that will bring you tremendous rewards."

Joyce Meyer has sold two million copies of her book, *The Battlefield of the Mind*. The many stories she tells of her life and ministry are remarkable. She also teaches amazing principles on her TV show, Enjoying Everyday Life, with such approachable authority that she rocks the mind into understanding and believing God's plan for you. "Where the mind goes, the man follows," she has said.

In *The Treasure Principle: Unlocking the Secret of Joyful Giving*, Randy Alcorn comments that "giving infuses life with joy. It interjects an eternal dimension into even the most ordinary day. That's just one reason you can't pay me enough not to give." So I exhort you to be a giver in business. Then you won't be a dead sea, because you'll have an outflow and where there's an outflow, there is room for an inflow.

THE POWER OF NETWORKING:
DECIDE TO NETWORK

IN CONCLUDING THIS CHAPTER, I offer this poem by Robert Muller, former assistant secretary-general of the United Nations:

Use every letter you write, use every conversation you have,

Every meeting you attend,

To express your fundamental beliefs and dreams.

Affirm to others the vision,

Of the world you want.

Network through thought,

Network through love, network through spirit.

You are the center of the network.

You are the center of the world.

You are a free, immensely powerful source,

Of life and goodness.

Affirm it. Spread it. Radiate it.

Think day and night about it,

And you will see a miracle happen:

The greatness of your own life.

Not in a world of big power,

Media and monopolies,

But of the five and a half billion individuals.

Networking is the new freedom, the new

democracy, a new form of happiness.

CHAPTER *nine*

Ideal Products

"Let food be your medicine and medicine be your food."

—Hippocrates

CHAPTER

IDEAL PRODUCTS

CENTURIES AGO, HIPPOCRATES CREATED the specialty of "nutritional medicine." Today, consumers practice food avoidance behavior when eating out, and they shop for food with a healthy purpose and function. Consumers choose to avoid pesticides, hormones, antibiotics, preservatives, food colorings, nitrates/nitrites, and genetically modified organisms (GMOs). At the same time, the movement for treating animals ethically influences product testing and encourages range-free/pasture-raised farming practices. Yet, consumers still demand the same qualities in functional foods: good taste, convenience, quality, premium ingredients, and value. The food industry and wellness entrepreneurs are responding with hundreds of new products that meet these criteria in each of ten functional food categories.

FUNCTIONAL FOODS

SINCE 2000, THE TOP ten functional food categories in this $50 billion U.S. industry are:

- Kids' foods

- 100 calorie-limited foods

- Phyto-solution foods

- Foods with multiple benefits

- Healthier fats

- Specialty food choices for the maturing populace

- Low glycemic index and gluten-free whole grains

- Organics

- Fun/novelty foods

- Performance-boosting beverages

THE PERFORMANCE-DRINK INDUSTRY reached almost $2 billion in sales in 2005 and is poised for more spectacular growth, because two-thirds of Americans say they are concerned about their energy levels. Those in the 18 to 25 age range are the biggest consumers of energy sports beverages, and 75 million Gen Y-ers will continue to drive this market upward to $5 billion by 2010. The unacceptable downside of this trend is the deleterious physiological effect on youth and adults who drink beverages extremely high in alcohol (Oteri, 2007), sugar, high-fructose corn syrup, and caffeine instead of eating a nutritious breakfast, lunch, and dinner. The alternative is a natural energy drink that is formulated with an exotic fruit juice of high antioxidant value that is also fortified with minerals. The youth make fabulous consumers and an even better sales force; baby boomers are also particularly strong users of ready-to-drink tea and coffee energy beverages.

Beverages now come in many formulations, and the future holds all kinds of new creative beverages. White and green teas have tremendous wellness properties provided by the major antioxidative polyphenols and epigallocatechin-gallate (EGCG). Caffeine is a stimulant of the central nervous system, respiratory system, and cardiac muscle. Coffee has around sixty polyphenolic antioxidant compounds. Guarana, a natural herbal source of guaranine, which is somewhat like caffeine, contains more milligrams per ounce of guaranine than coffee does caffeine and is an acceptable caffeine substitute.

TAURINE TIPS

MANY ENERGY DRINKS CONTAIN the new substrate for protein nutrition called taurine, which is the most abundant free amine in the intracellular compartment of the body. Taurine plays a functional role in stabilizing the electrical membrane potential of the cell, promotes calcium transport, exerts positive inotropic (contractile) effects on the heart, as well as maintains stable cardiac rhythm and normal blood pressure (Nittynen, 1999). Taurine is a fundamental nutritional supplement that assists the body to cope with the negative effects of catabolic stress (Merheb, 2007). Naturally sourced energy drinks made with standardized extracts of xanthone-rich fruit such as mangosteen, which are fortified with antioxidants, minerals, and such amines as taurine, provide energy as well as nutritional health benefits.

GENETICALLY MODIFIED ORGANISMS

THE INTERNATIONAL CENTER FOR Science and High Technology (ICS-UNIDO), a branch of United Nations Industrial Development Organization, meets regularly to discuss material pertaining to medicinal and aromatic plants (MAPs), because they are concerned that the industry is getting so large and is underregulated. At a meeting in May 2005 in Trieste, Italy, ICS-UNIDO announced that the global trade in MAPs and their wide spectrum of resulting health care products is steadily growing, exceeding $60 billion annually.

The United States' mission to ensure health practices and standards is expressed in the work of the National Institutes of Health. The NIH Office of Dietary Supplements (ODS) regulates the use of supplements, because there are numerous instances of problems with products, such as false contents and false claims. The FDA and USDA are up against difficult problems when it comes to our supply source of foods and drugs. The amount of food inspected is only 1% of the total imported. Many of our processed foods are made using food materials from other countries, especially China. More and more foods are processed by altering, adulterating, genetically cloning meats, and genetically manipulating our crops to suit the desires of the food production industries. Worldwide food marketplaces can be followed online and studied to raise your awareness; visit http://www.foodnavigator.com/.

To date, there have been numerous recalls and incidents of poisoning of foods with various types of bacteria. The loss of control of genetically modified corn and rice has also been reported. Mutated rice spreads geographically, thus contaminating other varieties of rice by cross-fertilization. These wild, mutant rice variants now have regulatory approval after the fact for use in the human food chain since the growers had lost control of the reproduction of the mutant strains of rice. More details can be read in Marc Gunther's article, "Attack of the Mutant Rice." Presumably, we have been viewing TV commercials for GMOs without disclaimers for some time now, since over a trillion GMO meals have been served.

Food labs have undertaken many studies to determine which essential oils could be used in food packaging to deter contamination by organisms of all classes. For example, there have been numerous cases of E. coli contamination of ground beef and spinach. Essential oils of basil and oregano can be used in plastic food packaging to suppress such pathogenic bacteria. In terms of animal husbandry, essential oils are also efficacious in the prevention of the gross infectious diseases, as well as in increasing productivity when the oils are added to feed of the animals penned in feed lots. Certain essential oils studied in vitro can also kill Clostridium botulinum and the salmonella bacteria, which have been determined to be contaminants of some recalled processed foods such as chili and peanut butter.

A publication of the CODEX Alimentarious Commission, a branch of the World Health Organization, enumerates guidelines for vitamins and mineral and food supplements. Purportedly, this guideline does not restrict access to vitamins and supplements but rather is designed to enhance international fair trade. As consumers, we need to remain aware and vocal about protecting our rights to convenient access to safe prescription medications, supplements, and food products.

WELLNESS PARADIGMS

CLEARLY, AS CONSUMERS, WE need new programs and studies to protect our interests and access to natural products and supplements that we can apply as we see fit. The ODS has undertaken numerous studies in conjunction with the National Institutes of Health. Their budget has grown from $3.5 million in 1999 to $27 million in 2006. Some of that money has been spent on studies of the relationship between aging and supplementation. Human studies with phytoestrogens, vitamin D, and osteoarthritis of the knee; chromium and enhancement of insulin signaling; modulation of autoimmunity by green tea phenolics; brain neuron modulator effects of ginkolides and bilobalides; and the mechanism of prostatic cancer prevention by lycopene have had mixed results.

Superior medicinal foods have health benefits that are exceedingly broad, affecting every organ system. Recent studies have shown saw palmetto and glucosamine/chondroitin to be less effective in relieving prostatic and arthritic symptoms as original studies suggested. A personal trial of these supplements is now recommended. It would be a good idea to verify whether or not you, the individual, experience a relief of symptoms through supplementation with saw palmetto or glucosamine/chondroitin.

AT LEAST AS LIKELY AS NOT

MOST PEOPLE AGREE WE need more substantial studies of all therapies, whether allopathic or CAM. Dr. Ted Gansler said the type of CAM used "is significantly influenced by gender, race, age, education, cancer type, and how far the cancer had spread." Younger, more affluent and more educated members of the group tend to be adopters of the therapies. Women were more likely than men to use energy techniques such as Yoga and Tai Chi (10.1 vs. 1.9%) and manipulative practices such as massage (16.9 vs. 3.9%). The difference between genders was less apparent for non-spiritual mind-body methods such as hypnosis, meditation and aromatherapy (58.6 vs. 42.8%) (Gansler, 2008).

An example, is is found with the use of black cohosh for a menopausal symptom of anxiety is the only herbal that has "statistically significant results" shown in a CAM study. Numerous other herbs, oils, and supplements have implied "at least as likely as not" quality of life improvement anecdotal relief of the symptoms of menopause known as hot flashes. A large percentage of in vitro (within the glass) research and in vivo (within the living) research has been published on all sorts of CAM medicines and practices outside the United States. The quality of all research is under clinical suspicion, whether undertaken as proof of principle, retrospectively, or as a prospectively designed research paper. That is why all research must be designed and written so as to be reproducible.

Recently, the United States Institute of Medicine has determined a link between Agent Orange and hypertension, and has recommended that the VA cover hypertension as well as the current list of diseases caused by the toxin. When my father was applying for disability through the VA system, the legal phrase used as a "means test" by the government stated that his exposure to Agent Orange in Vietnam had to meet the standard of "at least as likely as not" in order to be considered the cause of his physical disability. This phrase appeals to me as a means of evaluating supplement studies. Rather than casting aside all supplements for not providing statistically significant results, a more likely method of analysis could be that supplements are at least as likely as not the reason for improved health benefits.

OBSERVATIONAL AND INTERVENTIONAL

NEW FDA GUIDANCE PROVIDES details for analyzing an evidenced-based review system for the scientific evaluation of health claims, primarily using two types of studies. Observational studies measure associations between substance and disease, while intervention studies are randomized controlled studies. The nature of the fields of food supplements and evidence-based clinical aromatherapy would require more significant research, which is difficult to generate in order to reach the new FDA standards for substantiating health structure and function claims.

MEDICINAL FOODS

THINK FOR A MOMENT about which foods and supplements you put in your mouth. Now ask yourself, are they good for me? Could you classify your meals as "nutritional medicine"? Your answer should be yes if you want to live a long time in a healthy body. Therein lies the problem. Young people do not think of themselves as ever getting old. Many people give minimal thought to the long-lasting effects of daily food consumption.

Older people may not have been raised with the awareness that the quality and type of food counts in terms of aging well and general health matters. The foods in the following categories deliver a wealth of the nutritional elements that act as medicine for the human body.

FOOD AS MEDICINE

INFLAMMATION FIGHTERS	MUSCLE ENHANCERS	IMMUNITY BOOSTERS	BONE BUILDERS
Pineapples	Wild salmon	Ginger	Bok choy
Olive oil	Chocolate milk	Chili peppers	Alaskan king crab
Bing cherries	Quorn	White/Green tea	Dried plums
Dark chocolate	Greek-style yogurt	Blueberries	Oysters
Turmeric	Eggs	Cinnamon	Bananas
Wild fatty fish	Lentils	Sweet potatoes	Kiwis
Flaxseed	Tofu	Tomatoes	Broccoli
Almonds	Nonfat ricotta	Figs	Spinach
Apples	Grass-fed beef	Pomegranates	Leeks
Whole grains	Quinoa	Mushrooms (reiki, shiitake, maitake)	Artichokes
		Dark chocolate	Almonds

HEALTH PROBLEMS CAN BEGIN early or late in life and may progress to radically consume your health benefits and wealth assets. Consider all the obese children with diabetes and their predicted natural history of disease.

Diets work on paper but not in practice unless your daily diet is one of quality food as medicine. Alarming news reports have raised concerns about high-fructose corn syrup-containing beverages. These beverages can be eliminated from dietary consumption and substituted with others, such as white and green tea, fortified dietary smoothies and berry fruit juices, and natural energy drinks. Whole-grain Scottish oatmeal is a "medicinal" food and is noted for its cholesterol-lowering effect. An abundance of credible data suggests that juices from fruit and berries such as mangosteen, açaí, pomegranate, noni, wolfberry, and others have health benefits. The FDA process to obtain a claim as a medical food is lengthy and challenging. Subsequently, FDA-approved medical food designations are few.

MEDICAL FOODS

IN MAY 2007, THE FDA stated that a medical food is a food that is formulated to be consumed or administered internally under the supervision of a physician. A medical food is intended for the specific dietary management of a disease or condition for which distinctive nutritional requirements based on recognized scientific principles are established by medical evaluation. The medical food category is therefore very narrow. Medical foods are exempted from the labeling requirements for health claims and nutrient claims under the Nutrition Labeling and Education Act of 1990.

Food and drug safety laws enacted in the Prescription Drug User Fee Act IV change the way food and drugs will be advertised when brought to market. This legislation sets time frames for negotiating label changes, including the need for boxed warnings and additional information on contraindications, precautions, or adverse reactions. Pharmaceutical companies will pay increased annual fees to the FDA for these services. Stiffer fines and penalties are authorized for companies that fail to ensure the accuracy and fair balance of direct-to-consumer (DTC) drug advertising.

NUTRACEUTICALS OF THE NEW MILLENNIUM

MANY LIFESAVING AND LIFE-EMPOWERING compounds have been synthesized from plants, particularly antibiotics and narcotics. Recently, pharmaceutical companies have started producing nutraceuticals, a new class of prescription drugs. Limbrel (flavocoxid), is available by prescription and is classified as a new medical food by the FDA. Limbrel is a true dual inhibitor of inflammation that incorporates the COX1-2 and LOX anti-inflammatory aspects of bark and root extracts. Limbrel (flavocoxid), is a blend of concentrated flavonoids, primarily baicalin and catechin. The antioxidant resveratrol, from grapes, berry fruits, and wine, is now available as a nonprescription nutraceutical supplement.

Studies have verified that diets balanced in proper fats and rich in complex carbohydrates from fruits, vegetables, and grains are associated with less chronic disease. As the newly discovered phytomolecular components of plants and foods become FDA-approved and manufactured as nutraceuticals, one wonders what the dosage recommendations should be for treatment with these ideal products, since no long-term studies exist. Phytoestrogens in functional foods such as juices and essential oils inhibit hardening of the arteries (atherosclerosis) and carcinogenic processes. Research continues in the mechanisms of influence of estrogen agonist-antagonist receptor binding properties that affect many processes, including protein synthesis, cell differentiation, cell maturation, and cell death.

Aspirin, antibiotics, atropine, codeine, curare, digitalis, ephedrine, ergotamine, ipecac, morphine, papaverine, podophyline, quinine, senna, theophylline, and vinblastine were developed from the plant kingdom in the last century. A new Bayer aspirin has been released with the supplement phytosterols, claiming the added benefit of lowering the bad LDL cholesterol. Phytosterols block the absorption of cholesterol in the digestive track. This gives aspirin a two-pronged method of heart disease prevention. Perhaps those individuals who use essential oils and drink juices will become identified as the early adopters of the phytomolecular-based nutraceuticals from plants that function as the stimulants of healthy aging and cancer chemopreventative agents of the twenty-first century.

DIGESTING NUTRITION FROM PLANTS

THE HUMAN PHYSIOLOGY OF digestion and absorption of the phytomolecules from plants is complex. Plant lignans and isoflavonoid glycosides are transformed by intestinal bacteria into hormone-like compounds called phytosterols that become modulators of the hormonal system. The enterohepatic (intestine-liver) circulation actively processes the hydrolysis of isoflavonoid glycosides in the intestines using natural cultures of healthy probiotic bacteria, such as lactobacillus bacteroides and bifidobacteria. The isoflavones from digestion of plants become newly conjugated phytoestrogens in the liver and are reexcreted into bile for absorption in the small intestine. Isoflavone and anthocyanins are a subclass of flavonoids.

The isoflavones that are not reabsorbed are excreted mainly as monoglucuronides in urine. There is a statistically significant association between the intake of dietary fiber from berries and fruits and the urinary excretion of plant lignans. There is also low daily excretion of dietary lignans three months post jejunum-ileum (intestinal) bypass bariatric surgery due to malnutrition and malabsorption. One course of antibiotics eliminates the formation of intestinal phytoestrogen compounds for about three to four weeks before regaining pre-antibiotic levels.

RAINBOW-COLORED BEVERAGES

WE ARE DESIGNED TO eat foods that represent all the colors of the rainbow. The colors of the mangosteen and açaí juices are a brilliant orange and purple. The berry fruit juices have chemical properties that must be addressed in order to make the best juice product. Processing berries to make juices requires awareness of environmental and chemical composition of the juices in order to yield a more potent product that will look good and retain vital antioxidant properties when stored. The primary colors of the natural red, green, and blue copigmentation called anthocyanins are responsible for the antioxidant, anticarcinogenic, anti-inflammatory, antiangiogenic (making blood vessels), and cardiopreventative effects.

Juice anthocyanins react as antioxidants to absorb oxygen-free radicals, which are oxygen molecules with an unpaired electron. They also prevent oxidation of lipids and proteins in food products. Anthocyanins are highly susceptible to degradation and therefore are destabilized by pH acid-base alterations and storage temperature. Light is necessary for the biosynthesis of the anthocyanins pigments in plants; these pigments protect the living plant from too much harmful sun rays. While processing juice, light-induced degradation of anthocyanins is dependent on the presence of molecular oxygen causing direct or indirect oxidation. Proper utilization of the elements and light are fundamental to the growth of plants and production of juices.

There is an abundance of fruits, berries, and vegetables from which network marketing businesses can make juices. Berry fruit juices have extremely different tastes and are known by a variety of common names. What follows is a partial listing of genus and species names of berries that grow in the form of vines, bushes, shrubs, and trees. Mangosteen is a tree fruit. Luo han guo is a fruit of the vine. Blueberries come from flowering bushes. Açaí is a palm berry. Pomegranate is a shrub fruit.

COMMON NAMES, GENUS, AND SPECIES OF BERRIES: TAXONOMY OF THE PLANT KINGDOM

The world is ripe with species of berries that are studied in the laboratory in order to generate data that substantiates the health benefits of these fruits.

blackberry (Rubus spp.),

black raspberry (R. occidentalis),

blueberry (Vaccinium corymbosum),

cranberry (the American cranberry, V. macrocarpon,

European cranberry, V. oxycoccus),

red raspberry (R. idaeus),

strawberry (Fragaria × ananassa),

chokecherry (Prunus virginiana),

highbush cranberry (Viburnum trilobum),

serviceberry (Amelanchier alnifolia),

silver buffaloberry (Shepherdia argentea),

arctic bramble (R. articus),

bilberry, or bog whortleberry (Vaccinium myrtillus),

black currant (Ribes nigrum),

boysenberry (Rubus spp.),

cloudberry (Rubus chamaemorus),

crowberry (Empetrum nigrum, E. hermaphroditum),

elderberry (Sambucus spp.),

gooseberry (Ribes uva-crispa),

lingonberry (V. vitis-idaea),

loganberry (Rubus loganobaccus),

marionberry (Rubus spp.),

rowanberry (Sorbus spp.),

sea buckthorn (Hippophae rhamnoides)

pomegranate (Punica granatum),

goji berry, or wolfberry (Lycium barbarum),

mangosteen (Garcinia mangostana),

açaí berry (Euterpe oleraceae),

maqui berry (Aristotelia chilensis).

THE MEDICAL SCIENCE OF JUICES

THE BASIC MEDICINAL PROPERTIES of the juices exhibited by individual plants are similar and yet somewhat different, having specific attributes that are only beginning to be discovered. Different juices have different chemical variability and therefore different composition. The quality and quantity of the different classes of macronutrients, micronutrients, and phytomolecules present in fruit juices are highly variable. These qualifying factors are dependent on the physicality of each plant's unique biome in which it was grown and most especially, how the plant was processed and formulated with other juices and ingredients into the final beverage.

The rich colors of these fruits and berries are manifested through pigments, the proanthocyanidins and anthocyanins, which are light attenuators (decrease light) and powerful antioxidants (Kren ,2007). Anthocyanins are bound to simple sugars. The most common sugars are glucose, rhamnose, galactose, arabinose, and xylose. The most common di- and tri-saccharide sugars are rutinose, sophorose, sambubiose, and glucotutinose. Triglycolated (sugared) and acetylated anthocyanins are the most stable of these molecules, retaining their antioxidant values in higher percentages for a longer period of time. Juices can be synergistically mixed to bring out the best attributes of each juice to preserve color stability and antioxidant potency over time in storage. Many common juices, such as raspberry and strawberry, lose 99% of their anthocyanin potency during storage. Red wine about a year old may contain roughly 200 mg/l of anthocyanins, a decrease of about 50% from freshly crushed grape juice.

The combined influences of the various phytochemicals, polyphenols, anthrocyanins, and ellagitannins (tannin pigment) functioning with antioxidant and antiliperoxidant (lipid antioxidation) effects in pomegranate juice are complex and astounding (Zafra-Stona, 2007). Researching the antiatherosclerotic properties and cardiovascular benefits of pomegranate juice has yielded significant human studies showing decreased cholesterol in type 2 diabetics with hyperlipidemia (Esmailzadeh, 2006), reversing carotid artery intimal thickening and stenosis (Aviram, 2004); improved stress-induced myocardial ischemia in patients with coronary heart disease (Sumner, 2005); and inhibition of serum angiotensin converting enzyme activity, thus reducing blood pressure (Aviram, 2001). Pomegranate juice kills numerous bacteria and inhibits oral plaque formation (Menezes, 2006). Most natural plants with chemopreventative properties are antioxidative by nature. Studies have shown that cancer cells of the prostate gland have responded to several juices (e.g., pomegranate [Malik, 2005] and grapefruit). The phytomolecules of the juices remain in the system for hours after ingestion as metabolites. Some of the metabolites of the pomegranate ellagitannins persist in human urine for up to forty-eight hours, demonstrating prolonged effect (Seeram, 2006). Pomegranate has much higher concentrations of the isoflavonoids and lignans than citrus fruits such as lemon, orange, and grapefruit. Lignans are also found in the highest concentrations in the covering pericarp and testa layers of the mangosteen fruit.

Blueberries are beautiful and healthful. Twenty-first century research on blueberry and other juices from plants reminds me of the research conducted with plants in the last century that yielded so many types of medications, such as narcotics and antibiotics. Now the berries are being studied in laboratories worldwide for their cancer chemopreventative and cancer therapeutic actions (Hope, 2004). Jack LaLanne, the grandfather of fitness and power juicing, is the original early adopter of drinking juices. Jack is over ninety years young and started drinking juices as a teenager.

Early adopters of juice drinking may prove to be the truly forward thinkers and therefore healthiest of the boomers who reach their eighth and ninth decades of life in a uniquely healthy condition. Recently, researchers have observed the effectiveness of blueberries at reversing age-related deficits in memory. The flavenoids, in particular the anthrocyanins and flavanols of blueberry-induced memory improvements, are mediated by activation of signaling proteins via a specific pathway in the hippocampus, part of the brain that manages learning and memory (Williams, 2008).

Pterostilbene, an active constituent of blueberries and a natural methoxylated analogue of resveratrol, was evaluated for antioxidative potential. Resveratrol has three analogues: pterostilbene, piceatannol, and resveratrol trimethyl ether (Rimando, 2004). Resveratrol, a stilbenoid antioxidant found in grapes, wine, peanuts, and other berries, has been reported to have various properties, including aiding caloric restriction, cancer chemoprevention, and hypolipidemic (decrease lipids) as well as analgesic actions (Remsberg, 2008). Pterostilbene, a new agonist for the peroxisome proliferator-activated receptor alpha-isoform, lowers plasma lipoproteins and cholesterol in hypercholesterolemic hamsters (Rimando, 2005). Pterostilbene is cancer chemopreventative and is known to possess anti-inflammatory activity as well as induce apoptosis (cancer cell death) in various types of cancer cells. The effects of pterostilbene on cell viability in human gastric carcinoma melanoma and leukemia have been investigated (Ferrer, 2005; Tolomeo, 2005). Pterostilbene induces apoptosis and cell cycle arrest in human gastric carcinoma cells (Pan, 2007).

Resveratrol concentration is different in raw versus baked blueberries. Blueberries are often consumed after cooking, in pies for example. The effect of eighteen minutes of heating at 190 degrees Celsius resulted in between 17% and 46% degradation of the resveratrol. Therefore, the resveratrol content of baked or heat-processed blueberries should be expected to be lower than in the raw fruit. Although blueberries were found to contain resveratrol, the level of this chemoprotective compound was less than 10% of the amount present in grapes. Furthermore, cooking or heat processing of these berries contributes to the degradation of resveratrol.

Luo han guo is a fruit of the vine grown on mountain slopes in the southwestern Chinese province of Hunan. Traditionally, luo han guo has been suggested as an antitussive for cough and a cooling drink for quenching thirst and heat stroke. Anecdotally, people have noted increased energy after drinking the juice. Recent research has suggested it is effective against Epstein-Barr virus, a possible cause of chronic fatigue syndrome (Akihisa, 2007). The luo han guo fruit is rich in fiber, amino acids, manganese, and vitamin K. Luo han guo has a low glycemic index but is hundreds of times sweeter than sugar due to the presence of mogrosides, a group of triterpene-glycosides. It is an effective sugar substitute and has been utilized traditionally for diabetes and weight management. Luo han guo contains the glycoprotein momorgrosvin, which inhibits ribosomal protein synthesis and compounds that exert chemopreventative effects (Akihisa, 2007). Glycoproteins play an important role in cell-to-cell receptor-mediated communication for proper immune function.

The phenolics, flavenols, and catechins present in juices and teas are thought to be instrumental in the role of cancer prevention, prevention of hardening of the arteries, and coronary artery disease by various mechanisms. These phytomolecules are defined by the genetic makeup of each plant. The phytomolecules are instrumental to the proper human physiologic function at the cellular level, whether ingested as food, juice, teas, extracts, or essential oils. The human body has about eighty trillion cells, many of which are covered with molecular channels and G-protein receptors functioning as ionic pumps and regulators of biochemically triggered reactions, influenced by the phytomolecular components of plants. These phytomolecules participate actively as antioxidants and as selective induction agents of phase one and phase two metabolic pathways of liver enzymes involved in the detoxification of carcinogens and the metabolism and conjugation of medications.

P-glycoprotein (Pgp), a common chemical transporter of substances across cell membranes, is vulnerable to inhibition, activation, or induction by plant phytomolecules. A notable effect of two phytomolecular components of grapefruit juice (e.g., bergamottin and quercetin) is reported to modulate Pgp receptor activity and the bioavailability of various drugs (Zhou, 2004). Grapefruit juice increases the blood concentrations of two specific classes of medications: the calcium channels antagonists used for cardiac rhythm and blood pressure control, and the cholesterol lowering statins (Arayne, 2005). Pomegranate juice does not cause altered drug concentration or altered clearance of the anesthesia premedication and sedative midazolam when administered orally or intravenously (Farkas, 2007). Grapefruit juice impairs clearance and elevates plasma levels of oral midazolam (Goho, 2001).

Grapefruit juice has been found to be an inhibitor of the intestinal cytochrome P-450 3A4 systems, which are responsible for the first-pass metabolism of many drugs (Dahan, 2004). The Pgp pump, found in the brush border of the intestinal wall that transports many of these cytochrome P-450 3A4 substrates, has also been shown to be inhibited by grapefruit juice (Zhuo, 2004). Human cellular pumps, when activated by phytomolecules, induce secondary metabolic messengers that direct the metabolism of medications and synthesis of specialized proteins in the nucleus of the cell, which is defined by human DNA and messenger RNA.

TIME FOR TEA WITH WASHED LEMON

THE CALORIC RESTRICTION EFFECT of resveratrol (3, 5,4'-trihydroxy-trans-stilbene) is significant. If you are not drinking wine for the resveratrol and anthocyanins, then drink a berry fruit juice, such as white or green tea and blueberry, which can be found combined in some juice products. Green tea with epigallocathingallate (EGCG) is high in lignans but low in isoflavonoids, which are polyphenols. Both resveratrol and allocatechin-gallate, a major antioxidative green tea polyphenol, exert striking inhibitory effects on diverse cellular events associated with cancer of the prostate (Sartor, 2004; Stewart, 2003).

The wine industry has utilized essential oils of thyme, clove, cinnamon, and tea tree in concentrations ranging from 100 to 500 parts per million (ppm) to eliminate a wide range of postharvest pathogens on harvested grapes such as the fungus Botrytis cinerea (Arras, 2001). Some juice products contain essential oils of lemon and orange, sources of d-limonene that may inhibit tumor growth via inhibition of p21-dependent signaling and apoptosis resulting from induction of the transforming growth factor beta-signaling pathway (Kaji, 2001). D-limonene metabolites also cause G1 cell cycle arrest, inhibit posttranslational modification of signal transduction proteins, and cause differential expression of cell cycles. That means d-limonene helps regulate cells as they replicate in their life cycle to maintain the reproduction of healthy normal cells throughout the body (Reddy, 1997).

THE SOURCE AND THE POWER OF XANTHONES

THERE ARE NUMEROUS TWENTY-first-century scientific journal articles discussing xanthones and in particular, alpha mangostin, which is present in the mangosteen fruit's peel. The real story of the healing powers of mangosteen started centuries ago in Asia. The peel, called the pericarp, is where the powerful antioxidants and ligands are highly concentrated. The mangosteen pericarp is about one-quarter of an inch in thickness. It is green when unripe and dark purple when ripened. The powerful antioxidants are known as xanthones. There are about forty-plus xanthone phytomolecules in mangosteen pericarp that have remarkable healing properties. The medicinal properties of the mangosteen pericarp have been utilized by many generations of Asians and more recently by those seeking the benefits of the juice in products marketed today.

The standardized extracts of xanthones used in some formulation of mangosteen juices derived from the outer rind, or peel, not from the white "meat" inner part of the fruit. The rind of the partially ripened mangosteen fruit yields polyhydroxy-xanthone derivatives called mangostin and beta-mangostin. The pericarp of the fully ripe fruit also contains the xanthones gartanin, beta-disoxygartanin, and normangostin (Nguyen, 2005). There is considerable evidence linking prostaglandins with inflammation and pain mediated through arachidonic acid, which is blocked by xanthones (Nakatani, 2002). There is also induction of apoptosis (cancer cell death) by the xanthones present in the pericarp of the mangosteen fruit in vitro (Nagagawa, 2007). For more articles with conclusions like the ones listed here, search for the specific phytomolecules present in the pericarp of mangosteen using Google Scholar and PubMed.gov.

JUICE OF MANGOSTEEN AS A POTENTIAL MEDICINE

- Garcinia mangostana (mangosteen) has antioxdative and neuroprotective activities (Weecharangsan, 2006).

- Alpha-mangostin and garcinone B, are the anti-inflammatory xanthone phytomolecules present in the pericarp of the mangosteen fruit that inhibit cyclooxygenase and prostaglandin E2 synthesis in rat glioma cells (Yamakuni, 2005; Nakatani, 2004).

- Alpha-mangostin from mangosteen pericarp showed antibacterial activity against antibiotic-resistant, methicillin-resistant Staphylococcus aureus (MRSA) and vancomycin-resistant enterococci (VRE) and was also synergistic with antibiotics in vitro (Iqbal, 2007).

- Hardening of the arteries is caused in part by the oxidation of lipids in the blood stream. Garcinia mangostana (mangosteen) has xanthones that are phenolic phytomolecules with antioxidant activity, inhibiting the oxidation and damaging cardiovascular effects of low density lipids (Williams, 1995; Mahabusarakam, 2000).

THE CHEMICAL STRUCTURES OF the xanthones present in the mangosteen fruit are like the sesquiterpenes found in certain essential oils that also kill bacteria such as VRE and MRSA (Sakagami, 2005). Other berry fruit juices also kill bacteria (Voravunthunchai, 2005). The phytomolecules of mangosteen cause human leukemia cancer cell lines to die in the laboratory dish (Matsumoto, 2005). The xanthones of mangosteen induce cell death of human breast cancer cell lines (Moongkarndi, 2004). Translate the power of the greater than 40 xanthones of the mangosteen fruit into your own therapeutic CAM, fitness and wellness programs.

INTEGRATING JUICE THERAPY

PATIENTS AND THEIR DOCTORS should consider the following practical suggestions to help evaluate and adjust to normal changes possibly associated with the implementation of juice therapy. Drinking several ounces of juice from several types of fruit and berry beverages once or twice daily is recommended to see results. Each individual should prepare a written list of physical symptoms to refer to during the initial trial of juice therapy and should review them over several months. Often, people forget over time what subjective ailments are bothersome but readily recall previous pains or gastrointestinal symptoms that have disappeared, improved sleep habits, and increased energy when the list is revisited.

Initially, some individuals drinking the juices may experience loose bowel movements, possibly related to individual preexisting bowel flora interactions with the juices and variations in one's gastro-colic (stomach-colon) reflex mechanism. Proper digestion and the enterohepatic circulation of nutrients require particular intestinal bacteria that are killed by medications such as antibiotic therapy. Supplementation with probiotics to replenish intestinal flora is indicated after a course of antibiotics. Loose bowels movements, if experienced, should resolve quickly, and although possibly annoying, they should not be a cause for concern. It is not a significant enough reason to discontinue juice therapy, considering the possible long-term benefits.

Anecdotal testimonies of patients who suffer from idiopathic, autoimmune diseases and those nonresponders to medications prescribed for their symptoms have found juices that have improved the signs and symptoms of their illness. Physicians should allow patients to initiate juice therapy long before they reach this point in the natural history of the disease. Various juices, such as blueberry, pomegranate, and mineral-fortified mangosteen juice, boost and maintain elevated antioxidant values for hours after a single "dose" of juice. Continued dietary intake of mangosteen for weeks has been shown to positively affect immune T-helper cells and the CD4/CD8 ratio; decrease the biomarker of inflammation, C-reactive protein; and significantly increase the cytokine interleukin-1a, molecules of the immune system. The potential benefits outweigh the possibly minimal changes associated with initial therapy.

IDEAL RAINBOW-COLORED REMEDY

IN GENERAL, THE COMMONLY popular berry fruit juices build the body with protein, clean and detoxify, increase energy, relieve stress, promote prostate health, help limit retinopathy, improve glucose and lipid metabolism, and improve resistance to diseases such as virus fungus and bacterial infections. For centuries, orange-colored mangosteen has been used in the tropics to treat intestinal dysentery. Drinking essential juices improves digestive health, helping to eradicate bad breath and decrease symptoms of acid reflux, or GERD. These juices improve digestion by decreasing acid reflux, heal stomach ulcers by eliminating certain pathogenic bacteria such as H. pylori, and relieve symptoms of Crohn's disease and irritable bowel syndrome. The antioxidant capacity of the phenolic compounds found in the purple-colored açaí berry has been found to be an excellent defense against the free oxygen radical species peroxyl and good against the free oxygen radical species peroxynitrite, as compared to common fruit and vegetable juices, according to the study "Total Oxidant Scavenging Capacity (TOSC) of Euterpe oleracea (Acai) fruits" (Rodrigues, 2006). These rainbow-colored juice remedies are like a pot of gold at the end of the rainbow.

NATURAL WONDERS

THE FRUIT JUICES MADE from mangosteen and açaí are known for amazing nutritional properties. The açaí berry is similar to an egg in protein content. The berries have essential fatty acids like those of olive oil. Açaí has activity that lowers low density lipoproteins (LDL) cholesterol. It contains phytonutrients and antioxidants, plus anthocyanins as well as phytosterols for cardiovascular and prostate health. Açaí also has an abundance of B vitamins and minerals such as calcium, phosphorous, and potassium, as well as trace elements. Both fruits are rich in fiber and low in glycemic index, in contrast to the essential oils, which have virtually zero glycemic indexes because they are aromatic compounds without sugar content. These wonderful fruit juices bring the best combination of qualities to people of all ages to promote good health.

I attend network marketing conferences throughout the year. During these conferences a time is set aside to hear testimonies from participants regarding their experience and successes using various products. I vividly remember one mother describing the trials and tribulations her family, including their autistic child, had endured while seeking treatments. She spoke plainly yet with progressive emotion as she told about giving her child the same juice of mangosteen fortified with minerals that she was taking. One day the child said, "Mommy, I can think!" This simple dietary supplementation had remarkably changed everything after so many prescriptions and sessions of therapy had had very little impact.

ISLAND PEOPLE OF KUNA PANAMA

PEOPLE WITH A SWEET tooth like chocolate and so do the people of the Kuna Island tribe of Panama. This tribe has a remarkably low incidence of the various heart diseases, diabetes, and cancer in the older population. Interestingly, cocoa beverages are a principle portion of their diet. Researchers found that the risk of four out of the five most common killer diseases— cancer, diabetes, stroke, and heart failure—was reduced to less than 10% in the Kuna people, who drink up to forty cups of epicatechin-rich cocoa a week. This suggests that drinking cocoa rich in flavanols can positively affect blood sugar metabolism, cancer risk, and reverse impairment in the functioning of blood vessels, such as that caused by athcrosclerosis.

In a study published in the Journal of Cardiovascular Pharmacology (Hollenberg, 2006), male smokers, a group known to have problems with blood vessel function, were given cocoa drinks made with different levels of flavanol, ranging from 28 to 918 mg. In each group studied, the optimal effect of increased blood flow occurred after two hours. Blood vessel performance improved 50% with 179 mg of flavanols and continued to rise proportionately with increasing flavanol content.

The improvement in blood vessel function for the highest level of flavanol, 918 mg, was so great that it was equal to that found in a person with no known cardiovascular risk factors. The study was followed with a seven-day sustained trial, in which participants were given three drinks a day, totaling 918 mg. Blood vessel performance was monitored at intervals over the day, and then for a week after participants stopped taking the chocolate beverage.

The researchers said that blood vessel benefits from consuming the flavanol-rich cocoa for a week were comparable to "long-term drug therapy with statins," the cholesterol-lowering medication. A possible conclusion of the study is that the active ingredients in cocoa are so powerful that they should be classified as great a discovery as anesthesia and so beneficial that they should be called vitamins.

The power of the flavanol family of antioxidants is remarkable. Chocolate, with its high antioxidant content from flavanols such as epicatechin, translates into magnified oxygen radical absorbance capacity (ORAC) values that translate into less oxidative stress-induced free radical damage and thus much better health. Products offering the synergistic combination of a high ORAC content fruit, such as açaí berry and chocolate, could be considered even more potent. Entrepreneurs such as Little Girl Big Attitude Chocolates design and cater custom products of greater than 60% dark chocolate. (www. Littlegirlbigattitudechocolates.net)

BREAK THE FAST

IN THE UNITED STATES, major dietary arguments and observations are generated when various diets are compared. The study published in The Journal of the American Medical Association (Gardener, 2007) ranking the efficacy of the Atkins, Ornish, Zone, and Learn diets raises controversial claims and counterclaims that the subjects did not actually follow these diets, so how can they be legitimately ranked? The real controversy is that "science" still does not provide the definitive answer to the question, what makes people fat? Are there good and bad fats as well as good and bad carbohydrate calories that cause dysfunctional storage of fat? Good Calories, Bad Calories, written by Gary Taubes, offers an Atkins-like scientific presentation on this subject.

This we do know: A 15-year study of dietary fiber in morning cereals eaten by 15,000 doctors showed a significant decease in the doctors' developing heart failure over that time period. You can eat a fiber-rich breakfast like steel cut oatmeal to "break the fast" and have a healthier heart in fifteen years. Juices have significant quantities of both antioxidants and fiber. The combined antioxidant benefits of dark cocoa with a fiber-rich breakfast do have a daily impact that adds up over time.

There is an even greater rationale for caring enough to actually change what you ingest. Smell is a very significant part of eating. Perhaps you are snacking right now as you read this. Merely concentrating on what your food smells like and tastes like is a landmark for provoking change in food intake habits. Get involved in the smelling and chewing. This starts digestion. More chewing equals better absorption of the nutrients. That is the beginning of the method and mind. Now what about the quality of the material we ingest?

LOWEST-BID FOODS, COSMETICS, AND MEDICATIONS

AMERICANS AND BRITISH CONSUMERS' consumption of CAM-oriented health care goods and services has increased progressively year after year. Yet there are governmental regulatory movements in Europe to restrict the production and use of natural, herbal, and aromatic products. For example, pure natural essential oils as perfumes are in danger of being regulated out of existence, possibly because of poor science rather than specific health risks, such as allergies and the alleged photocarcinogenic and photomutagenic effects of furanocoumarins (mainly from citrus ingredients) contained within cosmetic preparations. Be aware and be informed by reading and supporting Cropwatch, the independent phytochemical industry watchdog, cofounded by Tony Burfield, found at http://cropwatch.org/.

Granted, governments have good reason to seek controls because of the multiple abuses and recalls from some manufacturers, mainly of Chinese origin. American corporations have been buying the cheapest source of ingredients from China to make drugs and processed food for American consumption. Some American corporations have had to recall or put a moratorium on some imported medications and food ingredients from China, due to contamination. Hopefully, bills before our Congress will be enacted, funded, and enforced to regulate the labeling and content of foods and products of foreign origination entering the United States.

SOLID REASONS TO DRINK LIQUIDS

STUDIES AND REPORTS HAVE shown that some bottles of manufactured pill and capsule supplements do not contain the quality and quantity of vitamins and minerals described on the label. For example, herbal supplements such as golden seal and echinacea have been falsely labeled for their content and potency. Worse yet, some "herbal" products have contained significant contaminants such as medications, drugs, toxic metals, and other compounds. Many of the ingredients of supplement-containing pills are damaged by acid pH in the stomach. Probiotics and digestive enzymes, for example, should be specially encapsulated to withstand stomach acid, which can readily reach a pH of 3.0. A chronic diet of lowest-bid foods and lack of quality bioavailable supplements produces marginal nutritional deficiencies that worsen over time. These are solid reasons to drink specially formulated juices with liquid supplements from known American manufacturers.

SOURCE OF SUPPLY MATTERS

THERAPEUTIC-GRADE BLENDS OF essential oils and specially blended juices from natural plants are available from many sources. There is tremendous product variety and variability in formulation, quality control, value, and ORAC from company to company. Whatever the brand, you must ascertain that the products are pure. The issue is quality assurance; not every company is on the alert, for solvents and toxic chemicals that might be present in the raw materials. It is critical that raw materials be thoroughly tested for impurities before they get into supplement products. Standardized extracts and preparations from Europe, India, and China have been sent to product manufacturers that test to ensure purity and find contaminants, necessitating the return of the product. These solvent contaminants have been encountered: green tea extract containing ethyl acetate, licorice extract containing 1,2 dichloroethane, and curcumin extract containing 1,2 dichloroethane.

Purchase products from companies that follow good manufacturing compliance (GMC) guidelines. Check statistics documenting purity and potency from independent laboratory studies. Brunswick and Consumer Labs offers certification of analysis to verify purity and potency from several perspectives. Athletes have concerns about World Anti-Doping Agency (WADA) banned substances. Consumers are concerned about ingesting pesticides. Essential oil products can be verified to be pesticide-free by means of gas chromatography (GC) analysis. Measuring the antioxidant ORAC value of juices and oils verifies increased potency, which translates to higher value and greater benefits. Certain essential oils and juices have the highest ORAC values known on the planet. It is possible that oils and juices taken together obtain a tremendous boost of nutrients and maximize your total dietary ORAC intake.

A diet rich in fruits, vegetables, and cereal grains is chemopreventative (i.e., reduces cancer risk), exemplified by the action of phytonutrients from plants such as lycopene, vitamins C and E, and beta-carotene. These chemopreventative properties coupled with the potentially additive and synergistic effect of the twenty-three thousand pure and mixed isoprenoids from plants, also found in certain essential oils, may further reduce risks of cancer. The oils rich in isoprenoids, such as d-limonene, are found in citrus, and geraniol is found in palmarosa, geranium, turmeric, and atlas cedar. The combination of naturally sourced products produced and tested by the right companies with the proper intended health benefits will deliver all the good health that you deserve.

THE OILMD

THE OILMD OFFERS AROMATHERAPY essential oil products to promote wellness through nature. Essential oils are a means to enhance preventative health care using nutritional medicine. These essential oils are derived from common plants, herbs, and spices that are generally regarded as safe (GRAS). The essential oils are supplied as premixed 10% dilutions in jojoba carrier oil using 9ml frosted roll-on ball dispensers for external applications.

The oilMD product descriptions are accompanied with links to abstracts that provide information on evidence-based clinical and laboratory references, available separately from the NIH Data Bank. These abstracts identify some positive, some inconclusive, and some negative results of numerous chemical, cellular, animal, and human studies. They also identify essential oils as well as the chemical constituents of essential oils, plants, and herbs to illustrate the emerging science of biologic mechanisms pertaining to aromatherapy. The National Center for Complementary and Alternative Medicine has also begun research into some clinical areas.

CONTINUING MEDICAL EDUCATION

HISTORICALLY, THERE HAS BEEN an underserved component in medical school curricula on the complex and demanding field of musculoskeletal diseases (Lynch, 2005). A primary care physician's ability to make accurate diagnoses and provide treatment using allopathic modalities is hampered by lack of support and knowledge for this particular subspecialty resulting in known patient demographic disconnects that limit thorough medical management of patients' musculoskeletal diseases (Lynch, 2006). Continuing education of postgraduate physicians is required to upgrade skills and develop awareness of new CAM techniques to integrate with allopathic modalities in the diagnosis and management of musculoskeletal diseases.

Integrative approaches to musculoskeletal diseases are advancing from the biomedical model to the biopsychosocial model (i.e., mind-body considerations) as well as the nutritional elements of medicine exemplified by the Wellness Revolution. Simultaneously, there is an increasing consumption of CAM goods and services, such as herbs, supplements, functional foods, berry fruit juice beverage products, and aromatherapy with essential oils, which have been chosen and managed by the patients themselves. These trends necessitate the health care provider's function as knowledgeable advocate and gatekeeper of nutritional medicine and CAM industries for their patients. Innovative research in the developing arenas of medical aromatherapy and the science of nutritional medical therapies with juices from the fruits and berries of plants from around the world presents challenges as well as new approaches to the management of musculoskeletal diseases faced by primary care providers.

TRIGGER POINT THERAPY

ALL OILMD PRODUCTS ARE Formulations of 10% natural, organic, therapeutic-grade essential oils blended in 90% jojoba carrier oil, a natural preservative with anti-inflammatory properties. These products are presented in bottles with roll-on balls for pulse point and trigger point therapy, a form of acupressure. Using the pulse point technique with the roll-on ball is innovative, allowing for direct application of essential oils at specific locations. Acupressure and the application of specialized essential oil blends to specific sites of nervous innervation and vascular blood flow (i.e., pulse points) is a unique combination of therapeutic modalities. The Trigger Point Therapy Workbook: Your Self-Treatment Guide for Pain Relief, by Clair Davies, describes the causes and symptoms of trigger points, plus therapeutic methods to find relief from pain (e.g., pain associated with fibromyalgia and myofascial syndromes).

AROMATHERAPY FOR WOMEN'S HEALTH

THE OILMD PRODUCT LINE of therapeutic-grade essential oils is unique. The first five blends are designed as aids for the general health and beauty of active women. Inhalation and dermal application of these blends promotes feminine wellness and well-being.

- Well-Balanced Lady for PMS, perimenopause syndrome, and menopause.

- Thigh Smoother for cellulite management.

- Appetite Tamer for appetite modification.

- Romantic Encounters for enhancement of your loving relationship.

- Bone Balancer for skeletal health.

THE OILMD PRODUCTS ARE provided in frosted glass, roll-on ball dispenser styles. Dermal applications using the roller ball dispensers achieve enhanced effectiveness for increased absorption and bioavailability.

ART OF AROMATHERAPY HORMONAL SYMPTOMS: WELL-BALANCED LADY

- The moment you feel the discomforts of PMS, perimenopause, or postmenopause, put Mother Nature to work. This blend of orange, sandalwood, jasmine, and ylang ylang essential oils is scientifically designed to enhance (not replace) your current approach to managing hormonal imbalance (Dayawansa, 2005). Inhale and massage often into wrist pulse points, neck, and palms. Mix in unscented body lotion and apply all over the body after your morning shower. Use it on your feet at bedtime. It's soothing, calming, and comforting to the body, mind, and spirit.

ESTHETIC AROMATHERAPY FOR NICE THIGHS: THIGH SMOOTHER

- Cellulite. Most women have it. And science has identified the culprits: tissue inflammation, low cellular metabolism, and poor circulation in the thigh area (Habashy, 2005). Thigh Smoother brings you an exquisite blend of lemon, grapefruit, ginger, patchouli, orange, cypress, juniper, and the increasingly rare helichrysum. Together they work to increase fat cell metabolism and promote healthier skin (Sekiya, 2004). In the morning, scrub your thighs in upward strokes with a dry brush or loofah sponge. Shower and then massage Thigh Smoother in an upward motion toward your heart. It's stimulating, invigorating, and safe.

HOLISTIC AROMATHERAPY FOR WEIGHT MANAGEMENT: APPETITE TAMER

- Most food aromas signal the brain to say, "I'm hungry." Appetite Tamer tells the brain to say "I'm full!" Inhale it and then absorb it into your palms and wrist pulse points right before meals and any time hunger pangs strike. Its lemon, and ginger oils are known to mildly modify appetite and stimulate metabolism (Nasel, 1994). What's more, it contains healthy fat, and that reduces your caloric intake while increasing the feeling of fullness. Reset your brain to help you manage weight. Take Appetite Tamer with you everywhere.

EDEN'S AROMATHERAPY FOR EROTIC PLEASURES: ROMANTIC ENCOUNTERS

- Ever since Queen Cleopatra's time, aromas have been used to stimulate the primal brain and bring the senses into states of desire and excitement (Masago, 2000). The oilMD's thoughtful blend of erotic oils is designed to safely elevate awareness, attraction, and the exchange of loving affection so needed by all humans. Massage and inhale the sandalwood, ylang ylang, ginger, and myrrh. Exotic. Irresistible. Magic.

INTEGRATIVE AROMATHERAPY FOR THE SKELETAL SYSTEM: BONE BALANCER

- Most people, even men, may start losing bone in their thirties. Many women wind up with osteoporosis. Here's safe and essential support to complement the exercise, calcium, soy, phytoestrogens and any prescription drugs in the battle against bone loss. This blend of sage, rosemary, thyme, juniper, pine, and eucalyptus oils was inspired by a study showing that these oils strongly inhibit the bone cell activity that causes bone reabsorption and loss (Muhlbauer, 2003). Regular use of this blend in a nonscented body lotion could potentially help preserve existing bone and facilitate new bone formation.

OPTIMAL AROMATHERAPY FOR THE EXERCISE MANDATE: SPORTS PERFORMANCE ENHANCER.

- Whether you're an athlete or must force yourself to exercise, both the body and the mind must cooperate. So this formula is essential. It elevates your attitude, energy, and heart rate (Haze, 2002). It even combats inflammation and the oxidative stress of exercise (Urso, 2003). Peppermint, black pepper, basil, rosemary, and ylang ylang—these are safe, natural stimulants for supercharged performance (Raudenbush, 2001). Feel strong. Feel confident. Feel motivated.

HEALING AROMATHERAPY FOR MINOR SPORTS INJURIES: SPORTS TRAUMA EASE

- This powerful blend of essential oils delivers a unique combination of healing qualities for sprains, bruises, and inflammation. Its centerpiece is the very therapeutic and rare oil of helichrysum—amazing for muscle and joint pain (Sala, 2003). Additionally, the blending of oils of myrrh, lavender, tea tree, basil, frankincense, ginger, and black pepper is an ingenious design of nature's best anti-inflammatory and pain-altering ingredients (Ghelardini, 2001). Add Sports Trauma Ease to your normal routines for managing minor sports injuries and other painful conditions. Feel treated well. Feel better sooner.

NATURE'S AROMATHERAPY FOR MUSCLES: MUSCLE WELLNESS

- Muscles have their own unique needs when overused. Scientific research shows that essential oils can be a rich source of restorative nutrient energy for muscle rejuvenation and recuperation (Peana, 2002). A yoga-like stretching routine in conjunction with Muscle Wellness blend following your workout is fabulous. Massage and inhalation brings you the soothing anti-inflammatory and pain-altering benefits of rosemary, orange, grapefruit, and peppermint. Combine with Sports Performance Enhancer to boost muscle strength. Feel restored, relaxed, refreshed.

GUIDED AROMATHERAPY FOR NAUSEA, ARTHRITIS, AND MIGRAINES: GINGERMD

- Here's the magic that makes the difference for anesthesia patients: an essential oil so correctly extracted from the ginger root that it can block the dreaded postop nausea. Unlike other ginger formulations, GingerMD retains the natural chemicals most effective for conquering nausea related to anesthesia (Geiger, 2005), chemotherapy (Hickok, 2007), pregnancy (Borrelli, 2005), and motion sickness (Grontved, 1988). Plus, it's been known to be a safe complementary therapy for migraine headaches and joint pain of arthritis (Altman, 2001). It's safe, effective, and amazing.

CHAPTER *ten*

Prescription for Success

"If we could give every individual the right amount of nourishment and exercise, not too little and not too much, we would have found the safest way to health."

—Hippocrates

CHAPTER

PRESCRIPTION FOR SUCCESS

FATHER'S DAY, 1968, WAS a major turning point in my understanding of success. It was the beginning of the summer prior to my junior year of high school and my father's departure to serve as a chest surgeon in the Vietnam War. Lt. Col. Geiger was also commodore of the Presidio Yacht Club, which is directly beneath the North Tower of the Golden Gate Bridge. On that day, with his crew of one—me—we entered the Aeolian Race to the Lightship located thirteen miles outside the Golden Gate, in our class B Cal twenty-foot sailboat, Gentoo. The well-outfitted sailboat was painted like a penguin, with a black hull and a white deck. We had practiced for this race, so we were ready.

THE GOLDEN GATEWAY

AT THE STARTING LINE just offshore the St. Francis Yacht Club in San Francisco, the morning sky was clear and the sea was calm. The contenders of the various boat classes jockeyed for position at the starting line. The starting gun fired every five minutes for each class, and soon the whole fleet of sailboats was sent off against a flood (incoming) tide. As we sailed west beneath the Golden Gate Bridge, the commodore elected to separate from the fleet and tack along the south side of the shipping channel, riding some residual ebb current out between the headlands of Marin County and San Francisco, toward the Lightship. Little did we know that tactical decision and the marking of two magnetic compass headings taken by my father would make all the difference between returning safely home and giving me an understanding of how to be victorious in the face of limited evidence of success.

I remember feeling seasick from the motion of the rolling ocean swells that got larger and larger as the day sailed by. This was long before I knew ginger helped seasickness. I vividly remember my father saying, "We will need to follow the compass heading east 85 degrees magnetic" so we could find the finish and reach home port when the fog came in. This was also long before GPS. When I awoke from my nap in the cockpit, as we rounded the

Lightship, a heavy coastal marine layer of fog came rolling over us, and soon we lost sight of the bright red Coast Guard cutter. We could see nothing except each other and the fog.

A SPOOKY RACE IN PEA SOUP FOG

A REPORTER WHO SAILED in the Lightship race headlined that race as "spooky, with pea soup fog" and very little wind. Plenty of foghorns sounded with steady, pulsating regularity all around us, but no sailboats could we see. Dad took us back wing on wing with the whisker pole on that compass heading of east 85 degrees magnetic that he had taken earlier. After many hours we found ourselves under the Golden Gate Bridge entering San Francisco Bay. We had persisted on that course with determination toward the finish line, which we could not see but knew existed somewhere ahead.

We had no idea where we were in relation to the rest of the fleet, but we knew we were getting closer to the finish line with each blast of the remarkably loud foghorns of the Golden Gate Bridge. As we crossed the finish line and the gun fired, we were both elated and exhausted. Competitors are well aware of that combination of feelings, but our elation had to be held somewhat in abeyance, because we still had to find our way home in pea soup fog. We headed back to our berth at the Presidio Yacht Club along the other compass heading of 300 degrees magnetic north, not knowing how we placed in that race until the following morning.

Monday morning, the San Francisco Chronicle published the race results along with a narrative of the race by the same reporter who had finished on another boat. The Gentoo had won first in our One Design class B and beat the class A boats with spinnakers as well, with a time much better than the sailboats with their huge spinnaker sails.

In 1968, a record fleet of 238 boats started the race but only 88 finished—a 60% dropout rate. In 2008, the Lightship race and rough seas took the lives of two sailors and their Cheoy Lee Offshore thirty-one-foot sailboat. Under different conditions, sheer strategy, two compass headings, and emotional belief helped my father and I beat faster boats with spinnakers on that twenty-six-mile round-trip race outside the Golden Gate Bridge into the Pacific Ocean, round the Lightship, and back into the San Francisco Bay, shrouded in dense fog, to reach our home port in Horseshoe Cove.

At the time, our circumstances had appeared hopeless. Downright hopelessly foggy, in fact, but with persistence, we had not only found our way home but had also won that long and challenging race. And we won in a way that means more to me now than ever before, since I have become increasingly aware of the importance of realizing one's passions through determining one's purpose, vision, and goals in advance. A detailed, well-planned strategy of one's passions determines the winner's prize. You can navigate the wayward winds of life's prevailing troubles by setting your sails on a course toward success. We won a book, *American Classical Navigator*, which has been prominently displayed on Dad's bookshelf and in his heart and mine for years.

When you get into a tight place and everything goes against you,
till it seems as though you could not hold on a minute longer, never give up then,
for that is just the place and time that the tide will turn.

—Harriet Beecher Stowe

COMPASS HEADING TOWARD YOUR
HEART'S PASSION

ON THE SURFACE IT would appear that the Gentoo's commodore is quite different from Captain Jack Sparrow, played by Johnny Depp, of the Pirates of the Caribbean movie franchise. Yet both men had purpose and far-reaching vision. And both men used a compass to reach their goal. Hollywood designed the compass in the movie to point toward the passion of the heart, which varied according to Jack Sparrow's purpose or predicament. That compass usually pointed in the direction of Captain Jack's passion, which was buried treasure.

At times Captain Jack was confused and misaligned with his purpose. He referred to a map, which is analogous to our own written purpose, vision, and goals. Our passion for our own prescription for success must be tuned to a frequency like a magnetized compass heading, and focused with the satellite precision of a GPS device, pointing to our goal, the finish line of our race. Personal growth is about leadership of self. Determine your purpose, your vision, and your goal based on the passions inside your heart. God gives you the desires of your heart so you can pursue godly dreams. Set your compass heading and your sails to work the winds of life, and don't let pea soup fog or the tidal changes of life impede your dreams. The following are some major waypoints on the oilMD's prescription for success.

THE OILMD'S PRESCRIPTION FOR SUCCESS

SUCCESS IS A STRUCTURED journey shaped by our responses to wins and failures, not a destination. Start with the seven major positive emotions from Napoleon Hill's *Think and Grow Rich* as a rich source of success principles that are navigated by autosuggestion through the subconscious mind. Mastery of the emotions of desire, faith, love, sexual desire, enthusiasm, romance, and hope unleash the creative powers so urgently needed and ardently desired by those who seek the sweet smell of success. Don't let happiness slip away at midlife, as a study concluded occurs to a majority of middle-aged people of all nations.

Decide to practice the fine art of thinking that creates happiness and then proceed on the path to attract health and wealth. Creating happiness can be learned. Make the following choices to be successful and break through to happiness: Successful people are nearly three times as likely to describe themselves as risk takers, nearly six times as likely to say they manage their time and activities well, and nearly three times as likely to say they are satisfied that they can successfully navigate the most challenging changes of life. Overall, successful people are more likely to take control and make freedom-oriented choices.

You cannot travel within and stand still without.

—James Allen

WHAT HAVE YOU GOT TO LOSE?

PHYSICIANS EMBRACE NEW PARADIGMS in health care education in the Wellness Revolution to promote weight loss and longevity, in books and on television shows such as Oprah. American doctors Mehmet C. Oz, MD, and Michael F. Roizen, MD, authors of *You: On A Diet*, have made education their passion, and are creating an immense impact by inspiring people to understand how to get a thinner, healthier, and younger body. A recent CD, *Live Younger…Die Older*, by Michael Roizen, MD, the author of *Real Age*, is powerful, educational, and inspirational. Dr Roizen co-authors yet another amazing book with Dr. Oz, titled *You: Staying Young: The Owner's Manual for Extending Your Warranty*. The impact of the excellent medical advice found in this series of books will be something to behold in years to come. (www.realage.com)

A TIME FOR CHANGE

THE COMMONLY PRACTICED, PURELY allopathic medical approach to health and wellness is inadequate by itself. That philosophy of medicine usually starts patients on the self-fulfilling cycle of "a pill a day for each new symptom" for the rest of their lives. The weight-gaining, obese patient usually is placed on medications for the constellations of bodily signs and symptoms associated with esophageal reflux, irritable bowel syndrome, asthma, depression, high blood sugar, high blood pressure, and painful syndromes such as osteoarthritis and fibromyalgia. The various prescriptions to treat these signs and symptoms become increasingly necessary to counteract the effects caused by fatty tissue that stores calories as triglycerides, which produces the hormones leptin, adiponectin, and resistin. The fat tissue secretes damaging inflammatory proteins called cytokines and produces the proatherogenic chemokines that instigate hardening of the arteries. In terms of acid reflux and gastroesphogeal reflux disease (GERD) associated with obesity, many people who are 5%, 10%, and 20% overweight with a BMI of 30 and above often suffer from GERD and may take proton pump inhibitors, which inhibit the production of stomach acid. Proper stomach acid is needed normally to help the body absorb calcium. There is an increased incidence in hip fractures among people taking certain proton pump inhibitors to treat GERD.

There are numerous medications for the multitude of symptoms of obesity, starting with the gastrointestinal tract: antacids for bloating and gas; antibiotics for ulcers secondary to H. pylori; proton pump inhibitors such as Protonix for GERD; metformin and insulin for diabetic blood sugar control; neurontin for the painful neuropathy of feet secondary to diabetes; Wellbutrin for psychological disorders like depression and obsessive-compulsive disorders (OCD); Warfarin and Plavix to prevent blood clots; nonsteroidals for osteoarthritis; enalapril for the high blood pressure. The list goes on and on. I see this trend frequently in the medical records of patients' charts, while consenting and preparing then for anesthesia prior to surgery.

Now you can see this process for yourself on television. The Learning Channel series Big Medicine shows details of surgery preparations for the morbidly obese person. This show is unique to our day and time. The controversial and successful world of bariatric surgery is multidisciplinary, offering services that change people's lives dramatically. Undergoing the laprosocpic adjustable gastric banding procedure is done now as commonly as other gastric bypass operations. Treatment with lavender aromatherapy in the post-anesthesia care unit after gastric banding reduces the requirement for pain medications in that setting (Kim, 2007). Obese patients have many coexisting diagnoses, medications, and histories of adverse drug reactions. The signs, symptoms, and diseases associated with obesity come at a price and develop over time, often years, and worsen over decades, which can result in devastating events such as those associated with worsening arterial circulation, potentially causing heart attack and stroke. This is what you can look forward to if you don't take care of yourself, no matter what your age and why a multidisciplinary approach of integrative medical management is necessary.

Practice caloric restriction and determine what your ideal weight should be. Use guided imagery to visualize yourself at that ideal weight as you take the actions necessary to get you there. The LifeSuccess Perfect Weight program will help you to place the perfect image of your ideal weight into your mind and body. Download and repeatedly listen to the free visualization MP3 product to guide your imagination toward a new mental image of your perfect weight and waistline. You may purchase this incredible program at http://www.bobproctorperfectweight.com/.

SUPPLEMENT WELL TO LIVE WELL

PROMOTING WELLNESS THROUGH NATURE Involves supplementing well with berry fruit juices, meal replacement diet smoothies, and healthy energy drinks, plus applications of essential oils designed to help augment and improve health. The honest, heartfelt testimonies about weight loss and healings that I have heard from people with significant medical problems who use essential oils and juices are too numerous and too sincere to be ignored. We should manage our own personal revolution of wellness, realizing that in certain respects, all we have to go on is personal experience, testimonies, and extrapolation from data of third-party literature. Supplement correctly, using essential oils and juice products for yourself. Prove to yourself what works. Consume natural berry fruit juices and essential oils for their health benefits and distribute these wonderful products of the Wellness Revolution for their wealth benefits to you and others in your sphere of influence. Supplementing lifestyle and diet with the extra nutritional ingredients to counteract the oxidative stressful events of daily living is more than advisable; it is essential, even lifesaving (O'Keefe, 2008). Many of these products are pure, even organically sourced, and have money-back guarantees. These innovative products are part of business programs designed to empower health and create wealth. Wellness Revolution entrepreneurs formulate weight loss shakes and energy drinks from juices and other plant-based sources to help promote wellness through nature.

DECREASE OXIDATIVE STRESS
TO AGE WELL

CHEMICAL STRESSES DUE TO dietary and environmental factors have negative effects, notably, acceleration of aging (Bonnefoy, 2002). As we age, body tissue, including fat, is oxidized by free radicals, which basically are chemicals with unpaired electrons exerting oxidizing, rustlike damage at the cellular level (Barja, 2004). The aging reaction of the body as a result of these combined negative energies is called "oxidative stress." Antioxidants protect the over eighty trillion body cells from oxidative stress by scavenging free radicals and binding them to render them harmless.

Aging is not a function. Aging can be defined as an endogenous (inside), progressive deterioration in age-specific components of fitness. It is a secondary effect of the decline in the force of the natural selection with age.

—James Fires

AGING HAS MANY COMPLICATING factors, not the least of which is disease and decreased state of mental awareness due to dementia. Those individuals who choose to age meaningfully can offer the wisdom of years, functioning as mentors to young and old alike. Mentoring activities serve to preserve mental agility. The use of neuroprotective supplements with broad-spectrum antioxidant ability may help with the mental and physical activities of daily living as people age. Consider that Alzheimer's disease will affect around 20% of the population by the year 2020. Preventative dietary measures can be undertaken now to ensure that you will age well. Seniors who are mentally agile can age meaningfully, functioning as volunteers and mentors.

Dementia and Alzheimer's disease are very serious problems caused by loss of neurons and the loss of excitatory amino acid neurotransmitters, coupled with damage from inflammatory mediators deposited within the neurological tissues of the brain. New recommendations of medications for the management of dementia and Alzheimer's such as memantine (Namenda) and the skin patch rivastigmine (Exelon) are effective. Use of nonsteroidal anti-inflammatory agents such as ibuprofen were initially studied and shown to be effective, but other research has shown otherwise. Different supplements that have been suggested for prevention of dementia and Alzheimer's disease, such as antioxidants, herbs, essential oils, the omega-3 fatty acid, DHA, alpha-lipoic acid and acetyl-L-carnitine (Bastianetto, 2002).

THE YOUTHFUL BRAIN

AGE REVERSAL HAS BEEN studied extensively in laboratories worldwide because people have a great interest in staying young. Stay younger longer using natural products from plants with antioxidants, such as red wine-derived resveratrol and its analogues that functionally mimic several of the biochemical effects of calorie restriction that promotes longevity. The flavenoid antioxidants have positive physiological effects on the brain, mitochondria, and the central nervous system (Miquel, 2002). Herbs have also been studied extensively because of the antioxidant properties they bring to the table. Brain-specific nutrients such as choline and taurine may cause memory improvement.

Neuron damage from deposition of the insoluble fibrous protein amyloid and damage caused by free radicals are considered extremely problematic to the aging brain. When rats ate the essential oil of thyme, they showed significant age-related improvement due to overall antioxidant activity from polyphenols distilled from the herb (Youdim, 1999). Laboratory findings suggest that creating a more favorable antioxidant capacity, in combination with maintaining higher levels of phospholipid polyunsaturated fatty acids in brain, heart, and liver tissues, during the life span of the rats resulted in longer life (Youdim, 1999). Epidemiology data on supplementation suggests that antioxidants and the proper balance of fatty acids may have a beneficial effect on many other age-related diseases, such as the chronic disease state cancer, neurodegenerative diseases such as dementia, and certain diseases of the eyes, such as macular degeneration.

Essential oils have shown benefits to the aged with dementia. A clinical trial of aromatherapy for agitation in nursing home patients with dementia was undertaken under the guidance of the famous heart surgeon, Michael DeBakey, MD, at the Houston Center for Quality of Care (Krause, 2008). It was determined that, because many elderly patients have an altered sense of olfactory function due to age-related changes or due to medications, essential oils needed to be applied cutaneously during massage for better effect (Soden, 2004). The elderly require a certain amount of sensory stimulation. Massage therapists and caregivers practicing healing touch techniques with essential oils can have significant beneficial effects on the elderly with mild, moderate, or severe dementia (Roberson, 2003).

Elderly nursing home residents experience sundowning syndrome, which is characterized by noisy disruptive behavior in the evening. Residents also have problems such as insomnia, loss of appetite, and resident-to-resident arguments, all of which are amenable to essential oil treatments. The Mattie C. Hall Health Care Center in Akin, South Carolina, is a recipient of the "Spirit of Caring" Best Practices Award, granted by the South Carolina Department of Health and Environmental Control, for the implementation and exemplary outcomes of their aromatherapy programs. The staff monitored residents for signs and symptoms observed during the use of essential oils for weight gain or loss; disruptive, combative, or resistive behavior; and the need for psychotropic drug prescriptions. The positive effects of aromatherapy were noteworthy and remarkable in that weight loss decreased from 23% of the residents to 7%, and the need for psychotropic medications decreased from 20% to 5%. The staff used simplistic methods to dispense the oils, such as spray bottles (hydrosols), compresses, bathwater, nebulizers, diffusers, and massage. The cost of the supplies was a few hundred dollars to the facility. The staff used essential oil blends with names like Wake Me and Feed Me, a blend of grapefruit and clove; Heaven's Scent, a blend of grapefruit and frankincense; Afternoon Delight, a blend of lavender and bergamot; and Stay Tuned, a mixture of bergamot, cinnamon, ylang ylang, and lemon. These magnificent successes are promoting meaningful aging for people with Alzheimer's disease. The clinical benefits from the practice of aromatherapy with essential oils are being realized by the clinical aromatherapist, Jackie Farnell, and her patients. (http://www.scentsiblesolutions.net/)

Other essential oils, such as Lavandula angustifolia (Lin, 2007) and Melissa officinalis (lemon balm) (Ballard, 2002), have been used to treat agitated behavior in dementia patients with good results (Snow, 2004), to the point of successfully weaned patients from their prescribed pharmaceuticals and showing significant results in improved behavior, fewer adverse drug reactions, and decreased formulary cost to the facility (Cohen-Manfield, 2007). As the number of elderly people living in extended-care nursing facilities and hospice settings rises, the role of aromatherapy and berry fruit juice therapy to provide phytomolecules and broad-spectrum antioxidants in the form of polyphenols and flavenoids could be instrumental in treating and alleviating the signs and symptoms of aging, dementia, and Alzheimer's disease (Campbell, 2001).

The stress of aging and oxidative stress in particular alters physiology profoundly. Growing areas of interesting research identify herbal remedies for disorders of attention span, perception, memory, and decision-making (Gold, 2001). The body's inability to cope with mental status-related problems associated with stress and aging may be due, in part, to a diet low in vitamins, minerals, trace elements, and antioxidants, which could result in marginal nutritional deficiencies as alluded to by the creator of orthomolecular medicine, Dr. Linus Pauling. Eat well to limit the oxidative stresses of life and live better longer.

WOMEN'S HEALTH

WOMEN HAVE UNIQUE HEALTH care needs throughout their lives that become more complex when they enter perimenopause and menopause. Numerous studies have been undertaken to elucidate these health care requirements and supplementation issues, specifically for women in the middle-age group. Emerging views regarding the efficacy of hormone treatment and the risk-benefit ratios associated with hormone replacement therapy (HRT) abound. Several studies have been undertaken for a combination of botanical treatments of menopausal symptoms, such as anxiety and hot flashes. The American Journal of Epidemiology has published results showing that the higher the percentage of body fat, the more likely a woman will experience hot flashes and night sweats (Thurston, 2008). Many women turn to natural products such as black cohosh and essential oils for natural HRT-like remedies to treat their symptoms. Women who have had gynecologic outpatient surgery associated with menopausal symptoms have found relief from aromatherapy.

Premenopausal women know that at a certain time of the month, they may have symptoms that are extremely difficult to bear. Women going through menopause have recurrent symptoms much more frequently, perhaps hourly. An office worker had hot flashes that were particularly distressing because they were impossible to predict or control, until she tried a blend of essential oils of orange, sandalwood, jasmine, patchouli, and ylang ylang. Repeated application of this blend of oils on the skin at her pulse points and the smell of the wonderful aromas not only decreased the number of hot flashes, but remarkably decreased the sweating and duration of each subsequent hot flash as well. She now keeps the blend of essential oils in her car, her purse, and at the bedside for fast and easy relief when a hot flash occurs.

Both women and men may begin developing osteoporosis in their thirties. Several essential oils may contribute to bone health: sage, juniper, pine, dwarf pine, and eucalyptus, as well as oils derived from common kitchen spices. Rosemary, thyme, and sage were noted to be effective due to their high monoterpene content. These oils work by inhibition of osteoclasts that remodel and tear down bone cells (Muhbauer, 2003). Remember that walking and repetitive training with light weights builds stronger bone by working the muscles attached to the bones by tendons.

IDEAL EXERCISE

EXERCISE IS ESSENTIAL TO women's health. Studies have shown that exercise at different "doses" of physical activity yields different responses in cardiorespiratory fitness among sedentary, overweight, and postmenopausal women with elevated blood pressure. Women who exercised to varying degrees experienced the positive changes of increased muscle mass and decreased fat, proportionally determined by how much they worked out. That is the ideal change in body composition induced by exercise. Increased muscle mass and decreased body fat resulting from a proper fitness program are preferred to poor dieting without an exercise program, which leads to decreased muscle mass and continued excess fat. Exercise not only builds muscle and burns fat; it also resets the body's resting metabolic rate to a higher set point, so you burn more calories when resting.

Walking is an ideal exercise, because it is low impact and still somewhat strenuous. Walking ten thousand pedometer-measured steps daily has been shown to create positive metabolic balance (i.e., weight loss). Normally, we walk about six thousand steps per day and need thirty minutes more of treadmill time to gain the remaining four thousand steps. Walking fewer than five thousand steps per day is considered a sedentary lifestyle, which results in a negative metabolic balance, or weight gain. Train your body to adapt to more and more exercise in order to build endurance and strengthen the heart, developing a more muscular build.

The body responds to cyles of light and dark with hormonal variations that exert circadian influences on the body's reaction to the stresses of exercise. Choosing the best type of exercise depends on age, sex, and time of day.

Women and men need daily walking and workouts with weights several times per week. The simple act of breathing causes physiological stress, because the air causes cellular oxidization, generating free radicals, which are the chemicals that age us. Breathing can also be used to treat stress. Humming produces nitric oxide in the sinuses. Nitric oxide is a potent dilator of blood vessels. Wind sprints are an excellent cardiovascular exercise. Regular daily wind sprints in any sport, fast walking, and stair climbing are great exercises. Oxidative stress occurs when we exercise, increasing with rising altitude, but the overall benefits of exercise far outweigh that stress.

EXERCISE IS MEDICINE

NEW BRAIN CELLS ARE created as we exercise. The wonderful Miracle Gro-like substance called brain-derived neutrotrophic factor (BDNF) induces growth of new neurons. Spark: The Revolutionary New Science of Science of Exercise and the Brain, by John Ratey, MD, has generated significant interest in new research supporting exercise as medicine for the brain. Exercise affects cognitive ability just as it affects muscles, making the brain better and smarter. These new BDNF-stimulated brain cells have increased capillary circulation and higher levels of the neurotransmitters dopamine, serotonin, and norepinephrine. These findings about exercise have led researchers to propose that exercise benefits memory. Paradoxically, exercise is remotely chemically akin to the combined antidepressant effects of taking Prozac and and the mental stimulation of taking Ritalin. Physical activity could become instrumental in preventing Alzheimer's disease, attention-deficit hyperactivity disorder (ADHD), and other cognitive disorders. No matter what your age, an active body is essential for an active mind and strong immune function (Jensen, 1999). Exercise is medicine for the mind and body.

IDEAL BRAIN EXERCISE

ALTHOUGH PLENTY OF STUDIES describe the ideal workout, little data defines the ideal workout for the brain. Exercise for many people often stops for good when it is no longer required as part of physical education class in school. Please realize that the better quality foods you eat and the more you exercise throughout all the decades of life, the more benefits you will gain from those endeavors, not just in building muscles but in preventing heart failure and brain failure.

Previously, a basic tenet of human physiology stated that the brain (i.e., the central nervous system, or CNS), does not regenerate when damaged, destroyed, or lost due to the aging process. Scientific events have shown that CNS cells can be regenerated. Stem cell research using skin cells and umbilical cord blood for therapy is accelerating worldwide. The cells of the nerve sheath of the first cranial nerve for olfaction have totipotent stem cell ability when surgically implanted into the spine. New research on BDNF shows why physical exercise is important to the brain. Scientists have preliminary observations that new nerve cells can be grown in the human brain simply by putting subjects on a three-month aerobic workout regimen! Physically and mentally challenging activities are currently approved prescriptions for success for people of all ages when modified and in moderation.

THOUGHTS ARE THINGS AND IDEAS BECOME EMOTIONS

MASTERY OF SELF IMPLIES mastering one's thought life. "Patient Fix Thyself," an article by Robert Langreth in Forbes (April 2007) describes how cognitive-behavioral therapy (CBT) is making great strides over traditional psychoanalysis in treating psychological illnesses. He emphasizes that CBT is at least as effective as drug therapy for nonpsychotic disorders. The success of CBT is based on the major tenet of CBT: Thinking has a powerful influence on symptoms. For instance, anxiety-producing ideas precede the emotions associated with anxiety. Robert Leahy, in The Worry Cure, expresses enthusiasm for CBT and the more than 140 encouraging studies that encompass behavioral issues such as depression, hypochondria, insomnia, suicide, anxiety, and panic attacks. Dr. Phil McGraw uses confrontational behavioral modification techniques that resemble CBT on television when he asks his guests, "What were you thinking?" and "How is that working out for you?" These techniques seem to be new and innovative.

In actuality, they are not so new, since Napoleon Hill in 1938 wrote that the seven negative emotions to avoid—fear, jealousy, hatred, revenge, greed, anger, and superstition—form the basis of most psychological disorders. Negative thoughts and negative emotions "voluntarily" inject themselves into the subconscious mind, whereas positive emotions must be thought purposefully to ensure placement in the subconscious mind.

Obsessive-compulsive disorder (OCD) is characterized by "invasive" anxiety-laden thoughts and accompanying repetitive behaviors that are enacted to reduce anxiety. The exact chemical basis for OCD is elusive. Hyperactivity of brain neurons is consistently seen in sections of an OCD brain. This hyperactivity is measured as the increased rate of glucose metabolism, as seen in an OCD patient's brain imaging, particularly in the caudate nucleus of the brain. Successful treatment with Prozac-like medications or CBT reverses those findings. Roughly 60% of OCD patients respond to medications like Prozac or to CBT, or a combination of both. One study showed essentially identical results when comparing CBT to Prozac-using positron emission tomography to measure the rate of glucose metabolism in the OCD brain after Prozac treatment alone and after CBT alone. Both types of treatments decreased the rate of glucose metabolism to levels seen in healthy people without OCD. The rate of decrease appeared proportional to the degree of improvement in their OCD symptoms. CBT is free of side effects and works on the brain in ways that are objective and measurable. A brain scan taken during CBT appears similar to that taken during a treatment with medication.

Every time we choose a good thought, we make a good investment.
—Raymond Holliwell

READING TRAINS THE BRAIN

THE HUMAN GENOME CONSISTS of thirty thousand genes, six thousand of which are expressed in the human brain. The following books about our brains expound and expand the empires of the mind. *Train Your Mind, Change Your Brain*, by Sharon Begley, emphasizes neuroplasticity as the brain's ability to remold itself. Five Minds of the Future, by Howard Gardner, defines five new categories of the mind: the disciplined mind, the synthesizing mind, the creating mind, the respectful mind, and the ethical mind, as well as their theoretical attributes. The trained mind of the future invokes new creative paradigms on everything from improved global health to paying forward wealth.

Psychoneuroimmunology explains the mind-body relationship in terms of thinking, emotions, the nervous system, cellular communication, and their effects on the immune system. Communicating along new frequencies facilitates creativity. Effective listening habits can be gained through practice and study. Neurolinguistic programming (NLP) is a learned technique that enables the listener to understand what another individual is actually communicating. In NLP terms, "success" is defined as getting what you want, and "happiness" is defined as wanting what you get.

Teens have their own special awareness of life that could benefit from increased education in the fine arts of goal setting and communication. These necessary skills rank high on the list of success principles. Bob Proctor's interactive online youth web community is accented with coaching modules that youth can work through at their own speed. The program, called Goal33, is designed to produce higher marks in school, improved social life, and career guidance. Couple that program with Sean Covey's book, *The Seven Habits of Highly Effective Teens*, and you definitely have material that youth and teens can sink their teeth into.

The Seven Habits of Highly Effective People, by Stephen R. Covey, delineates the "can do's" and "how to's" for having a victorious private and public life by applying thoughtful role-modeling exercises. True leadership derives from the fundamental art of leadership of self, which entails maintaining self-health and managing activities of daily living, including personal growth through study. It is vitally important to experience personal growth so that you can build strong interpersonal relationships, because the vast majority of what is really known as "success" is based on who you know and how you conduct yourself toward them.

PRICELESS RELATIONSHIP BUILDING

THE LAW OF SUCCESS In Sixteen Lessons was a course created and taught by Napoleon Hill in the early 1900s at the suggestion of the great Andrew Carnegie. A two-volume book is available that is well worth owning and reading. It summarizes life success principles succinctly in sixteen lessons, from the mastermind to the golden rule. The following quote from the introduction of the course brilliantly illuminates the truth of building deeply valued relationships because they fulfill the need for humans to live and work together. Only then can personal successes be valuable, even priceless, in your own life and legacy:

'Success in this world is always a matter of individual effort, yet you will only be deceiving yourself if you believe that you can succeed without the cooperation of other people. Success is a matter of individual effort only to the extent that each person must decide, in his or her own mind, what is wanted. This involves the use of the imagination. From this point on, achieving success is a matter of skillfully and tactfully inducing others to cooperate.'

— Napoleon Hill

YOUR RELATIONSHIP WITH THE DIVINE

THE DIVINE DESIRES YOU to manifest health, wealth, and happiness by impressing and embedding guided images of success and opulence into your subconscious mind. The divine mind is able to super abundantly bring to pass anything that you can ask or think, according to the power that works in you. Consider the profound nature of the last statement and the following passage written at the beginning of the last century by Thomas Troward, European philosopher and author of The Dore Lectures on Mental Sciences and The New Thought and the New Order:

My Mind is a center of Divine operation. The Divine operation is always for expansion and fuller expression and this means the production of something beyond what has gone before, something entirely new, not included in past experience, though proceeding out of it by an orderly sequence of growth. Therefore, since the Divine operation cannot change its inherent nature, it must operate in the same manner in me; consequently in my own special world, of which I am the center, it will move forward to produce new conditions, always in advance of any that have gone on before.

THE OILMD PRESCRIPTION FOR SUCCESS

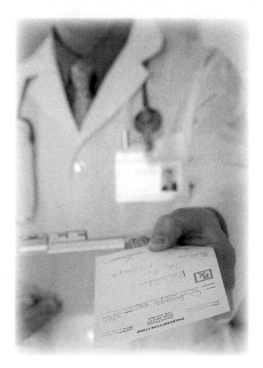

A DOCTOR'S PRESCRIPTION IS a medicolegal document that defines what is prescribed to the patient, how the pharmacist is to dispense it, and how the patient is to receive its intended benefit. The prescription forms a bond between patient and doctor. The following is the oilMD prescription for success:

- Use essential oils.

- Drink berry fruit juices.

- Eat well and exercise.

- Be happy and grateful.

- Subscribe to the oilMD Wellness News Network.

Because … a merry heart doeth good like a medicine
(Prov. 17:22) KJV

I sincerely hope that this edition of The Sweet Smell of Success: Health and Wealth Secrets will help you live and act in a way that brings you all the good that you deserve.

Watch the oilMD's videos on various websites, including YouTube. Subscribe to the educational courses offered on the oilMD Wellness Network.

www.oilmdwellnessnetwork.com

bibliography

Chapter 1: The Art of Aromatherapy

Cappello, G., Spezzaferro, M., Grossi, L., Manzoli, L., & Marzio, L. (2007). *Peppermint oil (Mintoil) in the treatment of irritable bowel syndrome: A prospective double blind placebo-controlled randomized trial. Dig Liver Dis., 39(6), 530-536.*

Inouye, S., & Yamaguchi H., (2001). *Antibacterial Activity of Essential Oils and Their Major Constituents Against Respiratory Tract Pathogens by Gaseous Contact. Journal of Antimicrobial Chemotherapy 47:565-73.*

Kline, R.M., Kline, J.J., Di Palma, J., & Barbero GJ. (2001). *Enteric-coated, pH-dependent peppermint oil capsules for the treatment of irritable bowel syndrome in children. J Pediatr. Jan;138(1):125-8.*

Lehrner J Marwinski, G. *Ambient Odors of Orange and Lavender Reduce Anxiety and Improve Mood in a Dental Office. (2005).Physiology of Behavior, 86, (1-2):92- 95.*

Srivasta, K.C., & Mustapha, T., (1992). *Ginger (Zingiber officinale) in Rheumatism and Musculoskeletal Disorders. Medical Hypotheses 39 (1992):342-8.*

Yip, Y.B., & Tam, A.C. (2009). *An experimental study on the effectiveness of massage with aromatic ginger and orange essential oil for moderate-to-severe knee pain among the elderly in Hong Kong. Complement Ther Med. Jun; 16(3):131-8.*

Chapter 2: Worthy Ideals

http://www.bobproctorlive.com

http://www.nightingale.com/

http://www.sgroilmd.com

http://www.vervemd.com

Kuriyama, H., Watanabe, S., Nakaya, T., Shigemori, I., Kita, M., Yoshida, N., Masaki, D., Tadai, T., Ozasa, K., Fukui, K., & Imanishi, J., (2005). Immunological and Psychological Benefits of Aromatherapy Massage. Evid Based Complement Alternat Med. Jun; 2 (2):179-184.

O'Keefe, J.H., Gheewala, N.M., & O'Keefe, J.O., (2008) Dietary strategies for improving post-prandial glucose, lipids, inflammation, and cardiovascular health. J Am Coll Cardiol. Jan 22; 51(3):249-55.

Chapter 3: Worldwide Wellness: A Doctor's Perspective

Berger, M.M., (2005). Can oxidative damage be treated nutritionally? Clin Nutr. Apr; 24(2):172-83.

Chandan, K., Savita, K., & Sashwati, R., (2006). Tocotrienols: Vitamin E Beyond Tocopherols. Life Sci. March 27; 78(18): 2088–2098.

Chapple, I.L., Milward, M.R., & Dietrich, T., (2007). The prevalence of inflammatory periodontitis is negatively associated with serum antioxidant concentrations. J Nutr. Mar; 137(3):657-64.

Costantino, V., Fattorusso, E., Menna, M., & Taglialatela-Scafati, O., (2004). Chemical diversity of bioactive marine natural products: an illustrative case study. Curr Med Chem. Jul; 11(13):1671-92.

Eaton, S., (2006) The biochemical basis of antioxidant therapy in critical illness. Proc Nutr Soc. Aug; 65(3):242-9.

Ebihara, T., Ebihara, S., Maruyama, M., Kobayashi, M., Itou, A., Arai, H., & Sasaki, H., (2006). A randomized trial of olfactory stimulation using black pepper oil in older people with swallowing dysfunction. J Am Geriatr Soc. Sep; 54(9):1401-6.

Edris, A.E., (2007). Pharmaceutical and therapeutic potentials of essential oils and their individual volatile constituents: a review. Phytother Res. Apr; 21(4):308-23.

Fine, D.H., Markowitz, K., Furgang, D., Goldsmith, D., Charles, C.H., Lisante, T.A., & Lynch, M.C., (2007). Effect of an essential oil-containing antimicrobial mouthrinse on specific plaque bacteria in vivo. J Clin Periodontol. Aug; 34(8):652-7.

Fine, D.H., Markowitz, K., Furgang, D., Goldsmith, D., Ricci-Nittel D., Charles, C.H., Peng, P., & Lynch, M.C.,(2007). Effect of rinsing with an essential oil-containing mouthrinse on subgingival periodontopathogens. J Periodontol. Oct; 78(10):1935-42.

Gordaliza, M., (2007). Natural products as leads to anticancer drugs. Clin Transl Oncol. Dec; 9(12):767-76.

Haefner, B., (2003). Drugs from the deep: marine natural products as drug candidates. Drug Discov Today. Jun 15; 8(12):536-44.

https://www.23andme.com/

http://www.berkshirehathaway.com/

http://www.gatesfoundation.org/default.htm

http://www.healthvault.com/

http://www.helpinghandsinafrica.com/donors/index.shtml

http://www.jcvi.org/

http://www.keepachildalive.org/

http://www.paulallen.com/?contentId-1

http://www.rjbuckle.com/index.html

http://www.revolutionhealth.com/

Imura, M., Misao, H., Ushijima, H., (2006). The psychological effects of aromatherapy-massage in healthy postpartum mothers. J Midwifery Womens Health. Mar-Apr; 51(2):e21-7.

Latham, J.R., Wilson, A.K., & Steinbrecher, R.A., (2006; 2006). The mutational consequences of plant transformation. J Biomed Biotechnol. (2):25376.

Muñoz, C.A., Kiger, R.D., Stephens, J.A., Kim, J., & Wilson, A.C., (2001). Effects of a nutritional supplement on periodontal status. Compend Contin Educ Dent. May; 22(5):425-8.

Nakao, Y., Fusetani, N., (2007). Enzyme inhibitors from marine invertebrates. J Nat Prod. Apr; 70(4):689-710.

Uemura, D., (2006). Bioorganic, Studies on marine natural products--diverse chemical structures and bioactivities. Chem Rec.; 6(5):235-48.

Zhao, J., (2007).Plant troponoids: chemistry, biological activity, and biosynthesis. Curr Med Chem.; 14(24):2597-621.

Zhao, J., (2007). Nutraceuticals, Nutritional Therapy, Phytonutrients, and Phytotherapy for Improvement of Human Health: A Perspective on Plant Biotechnology Application. Recent Patents on Biotechnology; 1, 75-97 75.

Chapter 4: Ideal Scents

Carroll, S.P., & Loye, J., (2006). PMD, a registered botanical mosquito repellent with deet-like efficacy. J Am Mosq Control Assoc., (2006) Sep; 22(3):507-14.

Chung, F., Yegneswaran, B., Liao, P., Chung, S., Vairavanathan, S., Islam, S., Khajehdehi, A., Shapiro, & Colin, M., (2008). STOP Questionnaire: A Tool to Screen Patients for Obstructive Sleep Apnea. Clinical Investigations Anesthesiology. May; 108(5):812-821.

Ebihara, T., Ebihara, S., Maruyama, M., Kobayashi, M., Itou, A., Arai, H., & Sasaki, H., (2006). A randomized trial of olfactory stimulation using black pepper oil in older people with swallowing dysfunction. J Am Geriatr Soc. 2006 Sep; 54(9):1401-6.

Elson, C.E., Underbakke, G.L., Hanson, P., Shrago, E., Wainberg, R.H., & Qureshi, A.A., (1989). Impact of lemongrass oil, an essential oil, on serum cholesterol. Lipids. Aug; 24(8):677-9.

Koch, C., Reichling, J., Schneele, J., & Schnitzler, P., (2008). Inhibitory effect of essential oils against herpes simplex virus type 2. Phytomedicine. Jan; 15(1-2):71-8.

Puhan, M.A., Suarez, A., Lo Cascio, C., Zahn, A., Heitz, M., & Braendli, O., (2006). Didgeridoo playing as alternative treatment for obstructive sleep apnoea syndrome: randomised controlled trial. BMJ. Feb 4; 332(7536):266-70.

Chapter 5: Medical Aromatherapy in the Twenty-first Century

Allen, W., (1929). Effect of Various Inhaled Vapors on Respiration and Blood Pressure in Anesthetized, Unanaesthetized, Sleeping and Anosmic Subjects. Am J Physiol.; 88: 620-632.

Ballard, C.G., O'Brien, J.T., Reichelt, K., & Perry, E.K., (2002). Aromatherapy as a safe and effective treatment for the management of agitation in severe dementia: the results of a double-blind, placebo-controlled trial with Melissa. J Clin Psychiatry. Jul; 63(7):553-8.

Beck, A., Salem, K., Krischak, G., Kinzl, L., Bischoff, M., & Schmelz, A., (2005), Nonsteroidal anti-inflammatory drugs (NSAIDs) in The Perioperative Phase in Traumatology and Orthopedics Effects on Bone Healing. Oper Orthop Traumatol. Dec;17(6):569-78.

Calcabrini, A., Stringaro, A., Toccacieli, L., Meschini, S., Marra, M., Colone, M., Salvatore, G., Mondello, F., Arancia, G., & Molinari, A., (2004). Terpinen-4-ol, The Main Component of Melaleuca Alternifolia (tea tree) Oil Inhibits the In Vitro Growth of Human Melanoma Cells. J Invest Dermatol. Feb; 122(2):349-60.

Cousins, L., (2002). Inflammation and Cancer. Nature. 420:860-867.

Eger, E.I., (2006). et al. Contrasting roles of the N-Methyl-D-Aspartate Receptor in the Production of Immobilization by Conventional and Aromatic Anesthetics. Anesthesia Analgesia; 102:1397-406.

Ferrini, A.M., Mannoni, V., Aureli, P., Salvatore, G., Piccirilli, E., Ceddia, T., Pontieri, E., Sessa R., & Oliva, B,. (2006). Melaleuca Alternifolia Essential Oil Possesses Potent Anti-Staphylococcal Activity Extended to Strains Resistant to Antibiotics. Int J Immunopathol Pharmacol. Jul-Sep; 19(3):539-44.

Geiger, J.L., (2005). The Essential Oil of Ginger, Zingiber officinale, and Anesthesia. The International Journal of Aromatherapy 15, 7-14.

Giordani, C., Molinari, A., Toccacieli, L., Calcabrini, A., Stringaro, A., Chistolini, P., Arancia, G., & Diociaiuti, M., (2006). Interaction of Tea Tree Oil with Model and Cellular Membranes. J Med Chem. Jul 27; 49(15):4581-8.

Goel, N., & Lao, R.P., (2006). Sleep changes vary by odor perception in young adults. Biol Psychol. Mar; 71(3):341-9.

Goel, N., & Grasso, D.J., (2004). Olfactory discrimination and transient mood change in young men and women: variation by season, mood state, and time of day. Chronobiol Int. Jul; 21(4-5):691-719.

Goel, N., Kim, H., & Lao, R.P., (2005). An olfactory stimulus modifies nighttime sleep in young men and women. Chronobiol Int.:22(5):889-904.

Haze. S., Sakai, K., & Gozu, Y., (2002). Effects of fragrance inhalation on sympathetic activity in normal adults. (2002). Jpn J Pharmacol. Nov; 90(3):247-53.

Henley, D.V., Lipson, N., Korach, K.S., & Bloch, C.A., (2007). Prepubertal Gynecomastia Linked to Lavender and Tea Tree Oils. N Engl J Med. Feb 1:356(5):479-85.

Holmes, C., Hopkins, V., Hensford C, MacLaughlin V, Wilkinson D, & Rosenvinge H. (2002). Lavender oil as a treatment for agitated behaviour in severe dementia: a placebo controlled study. Int J Geriatr Psychiatry. Apr; 17(4):305-8.

Howes, J.R., Houghton, P.J., & Barlow, D.J., (2002). Assessment of Estrogenic Activity in Some Common Essential Oil Constituents. Journal of Pharmacy & Pharmacology. 54:1521–1528. http://www.Nobelprize.org/medicine/laurates/2004.

Kim, J.T., Wajda, M., Cuff, G., Serota, D., Schlame, M., Axelrod, D.M., Guth, A.A., & Bekker, A.Y., (2006). Evaluation of Aromatherapy in Treating Postoperative Pain: A Pilot Study. Pain Pract. Dec; 6(4):273-7.

Klein, E., (2006). Genetic Susceptibility and Oxidative Stress in Prostate Cancer. Urology Vol 68: Number 6 Dec 1145-1151.

Komori, T., Matsumoto, T., Motomura, E., & Shiroyama, T., (2006). The sleep-enhancing effect of valerian inhalation and sleep-shortening effect of lemon inhalation. Chem Senses. Oct; 31(8):731-7.

Lee, A., Chui, P.T., Aun, C.S., Lau, A.S., & Gin, T., (2006). Incidence and Risk of Adverse Perioperative Events Among Surgical Patients Taking Traditional Chinese Herbal Medicines. Anesthesiology. Sep; 105(3):454-61.

Mehta, S., (1998). Use of Essential Oil to Promote Induction of Anesthesia in Children. Anesthesia: 53:720-1.

Moran, G.J., Amii, R.N., Abrahamian, F.M., & Talan, D.A., (2005). Methicillin-Resistant Staphylococcus Aureus in Community-Acquired Skin Infections. Emerg Infect Dis. Jun; 11(6):928-30.

Sano, A., Sei, H., Seno, H., Morita, Y., & Moritoki, H., (1998). Influence of cedar essence on spontaneous activity and sleep of rats and human daytime nap. Psychiatry Clin Neurosci. Apr;52(2):133-5.

Santoro, G.F., das Gracas Cardoso, M., Guimaraes, L.G., Salgado, A.P., Menna-Barreto, R.F., & Soares, M.J., (2007). Effect of Oregano (Origanum vulgare L.) and Thyme (Thymus vulgaris L.) Essential Oils on Trypanosoma Cruzi (Protozoa: Kinetoplastida) Growth and Ultrastructure. Parasitol Res. Mar; 100(4):783-90.

Shen, J., (2007). Mechanisms of changes induced in plasma glycerol by scent stimulation with grapefruit and lavender essential oils. Neuroscience Letter.Apr 18; 416(3):241-6.

Sherry, E., Boeck, H., & Warnke, P.H., (2001). Percutaneous Treatment of Chronic MRSA Osteomyelitis with a Novel Plant-Derived Antiseptic. BMC Surg.; 1:1. Epub 2001 May 16.

Sherry, E., Reynolds, M., Sivananthan, S., Mainawalala, S., & Warnke, P.H., (2004). Inhalational Phytochemicals as Possible Treatment for Pulmonary Tuberculosis: Two Case Reports. Am J Infect Control. Oct; 32(6):369-70.

Sherry. E., Sivananthan, S., Warnke, P.H., & Eslick, G.D., (2003). Topical Phytochemicals Used to Salvage the Gangrenous Lower Limbs of Type 1 Diabetic Patients. Diabetes Res Clin Pract. Oct; 62(1):65-6.

Smith, C., Crowther, C., Willson, K., Hotham, N., & McMillian, V., (2004). A Randomized Controlled Trial of Ginger to Treat Nausea and Vomiting in Pregnancy. Obstet Gynecol. Apr; 103(4):639-45.

Surh, Y., (1999). Molecular Mechanisms of Chemopreventive Effects of Selected Dietary and Medicinal Phenolic Substances. Mutat Res. Jul 16; 428(1-2):305-27.

Talpur, N., (2005), Effects of a novel formulation of essential oil on glucose-insulin metabolism in diabetic hypertensive rats: A pilot Effects of a Novel Formulation of Essential Oil on Glucose-Insulin Metabolism in Diabetic Hypertensive Rats: A Pilot Study. Diabetes, Obesity and Metabolism, 7, 2005, 193-199.

Tanida, M., (2005). Olfactory stimulation with Scent of essential oil of grapefruit affects autonomic neurotransmission and blood pressure. Brain Res. Oct 5; 1058(1-2):44-55.

Tipton, D.A., & Hamman, N.R., Dabbous MK. (2006). Effect of Myrrh Oil on IL-1beta Stimulation of NF-kappaB Activation and PGE(2) Production in Human Gingival Fibroblasts and Epithelial Cells. Toxicol In Vitro. Mar; 20(2):248-55.

Warnke, P.H., Sherry, E., Russo, P.A., Acil, Y., Wiltfang, J., Sivananthan, S., Sprengel, M., Roldan, J.C., Schubert, S., Bredee, J.P., & Springer, I.N., (2006). Antibacterial Essential Oils in Malodorous Cancer Patients: Clinical Observations in 30 Patients. Phytomedicine. Jul; 13(7):463-7.

Chapter 6: Ideal Anesthesia

Allen, W., Am. (1929). Effect of various inhaled vapors on respirations and blood pressure in anesthetized, anaesthetized, sleeping and anosmic subjects. J. of Physiology., 88:620-632.

Eger, E.I. 2nd, Liao, M., Laster, M.J., Won, A., Popovich, J., Raines, D.E., Solt, K., Dutton, R.C., Cobos, F.V. 2nd, & Sonner, J.M., (2006). Contrasting roles of the N-methyl-D-aspartate receptor in the production of immobilization by conventional and aromatic anesthetics. Anesth Analg. May; 102(5):1397-406.

Chung, F., Yegneswaran, B., Liao, P., Chung, S.A., Vairavanathan, S., Islam, S., Khajehdehi, A., & Shapiro, C.M., (2008). STOP questionnaire: a tool to screen patients for obstructive sleep apnea. Anesthesiology. May; 108(5):812-21.

Naguib, M., (2007). Melatonin and Anesthesia: A Clinical Perspective. Journal of Pineal Research; 42:12-21.

Orser, B., (2007). "Lifting the Fog Around Anesthesia." Scientific American, June. 54-61.

Tekbas, O.F., Ogur, R., Korkmaz, A., Kilic, A., & Reiter, R.J., (2008). Melatonin as an antibiotic: new insights into the actions of this ubiquitous molecule. J Pineal Res. Mar; 44(2):222-6.

Theusinger, O.M., Leyvraz, P.F., Schanz, U., Seifert, B., & Spahn, D.R., (2007). Treatment of iron deficiency anemia in orthopedic surgery with intravenous iron: efficacy and limits: a prospective study. Anesthesiology. Dec; 107(6):923-7.

Chapter 7: Ginger and Anesthesia

Altman, R.D., & Marcussen, K.C., (2001). Effects of a Ginger Extract on Knee Pain in Patients with Osteoarthritis. Arthritis Rheum. M Nov; 44(11):2531-8.

Anderson, L.A., & Gross, J.B., (2004). Aromatherapy with Peppermint, Isopropyl Alcohol, or Placebo is Equally Effective in Relieving Postoperative Nausea. J Perianesth Nurs. Feb; 19(1):29-35.

Andrade, J., (1995). Learning During Anaesthesia: A Review. Br J Psychol. Nov; 86:479-506.

Arnberger, M., Stadelmann, K., Alischer, P., Ponert, R., Melber, A., & Greif, R., (2007). Monitoring of neuromuscular blockade at the P6 acupuncture point reduces the incidence of postoperative nausea and vomiting. Anesthesiology. Dec; 107(6):903-8.

Apfel, C., (2004). A Factorial Trial of Six Interventions for the Prevention of Postoperative Nausea and Vomiting. N Engl. J of Med. June 350; 24:2441-2512.

Apfel, C., & Roewer, N,.(2003). Risk Assessment of Postoperative Nausea and Vomiting. Int Anesthesiol Clin.; 41(4):13-32.

Bonati, A., (1991). How and Why Should We Standardize Phytopharmaceutical Drugs for Clinical Validation. Ethnophamacol. Apr; 32(1-3):195-7.

Bone, M.E., Wilkinson, D.J., Young, J.R., McNeil, J., & Charlton, S., (1990). Ginger Root—A New Antiemetic. The Effect of Ginger Root on Postoperative Nausea and Vomiting After Major Gynaecological Surgery. Anaesthesia. Aug; 45(8):669-71.

Buck, L.B., (1992). The Olfactory Multigene Family. Current Opinion Neurobiology. June; 2(3):282-8.

Cantor, R.S., (2001). Breaking the Meyer-Overton Rule: Predicted Effects of Varying Stiffness and Interfacial Activity on the Intrinsic Potency of Anesthetics. Biophys J. May; 80(5):2284-97.

Chen, W.R., Xiong, W., & Shepherd, G.M,. (2000). Analysis of Relations Between NMDA Receptors and GABA Release at Olfactory Bulb Reciprocal Synapses. Neuron. Mar; 25(3):625-33.

da Silva, J.M., Mapleson, W.W., & Vickers, M.D., (1997) Quantitative Study of Lowe's Square-Root-of-Time Method of Closed System Anesthesia. Br J Anaesth. Jul ;(1):103-12.

Dando, T.M., & Perry, C.M., (2004). Aprepitant: A Review of Its Use in the Prevention of Chemotherapy-Induced Nausea and Vomiting. Drugs. 64(7):777-94.

Darkow, T., Gora-Harper, M.L., & Goulson, D.T., (2001). Record KE. Impact of Antiemetic Selection on Postoperative Nausea and Vomiting and Patient Satisfaction. Pharmacotherapy. May; 21(5):540-8.

Eberhart, L.H., Mayer, R., Betz, O., Tsolakidis, S., Hilpert, W., Morin, A.M., Geldner, G., Wulf, H., & Seeling, W., (2003). Ginger Does Not Prevent Postoperative Nausea and Vomiting after Laparoscopic Surgery. Anesth Analg. Apr; 96(4):995-8.

Eger, E.I., (1998). Current and Future Perspectives on Inhaled Anesthetics. Pharmacotherapy. Sep-Oct; 18(5):895-910.

Ernst, E., & Pittler, M.H., (2000). Efficacy of Ginger for Nausea and Vomiting: a Systematic Review of Randomized Clinical Trials. Br J Anaesth. Mar; 84(3):367-71.

Firestein, S., (2004). A Code in the Nose. Sci STKE. Mar 30; 2004(227):pg15.

Gidron, Y., Barak, T., Henik, A., Gurman, G., & Stiener, O., (2002). Implicit Learning of Emotional Information Under Anesthesia. Neuroreport. Jan 21; 13(1):139-42.

Guh, J.H., Ko, F.N., Jong, T.T., & Teng, C.M., (1995). Antiplatelet Effect of Gingerol Isolated from Zingiber officinale. J Pharm Pharmacol. Apr ;(4):329-32.

Gupta, A., Wu, C.L., Elkassabany, N., Krug, C.E., Parker, S.D., & Fleisher, L.A., (2003). Does the Routine Prophylactic Use of Antiemetics Affect the Incidence of Post Discharge Nausea and Vomiting Following Ambulatory Surgery? A Systematic Review of Randomized Controlled Trials. Anesthesiology. Aug; 99(2):488-95.

Habib, A.S., & Gan, T.J., (2003). Food and Drug Administration Black Box Warning on the Perioperative Use of Droperidol: A Review of the Cases. Anesth Analg. May; 96(5):1377-9.

Habib, A.S., Gan, T.J., (2004). Evidence-Based Management of Postoperative Nausea and Vomiting: A Review. Can J Anaesth. Apr; 51(4):326-41.

Hameroff, S., (2006). The Entwinded Mysteries of Anesthesia and Consciousness. Is There a Common Underlying Mechanism? Anesthesiology; 105:400-12.

Hodges, P.J., & Kam, P.C., (2002). The Perioperative Implications of Herbal Medicines. Anaesthesia. Sep; 57(9):889-99.

http://Nobelprize.org/medicine/laureates/2004/

Huang, Q., Matsuda, H., Sakai, K., Yamahara, J., & Tamai, Y., (1990) The Effect of Ginger on Serotonin Induced Hypothermia and Diarrhea. Yakugaku Zasshi. Dec; 110(12):936-42.

Huang, Q.R., Iwamoto, M., Aoki, S., Tanaka, N., Tajima, K., Yamahara, J., Takaishi, Y., Yoshida, M., Tomimatsu, T., & Tamai, Y., (1991). Anti-5-hydroxytryptamine 3 effect of galanolactone, diterpenoid isolated from ginger. Chem Pharm Bull (Tokyo). Feb; 39(2):397-9.

Jäger, W., (1992). Percutaneous absorption of lavender oil from massage oil. Journal of the Society of Cosmetic Chemists, 43:49-54.

Janssen, P.L., Meyboom, S., van Staveren, W.A., de Vegt, F., & Katan, M.B., (1996) Consumption of Ginger (Zingiber officinale roscoe) Does Not Affect Ex Vivo Platelet Thromboxane Production in Humans. Eur J Clin Nutr. Nov; 50(11):772-4.

Kawai, T., Kinoshita, K., Koyama, K., & Takahashi, K., (1994).Anti-Emetic Principles of Magnolia Obovata Bark and Zingiber Officinale Rhizome. Planta Med. Feb; 60(1):17-20.

Keating, A., & Chez, R.A., (2002). Ginger Syrup as an Antiemetic in Early Pregnancy. Altern Ther Health Med. Sep-Oct; 8(5):89-91.

Kobayashi, M., Ishida, Y., Shoji, N., & Ohizumi, Y., (1988). Cardiotonic Action of [8]-gingerol, an Activator of the Ca++-pumping Adenosine Triphosphatase of Sarcoplasmic Reticulum, in Guinea Pig Atrial Muscle. J Pharmacol Exp Ther. Aug; 246(2):667-73.

Lamb, A.B., (1994) Effect of Dried Ginger on Human Platelet Function. Thromb Haemost. Jan; 71(1):110-1.

Martins, A.P., Salgueiro, L., Goncalves, M.J., da Cunha, A.P., Vila, R., Canigueral, S., Mazzoni,V., Tomi, F., & Casanova, J., (2001). Essential Oil Composition and Antimicrobial Activity of Three Zingiberaceae from S.Tome e Principe. Planta Med. Aug; 67(6):580-4.

Mayer, M., Doenicke, A., Nebauer, A.E., & Hepting, L., (1996). Propofol and Etomidate-Lipuro for Induction of General Anesthesia. Hemodynamics, Vascular Compatibility, Subjective Findings and Postoperative Nausea. Anaesthesist. Nov; 45(11):1082-4.

Mehta, S., (1998). Use of Essential Oil to Promote Induction of Anaesthesia in Children. Anaesthesia, 53 pages 720-21.

Moneret-Vautrin, D.A., Morisset, M., Lemerdy, P., Croizier, A., & Kanny, G., (2002). Food Allergy and IgE Sensitization Caused by Spices: CICBAA data (based on 589 cases of food allergy). Allerg Immunol (Paris). Apr; 34(4):135-40.

Morin, A.M., Betz, O., Kranke, P., Geldner, G., Wulf, H., & Eberhart, L.H., (2004). Is Ginger a Relevant Antiemetic for Postoperative Nausea and Vomiting? Anasthesiol Intensivmed Notfallmed Schmerzther. May; 39(5):281-5.

Mustafa, T., & Srivastava, K.C., (1990). Ginger (Zingiber officinale) in Migraine Headache. J Ethnopharmacol. Jul; 29(3):267-73.

Myles, P.S., & Tan, N., (2003). *Reporting of Ethical Approval and Informed in Clinical Research Published in Leading Anesthesia Journals. Anesthesiology.* Nov; 99(5):1209-13.

Olowe, S.A., & Ransome-Kuti, O., (1980). *The Risk of Jaundice in Glucose-6-Phosphate Dehydrogenase Deficient Babies Exposed to Menthol. Acta Paediatr Scand.* May; 69(3):341-5.

Onogi, T., Minami, M., Kuraishi, Y., & Satoh, M., (1992).*Capsaicin-like Effect of (6)-shogaol on Substance P-Containing Primary Afferents of Rats: A Possible Mechanism of Its Analgesic Action. Neuropharmacology.* Nov; 31(11):1165-9.

Ostman, P.L., Faure, E., Glosten, B., Kemen, M., Robert, M.K., & Bedwell, S., (1990). *Is the Antiemetic Effect of the Emulsion Formulation of Propofol Due to the Lipid Emulsion? Anesth Analg.* Nov; 71(5):536-40.

Phillips, S., Ruggier, R., & Hutchinson, S.E., (1993). *Zingiber officinale (ginger)--An Antiemetic for Day Case Surgery. Anaesthesia.* Aug; 48(8):715-7.

Portnoi, G., Chng, L.A., Karimi-Tabesh, L., Koren, G., Tan, M.P., & Einarson, A., (2003). *Prospective Comparative Study of the Safety and Effectiveness of Ginger for the Treatment of Nausea and Vomiting in Pregnancy. Am J Obstet Gynecol.* Nov: 189(5):1374-7.

Qian, D.S., Liu, Z.S., (1992). *Pharmacologic Studies of Antimotion Sickness Actions of Ginger. Zhongguo Zhong Xi Yi Jie He Za Zhi.* Feb; 12(2):95-8, 70.

Savic, I., & Berglund, H., (2000). *Right-Nostril Dominance in Discrimination of Unfamiliar, But Not Familiar, Odours. Chem Senses.* Oct; 25(5):517-23.

Scuderi, P.E., & James, R.L., (2000). *Harris L et al. Multimodality Antiemetic Management Prevents Early Postoperative Vomiting after Outpatient Laparoscopy. Anesthesia Analgesia;* 91:1408-14.

Smith, C., Crowther, C., Willson, K., Hotham, N., & McMillian, V., (2004). *A Randomized Controlled Trial of Ginger to Treat Nausea and Vomiting in Pregnancy. Obstet Gynecol.* Apr; 103(4):639-45.

Spickard, A., & Hirschmann, J.V., (1994). *Exogenous Lipoid Pneumonia. Med.* Mar 28; 154(6):686-92.

Sripramote, M., & Lekhyananda, N.A., (2003). *Randomized Comparison of Ginger and Vitamin B6 in the Treatment of Nausea and Vomiting of Pregnancy. Med Assoc Thai.* Sep; 86(9):846-53.

Stevenson, R.J., & Boakes, R.A., (2003). *A Mnemonic Theory of Odor Perception. Psychol Rev.* Apr; 110(2):340-64.

Surh, Y., Park ,K., Chun, K., Lee, L., Lee, E., & Lee, S., (1999). *Anti-Tumor Promoting Activities of Selected Pungent Phenolic Substances Present in Ginger. J Environ Pathol Toxicol Oncol.;* 18(2):131-9.

Tate, S., (1997). *Peppermint Oil: A Treatment for Postoperative Nausea. Journal of Advanced Nursing* Sep; 26(3):543-9.

Turin, L., (1996). *A Spectroscopic Mechanism for Primary Olfactory Reception. Chem Senses.* Dec; 21(6):773-91.

Ueda, I., (2001). *Molecular Mechanisms of Anesthesia. Keio J Med.* Mar; 50(1):20-5.

Visalyaputra., S., Petchpaisit, N., Somcharoen, K., & Choavaratana, R., (1998). *The Efficacy of Ginger Root in the Prevention of Postoperative Nausea and Vomiting After Outpatient Gynaecological Laparoscopy. Anaesthesia.* May; 53(5):506-10.

Vishwakarma, S.L., Pal, S.C., Kasture, V.S., & Kasture, S.B., (2002). *Anxiolytic and Antiemetic Activity of Zingiber Officinale. Phytother Res.* Nov; 16(7):621-6.

Wang, J., Luthey-Schulten, Z.A., & Suslick, K.S., (2003). *Is the Olfactory Receptor a Metalloprotein? Proc Natl Acad Sci USA.* Mar 18; 100(6):3035-9.

Wang, S.M., & Kain, Z.N., (2002). *P6 Accupoint Injections Are as Effective as Droperidol in Controlling Early Postoperative Nausea and Vomiting in Children. Anesthesiology;* 97:359-66.

Yamakura, T., Bertaccini, E., Trudell, J.R., & Harris, R.A., (2001). *Anesthetics and ion Channels: Molecular Models and Sites of Action. Annu Rev Pharmacol Toxicol.;* 41:23-51.

Yurtseven, N., Karaca, P., Kaplan, M., Ozkul, V., Tuygun, A.K., Aksoy, T., Canik, S., & Kopman, E., (2003). *Effect of Nitroglycerin Inhalation on Patients with Pulmonary Hypertension Undergoing Mitral Valve Replacement Surgery. Anesthesiology.* Oct; 99(4):855-8.

Chapter 8: Ideal Business

http://www.2nerve2verve.com

http://dietshakedr.com

http://www.geigervideo.com

http://www.idealscentsllc.com

http://idealscents.newvision.net/

http://www.myvemma.com/juicermd

http://www.myverve.com/juicermd

http://www.oilmdwellnessnetwork.com

http://www.oilmd.com/

http://www.pr.com/company-profile/overview/4915

http://www.thesweetsmellofsuccessbook.com

http://www.yourentitysolution.com

http://www.youtube.com/user/myoilmd

Chapter 9: Ideal Products

Abebe, W., (2002).*Herbal Medication: Potential for Adverse Interactions with Analgesic Drugs. J Clin Pharm Ther. Dec; 27(6):391-401.*

Aggarwal A, Ades PA. *Interactions of Herbal Remedies with Prescription Cardiovascular Medications. Coron Artery Dis. 2001 Nov; 12(7):581-4.*

Akihisa, T., Hayakawa, Y., Tokuda, H., Banno, N., Shimizu, N., Suzuki, T., & Kimura, Y., (2007).*Cucurbitane glycosides from the fruits of Siraitia gros venorii and their inhibitory effects on Epstein-Barr virus activation. J Nat Prod. 2007 May; 70(5):783-8.*

Akihisa, T., Higo, N., Tokuda, H., Ukiya, M., Akazawa, H., Tochigi, Y., Kimura, Y., Suzuki, T., & Nishino, H., (2007). *Cucurbitane-type triterpenoids from the fruits of Momordica charantia and their cancer chemopreventive effects. J Nat Prod. 2007 Aug; 70(8):1233-9.*

Arayne MS, Sultana N, & Bibi Z. (2005). *Grape fruit juice-drug interactions. Pak J Pharm Sci. Oct;18(4):45-57.*

Arras, G., & Usai, M., (2001). *Fungitoxic activity of 12 essential oils against four postharvest citrus pathogens: chemical analysis of thymus capitatus oil and its effect in subatmospheric pressure conditions. J Food Prot. Jul; 64(7):1025-9.*

Aviram, M.,& Dornfeld, L., (2001). *Pomegranate juice consumption inhibits serum angiotensin converting enzyme activity and reduces systolic blood pressure. Atherosclerosis. Sep; 158(1):195-8.*

Aviram, M., Rosenblat, M., Gaitini, D., Nitecki, S., Hoffman, A., Dornfeld, L., Volkova, N., Presser, D., Attias, J, Liker, H., & Hayek, T., (2004). *Pomegranate juice consumption for 3 years by patients with carotid artery stenosis reduces common carotid intima-media thickness, blood pressure and LDL oxidation. Clin Nutr. Jun; 23(3):423-33.*

Chairungsrilerd, N., Furukawa, K., Ohta, T., Nozoe, S., & Ohizumi, Y., (1996). *Histaminergic and Serotonergic Receptor Blocking Substances from the Medicinal Plant Garcinia Mangostana. Planta Med. Oct; 62(5):471-2.*

Chanarat, P., Chanarat, N., Fujihara, M., & Nagumo, T., (1997). Immunopharmacological Activity of Polysaccharide from the Pericarb of Mangosteen Garcinia: Phagocytic Intracellular Killing Activities. J Med Assoc Thai. Sep; 80 Suppl 1:S149-54.

Chomnawang, M.T., Surassmo, S., Nukoolkarn, V.S., & Gritsanapan, W., (2007). Effect of Garcinia Mangostana on Inflammation Caused by Propionibacterium Acnes. Fitoterapia. Sep; 78(6):401-8.

Dansinger, M.L., Gleason, J.A., Griffith, J.L., Selker, H.P., & Schaefer, EJ., (2005). Comparison of the Atkins, Ornish, Weight Watchers, and Zone diets for weight loss and heart disease risk reduction: a randomized trial. JAMA. Jan 5; 293(1):43-53.

Dahan, A., & Altman, H., (2004).Food-drug interaction: grapefruit juice augments drug bioavailability--mechanism, extent and relevance. Eur J Clin Nutr. Jan; 58(1):1-9.

Esmaillzadeh, A., Tahbaz, F., Gaieni, I., Alavi-Majd, H., Azadbakht, L., (2006). Cholesterol-lowering effect of concentrated pomegranate juice consumption in type II diabetic patients with hyperlipidemia. Int J Vitam Nutr Res. May; 76(3):147-51.

Farkas, D., Oleson, L.E., Zhao, Y., Harmatz, J.S., Zinny, M.A., Court, M.H., & Greenblatt, D.J., (2007). Pomegranate juice does not impair clearance of oral or intravenous midazolam, a probe for cytochrome P450-3A activity: comparison with grapefruit juice. J Clin Pharmacol. Mar; 47(3):286-94.

Ferrer, P., Ortega, A., Benlloch, M., Obrador, E., Varea, M.T., Asensio, G., Jordá, L., & Estrela, J.M., (2005). Association between pterostilbene and quercetin inhibits metastatic activity of B16 melanoma. Neoplasia. Jan; 7(1):37-47.

Gansler, T., Kaw, C., Crammer, C., & Smith, T., (2008). A population-based study of prevalence of complementary methods use by cancer survivors: a report from the American Cancer Society's studies of cancer survivors. Cancer. Aug 4.

Gardner, C.D., Kiazand, A., Alhassan, S., Kim, S., Stafford, R.S., Balise, R.R., Kraemer, H.C., & King, A.C., (2007). Comparison of the Atkins, Zone, Ornish, and LEARN diets for change in weight and related risk factors among overweight premenopausal women: the A TO Z Weight Loss Study: a randomized trial. JAMA. Mar 7; 297(9):969-77.

Goho, C., (2001). Oral midazolam-grapefruit juice drug interaction. Pediatr Dent. Jul-Aug; 23(4):365-6.

Ho, C.K., Huang, Y.L., Chen, C.C., & Garcinone, E., (2002). A Xanthone Derivative, has Potent Cytotoxic Effect Against Hepatocellular Carcinoma Cell Lines. Planta Med. Nov; 68(11):975-9.

Hollenberg, K., & Norman, M., (2006).Vascular Action of Cocoa Flavanols in Humans: The Roots of the Story. Journal of Cardiovascular Pharmacology. 47 Supplement 2:S99-S102, June.

Hope, Smith, S., Tate, P.L., Huang, G., Magee, J.B., Meepagala, K.M., Wedge, D.E., & Larcom, L.L., (2004). Antimutagenic activity of berry extracts. J Med Food. 2004 Winter; 7(4):450-5.

Iqbal, A., Farrukh, A., & Mohammad, O., (2007). Modern Phytomedicine: Turning Medicinal Plants into Drugs.

Jung, H.A., Su, B.N., Keller, W.J., Mehta, R.G., & Kinghorn, A.D. (2006). Antioxidant Xanthones from the Pericarp of Garcinia Mangostana (Mangosteen). J Agric Food Chem. Mar 22; 54(6):2077-82.

Kaji, I., (2001). Et al. Inhibition by d-limonene of experimental hepatocarcinogenesis in Sprague-Dawley rats does not involve p21 (ras) plasma membrane association. Int J Cancer; 93:441-4.

Krenn, L., Steitz, M., Schlicht, C., Kurth, H., & Gaedcke, F., (2007). Anthocyanin- and proanthocyanidin-rich extracts of berries in food supplements--analysis with problems. Pharmazie. Nov; 62(11):803-12.

Lynch, J.R., Gardner, G.C., & Parsons, R.R., (2005). Musculoskeletal workload versus musculoskeletal clinical confidence among primary care physicians in rural practice. Am J Orthop. Oct; 34(10):487-91, discussion 491-2.

Lynch, J.R., Schmale, G.A., Schaad, D.C., & Leopold, S.S., (2006). Important demographic variables impact the musculoskeletal knowledge and confidence of academic primary care physicians. J Bone Joint Surg Am. Jul; 88(7):1589-95.

Matsumoto, K., Akao, Y., Kobayashi, E., Ohguchi, K., Ito, T., Tanaka, T., Iinuma, M., & Nozawa, Y., (2003). Induction of Apoptosis by Xanthones from Mangosteen in Human Leukemia Cell Lines. J Nat Prod. Aug; 66(8):1124-7.

Mahabusarakam, W., Proudfoot, J., Taylor, W., & Croft, K., (2000). Inhibition of lipoprotein oxidation by prenylated xanthones derived from mangostin. Free Radic Res. Nov; 33(5):643-59.

McCullough, M., Chevaux, K., Jackson, L., Preston, M., Martinez, G., Schmitz, H., Coletti, C., Campos, H., & Hollenberg, N., (2006). Hypertension, the Kuna, and the Epidemiology of Flavanols. Journal of Cardiovascular Pharmacology. 47 Supplement 2:S103-S109, June.

Menezes, S.M., Cordeiro, L.N., & Viana, G.S., (2006). Punica granatum (pomegranate) extract is active against dental plaque. J Herb Pharmacother.; 6(2):79-92.

Merheb, M., Daher, R.T., Nasrallah, M., Sabra, R., Ziyadeh, F.N., & Barada, K., (2007). Taurine Intestinal Absorption and Renal Excretion Test in Diabetic Patients. Diabetes Care. Oct; 30 (10): 2652-4.

Moongkarndi, P., Kosem, N., Kaslungka, S., Luanratana, O., Pongpan, N., & Neungton, N., (2004). Antiproliferation, Antioxidation and Induction of Apoptosis by Garcinia Mangostana (mangosteen) on SKBR3 Human Breast Cancer Cell Line. J Ethnopharmacol. Jan; 90(1):161-6.

Moongkarndi, P., Kosem, N., Luanratana, O., Jongsomboonkusol, S.,& Pongpan, N., (2004). *Antiproliferative Activity of Thai Medicinal Plant Extracts on Human Breast Adenocarcinoma Cell Line. Fitoterapia. Jun; 75(3-4):375-7.*

Nabandith, V., Suzui, M., Morioka, T., Kaneshiro, T., Kinjo, T., Matsumoto, K., Akao, Y., Iinuma, M., Yoshimi, N., (2004). *Inhibitory Effects of Crude Alpha-Mangostin, a Xanthone Derivative, on Two Different Categories of Colon Preneoplastic Lesions Induced by 1, 2-dimethylhydrazine in the Rat. Asian Pac J Cancer Prev. Oct-Dec; 5(4):433-8.*

Nakagawa, Y., Iinuma, M., Naoe, T., Nozawa, Y., & Akao, Y., (2007). *Characterized Mechanism of Alpha-Mangostin-Induced Cell Death:Caspase-Independent Apoptosis with Release of Endonuclease-G from Mitochondria and Increased miR-143 Expression in Human Colorectal Cancer DLD-1 cells. Bioorg Med Chem. Aug 15; 15(16):5620-8.*

Nakatani, K., Atsumi, M., Arakawa, T., Oosawa, K., Shimura, S., Nakahata, N., & Ohizumi, Y., (2002). *Inhibitions of Histamine Release and Prostaglandin E2 Synthesis by Mangosteen, a Thai Medicinal Plant. Biol Pharm Bull. Sep; 25(9):1137-41.*

Nakatani, K., Nakahata, N., Arakawa, T., Yasuda, H., & Ohizumi, Y., (2002). *Inhibition of Cyclooxygenase and Prostaglandin E2 Synthesis by Gamma-Mangostin, a Xanthone Derivative in Mangosteen, in C6 rat glioma cells. Biochem Pharmacol. Jan 1; 63(1):73-9.*

Nakatani, K., Yamakuni, T., Kondo, N., Arakawa, T., Oosawa, K., Shimura, S., & Inoue, H., Ohizumi, Y., (2004). *gamma-Mangostin inhibits inhibitor-kappaB kinase activity and decreases lipopolysaccharide-induced cyclooxygenase-2 gene expression in C6 rat glioma cells. Mol Pharmacol. Sep; 66(3):667-74.*

Nguyen, L.H., Venkatraman, G., Sim, K.Y., Harrison, L.J., (2005). *Xanthones and Benzophenones from Garcinia Griffithii and Garcinia Mangostana. Phytochemistry. Jul; 66(14):1718-23.*

Nittynen, L., Nurminen, M.L., Korpela, R., Vapaatalo, H., (1999). *Role of arginine, taurine and homocysteine in cardiovascular diseases. Ann Med. Oct; 31(5):318-26.*

Oteri, A., Salvo, F., Caputi, A.P., & Calapai, G., (2007). *Intake of Energy Drinks in Association With Alcoholic Beverages in a Cohort of Students of the School of Medicine of the University of Messina. Alcohol Clin Exp Res. Jul 25.*

Pan, M.H., Chang, Y.H., Badmaev, V., Nagabhushanam, K., & Ho, C.T., (2007). *Pterostilbene induces apoptosis and cell cycle arrest in human gastric carcinoma cells. J Agric Food Chem. Sep 19; 55(19):7777-85.*

Rassameemasmaung, S., Sirikulsathean, A., Amornchat, C., Hirunrat, K., Rojanapanthu, P., Gritsanapan, W., (2007). *Effects of Herbal Mouthwash Containing the Pericarp Extract of Garcinia Mangostana L on Halitosis, Plaque and Papillary Bleeding Index. J Int Acad Periodontol. Jan; 9(1):19-25.*

Reddy, B.S., (1997).et al. *Chemoprevention of colon carcinogenesis by dietary perillyl alcohol. Cancer Res; 57:420-5.*

Remsberg, C.M., Yáñez, J.A., Ohgami, Y., Vega-Villa, K.R., Rimando, A.M., & Davies, N.M., (2008). *Pharmacometrics of pterostilbene: preclinical pharmacokinetics and metabolism, anticancer, anti-inflammatory, antioxidant and analgesic activity. Phytother Res. Feb; 22(2):169-79.*

Rimando, A.M., Kalt, W., Magee, J.B., Dewey, J., Ballington, J.R., (2004). *Resveratrol, pterostilbene, and piceatannol in vaccinium berries. J Agric Food Chem. Jul 28; 52(15):4713-9.*

Rimando, A.M., Nagmani, R., Feller, D.R., & Yokoyama, W., (2005). *Pterostilbene, a new agonist for the peroxisome proliferator-activated receptor alpha-isoform, lowers plasma lipoproteins and cholesterol in hypercholesterolemic hamsters. J Agric Food Chem. May 4; 53(9):3403-7.*

Rodrigues, R.B., Lichtenthäler, R., Zimmermann, B.F., Papagiannopoulos, M., Fabricius, H., Marx, F., Maia, J.G., & Almeida, O., (2006). *Total oxidant scavenging capacity of Euterpe oleracea Mart. (açaí) seeds and identification of their polyphenolic compounds. J Agric Food Chem. Jun 14; 54(12):4162-7.*

Sakagami, Y., Iinuma, M., Piyasena, K.G., & Dharmaratne, H.R., (2005). *Antibacterial Activity of Alpha-Mangostin Against Vancomycin Resistant Enterococci (VRE) and Synergism with Antibiotics. Phytomedicine. Mar; 12(3):203-8.*

Sartor, L., Pezzato, E., Donà, M., Dell'Aica, I., Calabrese, F., Morini, M., Albini, A., & Garbisa, S., (2004). *Prostate carcinoma and green tea: (-) epigallocatechin-3-gallate inhibits inflammation-triggered MMP-2 activation and invasion in murine TRAMP model. Int J Cancer. Dec 10; 112(5):823-9.*

Seeram, N.P., (2008). *Berry fruits: compositional elements, biochemical activities, and the impact of their intake on human health, performance, and disease. J Agric Food Chem. Feb 13; 56(3):627-9.*

Seeram, N.P., Henning, S.M., Zhang, Y., Suchard, M., Li, Z., & Heber, D., (2006). *Pomegranate juice ellagitannin metabolites are present in human plasma and some persist in urine for up to 48 hours. J Nutr. Oct;136(10):2481-5.*

Suh, N., Paul, S., Hao, X., Simi, B., Xiao, H., Rimando, A.M., & Reddy, B.S., (2007). *Pterostilbene, an active constituent of blueberries, suppresses aberrant crypt foci formation in the azoxymethane-induced colon carcinogenesis model in rats. Clin Cancer Res. Jan 1; 13(1):350-5.*

Suksamrarn, S., Suwannapoch, N., Phakhodee, W., Thanuhiranlert, J., Ratananukul, P., & Chimnoi, N., (2003). Suksamrarn A. *Antimycobacterial Activity of Prenylated Xanthones from the Fruits of Garcinia Mangostana. Chem Pharm Bull (Tokyo). Jul; 51(7):857-9.*

Sumner, M.D., Elliott-Eller, M., Weidner, G., Daubenmier, J.J., Chew, M.H., Marlin, R., Raisin, C.J., & Ornish, D., (2005). Effects of pomegranate juice consumption on myocardial perfusion in patients with coronary heart disease. Am J Cardiol. Sep 15; 96(6):810-4.

Sundaram, B.M., Gopalakrishnan, C., Subramanian, S., Shankaranarayanan, D., & Kameswaran, L., (1983). Antimicrobial Activities of Garcinia Mangostana. Planta Med. May; 48(5):59-60.

Stewart, J.R., Artime, M.C., & O'Brian, C.A., (2003). Resveratrol: a candidate nutritional substance for prostate cancer prevention. J Nutr. 2003 Jul; 133(7 Suppl):2440S-2443S.

Tolomeo, M., Grimaudo, S., Di Cristina, A., Roberti, M., Pizzirani, D., Meli, M., Dusonchet, L., Gebbia, N., Abbadessa, V., Crosta, L., Barucchello, R., Grisolia, G., Invidiata, F., & Simoni, D., (2005). Pterostilbene and 3'-hydroxypterostilbene are effective apoptosis-inducing agents in MDR and BCR-ABL-expressing leukemia cells. Int J Biochem Cell Biol. Aug; 37(8):1709-26.

Voravuthikunchai, S.P., Kitpipit, L., (2005). Activity of Medicinal Plant Extracts Against Hospital Isolates of Methicillin-Resistant Staphylococcus Aureus. Clin Microbiol Infect. Jun; 11(6):510-2.

Weecharangsan, W., Opanasopit, P., Sukma, M., Ngawhirunpat, T., Sotanaphun, U., & Siripong, P., (2006). Antioxidative and Neuroprotective Activities of Extracts from the Fruit Hull of Mangosteen (Garcinia mangostana Linn.). Med Princ Pract.; 15(4):281-7.

Williams, C.M., El Mohsen, M.A., Vauzour, D., Rendeiro, C., Butler, L.T., Ellis, J.A., Whiteman, M., & Spencer, J.P., (2008). Blueberry-induced changes in spatial working memory correlate with changes in hippocampal CREB phosphorylation and brain-derived neurotrophic factor (BDNF) levels. Free Radic Biol Med. Aug 1; 45(3):295-305.

Williams, P., Ongsakul, M., Proudfoot, J., Croft, K., & Beilin, L., (1995). Mangostin inhibits the oxidative modification of human low density lipoprotein. Free Radic Res.Aug;23(2):175-84.

Yamakuni, T., Aoki, K., Nakatani, K., Kondo, N., Oku, H., Ishiguro, K., & Ohizumi, Y., (2005). Garcinone B reduces prostaglandin E2 release and NF-kappaB-mediated transcription in C6 rat glioma cells. Neurosci Lett. Feb 20; 394(3):206-10.

Yeh, A.C., Franko, O., & Day, C.S., (2008). Impact of clinical electives and residency interest on medical students' education in musculoskeletal medicine. J Bone Joint Surg Am. Feb; 90(2):307-15.

Zafra-Stone, S., Yasmin, T., Bagchi, M., Chatterjee, A., Vinson, J.A., Bagchi, D., (2007). Berry anthocyanins as novel antioxidants in human health and disease prevention. Mol Nutr Food Res. Jun; 51(6):675-83.

Zhou, S., Lim, L.Y., & Chowbay, B., (2004). Herbal modulation of P-glycoprotein. Drug Metab Rev. 2004 Feb; 36(1):57-104.

Art of aromatherapy featuring Well-Balanced Lady for hormonal symptoms:

Dayawansa, S., Umeno, K., Takakura, H., Hori, E., Tabuchi, E., Nagashima, Y., Oosu, H., Yada, Y., Suzuki, T., Ono, T., & Nishijo, H., (2003).Autonomic responses during inhalation of natural fragrance of Cedrol in humans. Auton Neurosci. Oct 31; 108(1-2):79-8.

Faure, E.D., Chantre, P., Mares, P., (2002). Effects of a standardized soy extract on hot flushes: a multicenter, double-blind, randomized, placebo-controlled study. Menopause. Sep-Oct; 9(5):329-34.

Murakami, S., Shirota, T., Hayashi, S., & Ishizuka, B., (2005). Aromatherapy for outpatients with menopausal symptoms in obstetrics and gynecology. J Altern Complement Med. Jun; 11(3):491-4.

Petrini, O., (2002). Clinical development of phytopharmaceuticals. Wien Med Wochenschr.;152(7-8):204-8.

Philp, H.A., (2003). Hot flashes--a review of the literature on alternative and complementary treatment approaches. Altern Med Rev. Aug; 8(3):284-302.

Schiffman, S.S,,Sattely-Miller, E.A., Suggs, M.S., & Graham, B.G., (1995). The effect of pleasant odors and hormone status on mood of women at midlife. Brain Res Bull.; 36(1):19-29.

Tice, J.A., Ettinger, B., Ensrud, K., Wallace, R., Blackwell, T., Cummings, S.R., (2003). Phytoestrogen supplements for the treatment of hot flashes: the Isoflavone Clover Extract (ICE) Study: a randomized controlled trial. JAMA. Jul 9; 290(2):207-14.

http://nccam.nih.gov/health/hotflashes/hotflash_summ.htm

http://nccam.nih.gov/health/hotflashes/pdf/hotflashessumm.pdf#self

Esthetic aromatherapy featuring Thigh Smoother for nice thighs:

Balchin, M., Parallel placebo controlled clinical study of a mixture of herbs sold as a remedy for cellulite.Lis- Phytother Res.199 Nov; 13(7):627-9.

Birnbaum, L., (2001). Addition of conjugated linoleic acid to a herbal anticellulite pill. Adv Ther. Sep-Oct; 18(5):225-9.

Habashy, R.R., Abdel- Naim, A.B., Khalifa, A.E., Al-Azizi, M.M., (2005). Anti-inflammatory effects of jojoba liquid wax in experimental models. Pharmacol Res. Feb; 51(2):95-105.

Hexsel D, Orlandi C, Zechmeister do Prado D. Botanical extracts used in the treatment of cellulite. Dermatol Surg. 2005 Jul; 31(7 Pt 2):866-72.

Rosenbaum, M., Prieto, V., Hellmer, J., Boschmann, M., Krueger, J., Leibel, R.L., & Ship, A.G., (1998). An exploratory investigation of the morphology and biochemistry of cellulite. Plast Reconstr Surg. Jun; 101(7):1934-9.

Sainio, E.L., Rantanen, T., & Kanerva, L., (2000). Ingredients and safety of cellulite creams. Eur J Dermatol. Dec; 10(8):596-603.

Sekiya, K., Ohtani, A., & Kusano, S., (2004). Enhancement of insulin sensitivity in adipocytes by ginger. Biofactors.; 22(1-4):153.

Holistic aromatherapy featuring Appetite Tamer for weight management:

Gidley, M.J., (2004). Naturally functional foods - challenges and opportunities. Asia Pac J Clin Nutr. Aug; 13(Suppl):S31.

Henry, C.J., & Emery, B., (1986). Effect of spiced food on metabolic rate. Hum Nutr Clin Nutr. Mar; 40(2):165-8.

Kris-Etherton, P.M., Hecker, K.D., Bonanome, A., Coval, S.M., Binkoski, A.E., Hilpert, K.F., Griel, A.E., & Etherton, T.D., (2002). Bioactive compounds in foods: their role in the prevention of cardiovascular disease and cancer. Am J Med. Dec 30; 113 Suppl 9B:71S-88S.

Niijima, A., & Nagai, K., (2003) .Effect of olfactory stimulation with flavor of grapefruit oil and lemon oil on the activity of sympathetic branch in the white adipose tissue of the epididymis. Exp Biol Med (Maywood). Nov; 228(10):1190-2.

Marques-Lopes, I., Forga, L., & Martinez, J.A., (2003). Thermogenesis induced by a high-carbohydrate meal in fasted lean and overweight young men: insulin, body fat, and sympathetic nervous system involvement. Nutrition. Jan; 19(1):25-9.

Matsumoto, T., Miyawaki, C., Ue, H., Yuasa, T., Miyatsuji, A., & Moritani, T., (2000). Effects of capsaicin-containing yellow curry sauce on sympathetic nervous system activity and diet-induced thermogenesis in lean and obese young women. J Nutr Sci Vitaminol (Tokyo). Dec; 46(6):309-15.

Naderi, G.A., Asgary, S., Ani, M., Sarraf-Zadegan, N, & Safari, M.R., (2004). Effect of some volatile oils on the affinity of intact and oxidized low-density lipoproteins for adrenal cell surface receptors. Mol Cell Biochem. Dec; 267(1-2):59-66.

Nasel, C., Nasel, B., Samec, P, Schindler, E., & Buchbauer, G., (1994). Functional imaging of effects of fragrances on the human brain after prolonged inhalation. Chem Senses. Aug; 19(4):359-64.

Sekiya, K,,Ohtani, A., & Kusano, S., (2004). Enhancement of insulin sensitivity in adipocytes by ginger. Biofactors.; 22(1-4):153-6.

Shannon, M., (1993). An empathetic look at overweight. Family Found. Nov-Dec; 20(3):3, 5.

Shen, J., Niijima, A., Tanida, M., Horii, Y., Maeda, K., & Nagai, K., (2005). Olfactory stimulation with scent of grapefruit oil affects autonomic nerves, lipolysis and appetite in rats. Neurosci Lett. Jun 3;380(3):289-94.

Teissedre, P.L., & Waterhouse, A.L., (2000). Inhibition of oxidation of human low-density lipoproteins by phenolic substances in different essential oils varieties. J Agric Food Chem. Sep; 48(9):3801-5.

Verma, S.K., & Bordia, A., (2001). Ginger, fat and fibrinolysis. Indian J Med Sci. Feb; 55(2):83-6.

Eden's aromatherapy featuring Romantic Encounters for erotic pleasures:

Cutler, W.B., & Genovese, E., (2002). Pheromones, Sexual Attractiveness and Quality of Life in Menopausal Women. Climacteric. Jun; 5(2):112-21.

Cutler, W.B., & Genovese-Stone, E., (1998), Wellness in Women After 40 Years of Age: The Role of Sex Hormones and Pheromones. Dis Mon. Sep; 44(9):421-546.

Giraldi, A.G., & Victor, J., (2002). Ugeskr Laeger. Female Sexual Dysfunction as Adverse Effect of Pharmacological Treatment. Oct 7; 164(41):4757-60.

Hongratanaworakit, T., Heuberger, E., & Buchbauer, G., (2004). Evaluation of the Effects of East Indian Sandalwood Oil and Alpha-Santalol on Humans After Transdermal Absorption. Planta Med. Jan; 70(1):3-7.

Levine, S.B., (2002). Reexploring the Concept of Sexual Desire. J Sex Marital Ther. Jan-Feb; 28(1):39-51.

Marthol, H., & Hilz, M.J., (2004). Female Sexual Dysfunction: A Systematic Overview of Classification, Pathophysiology, Diagnosis and Treatment Fortschr Neurol Psychiatr. Mar; 72(3):121-35.

Masago, R., Matsuda, T., Kikuchi, Y., Miyazaki, Y., Iwanaga, K., Harada, H., & Katsuura, T., (2000). Effects of Inhalation of Essential Oils on EEG Activity and Sensory Evaluation. J Physiol Anthropol Appl Human Sci. Jan; 19(1):35-42.

Sandroni, P., (2001). Aphrodisiacs Past and Present: A Historical Review. Clin Auton Res. Oct; 11(5):303-7.

Smith, P.J., & Talbert, R.L., (1986). Sexual Dysfunction with Antihypertensive and Antipsychotic Agents. Clin Pharm. May; 5(5):373-84.

Wilson, B., (1991). The Effect of Drugs on Male Sexual Function and Fertility. Nurse Pract. Sep; 16(9):12-7, 21-4.

Integrative aromatherapy featuring Bone Balancer for the skeletal system:

Barnes, S., (2003).Phyto-oestrogens and osteoporosis: what is a safe dose? Br J Nutr. Jun;89 Suppl 1:S101-8.

Cassidy, A., (2003). Potential risks and benefits of phytoestrogen-rich diets. Int J Vitam Nutr Res. Mar; 73(2):120-6.

Davis, S.R., O'Neill, S.M., Eden, J., Baber, R., Ekangaki, A., Stocks, J.M., & Thiebaud, D., (2004). Transition from estrogen therapy to raloxifene in postmenopausal women: effects on treatment satisfaction and the endometrium-a pilot study. Menopause. Mar-Apr; 11(2):167-75.

Eden, JA. (2001). Managing the menopause: phyto-oestrogens or hormone replacement therapy? Ann Med. Feb; 33(1):4-6.

Gallagher, J.C., (1999).Moderation of the daily dose of HRT: prevention of osteoporosis. Maturitas. Nov; 33 Suppl 1:S57-63.

Howes, M.J., Houghton, P.J., Barlow, D.J., Pocock, V.J., & Milligan, S.R., (2002). Assessment of estrogenic activity in some common essential oil constituents. J Pharm Pharmacol. Nov; 54(11):1521-8.

Kardinaal, A.F., Morton, M.S., Bruggemann-Rotgans, I.E., & van Beresteijn, E.C., (1998).Phyto-oestrogen excretion and rate of bone loss in postmenopausal women. Eur J Clin Nutr. Nov; 52(11):850-5.

Muhlbauer, R.C., Lozano, A., Palacio, S., Reinli, A., & Felix, R., (2003).Common herbs, essential oils, and monoterpenes potently modulate bone metabolism. Bone. Apr;32(4):372-80.

Santoyo, S., Cavero, S., Jaime, L., Ibanez, E., Senorans, F.J., & Reglero, G., (2005). Chemical composition and antimicrobial activity of Rosmarinus officinalis L. essential oil obtained via supercritical fluid extraction. J Food Prot. Apr; 68(4):790-5.

Singh, B., Bhat, T.K., & Singh, B., (2003). Potential therapeutic applications of some antinutritional plant secondary metabolites. J Agric Food Chem. Sep 10; 51(19):5579-97.

Tabanca, N., Khan, S.I., Bedir, E., Annavarapu, S., Willett, K., Khan, I.A, Kirimer N., Husnu, Can Baser K., (2004). Estrogenic activity of isolated compounds and essential oils of Pimpinella species from Turkey, evaluated using a recombinant yeast screen. Planta Med. Aug; 70(8):728-35.

Waddell, W.J., (2002). Thresholds of carcinogenicity of flavors. Toxicol Sci. Aug; 68(2):275-9.

Zhang, D., & Zhang, R.J., (2005). Ozonolysis of alpha-pinene and beta-pinene: Kinetics and mechanism. Chem Phys. Mar; 122(11):114308.

Optimal aromatherapy featuring Sports Performance Enhancer for the exercise mandate:

Bailey, D.M., Davies, B., (2001). *Acute mountain sickness; prophylactic benefits of antioxidant vitamin supplementation at high altitude. High Alt Med Biol. Spring; 2(1):21-9.*

Clarkson, P.M., & Thompson, H.S., (1997). *Drugs and sport. Research findings and limitations. Sports Med. Dec; 24(6):366-84.*

Cronin, J., & Sleivert, G., (2005). *Challenges in understanding the influence of maximal power training on improving athletic performance. Sports Med.; 35(3):213-34.*

Faria, E.W., Parker, D.L., & Faria, I.E., (2005). *The science of cycling: physiology and training - part 1. Sports Med.; 35(4):285-312.*

Faria, E.W., Parker, D.L., & Faria, I.E., (2005). *The science of cycling: factors affecting performance - part 2. Sports Med.; 35(4):313-37.*

Grissom, C.K., Richer, L.D., Elstad, M, R., (2005). *The effects of a 5-lipoxygenase inhibitor on acute mountain sickness and urinary leukotriene e4 after ascent to high altitude. Chest. Feb; 127(2):565-70.*

Haze, S., Sakai, K., & Gozu, Y., (2002). *Effects of fragrance inhalation on sympathetic activity in normal adults.Jpn J Pharmacol. Nov; 90(3):247-53.*

Hongratanaworakit, T., & Buchbauer, G.,(2004). *Evaluation of the harmonizing effect of ylang-ylang oil on humans after inhalation. Planta Med. Jul; 70(7):632-6.*

Juhn, M., (2003). *Popular sports supplements and ergogenic aids. Sports Med.; 33(12):921-39.*

Komarow, H.D., (2005). *Postolache TT. Seasonal Allergy and Seasonal Decrements in Athletic Performance. Clin Sports Med. Apr; 24(2):e35-e50.*

Kuipers, H., & Hartgens, F., (1997). *The use of drugs to improve athletic performance. Ned Tijdschr Geneeskd. Oct 11; 141(41):1965-8.*

Lim, K., Yoshioka, M., Kikuzato, S., Kiyonaga, A., Tanaka, H., Shindo, M., & Suzuki, M., (1997). *Dietary red pepper ingestion increases carbohydrate oxidation at rest and during exercise in runners. Med Sci Sports Exerc. Mar; 29(3):355-61.*

Madigan, R., Frey, R.D., & Matlock, T.S., (1992). *Cognitive strategies of university athletes. Can J Sport Sci. Jun; 17(2):135-40.*

Marsh, S.A., Coombes, J.S., (2005). *Exercise and the endothelial cell. Int J Cardiol. Mar 18; 99(2):165-9.*

Mittal, R. Gupta, R.L., (2000). *In vitro antioxidant activity of piperine. Methods Find Exp Clin Pharmacol. Jun; 22(5):271-4.*

Nair, B., (2001). Final report on the safety assessment of Mentha Piperita (Peppermint) Oil, Mentha Piperita (Peppermint) Leaf Extract, Mentha Piperita (Peppermint) Leaf, and Mentha Piperita (Peppermint) Leaf Water. Int J Toxicol.; 20 Suppl 3:61-73.

Raudenbush, B., (2001). Enhancing Athletic Performance through the Administration of Peppermint Odor. Journal of Sport & Exercise Psychology,, 23,156-160.

Satoh, T., & Sugawara, Y., (2003). Effects on humans elicited by inhaling the fragrance of essential oils: sensory test, multi-channel thermometric study and forehead surface potential wave measurement on basil and peppermint. Anal Sci. Jan; 19(1):139-46.

Subudhi, A.W., Jacobs, K.A., Hagobian, T.A., Fattor, J.A., Fulco, C.S., Muza, S.R., Rock, P.B., Hoffman. A.R., Cymerman, A., & Friedlander, A.L., (2004). Antioxidant supplementation does not attenuate oxidative stress at high altitude. Aviat Space Environ Med. Oct; 75(10):881-8.

Urso, M.L., & Clarkson, P.M., (2003). Oxidative stress, exercise, and antioxidant supplementation. Toxicology. Jul 15; 189(1-2):41-54.

Venkatraman, J.T., & Pendergast, D.R., (2002). Effect of dietary intake on immune function in athletes. Sports Med.; 32(5):323-37.

Healing aromatherapy featuring Sports Trauma Ease for minor sports injuries:

Buckle, J., (1999). Use of aromatherapy as a complementary treatment for chronic pain. Altern Ther Health Med. Sep; 5(5):42-51.

Galeotti, N., Ghelardini, C., Mannelli, L., Mazzanti, G., Baghiroli, L., & Bartolini, A., (2001). Local anaesthetic activity of (+) - and (-)-menthol. Planta Med. Mar;67(2):174-6.

Gedney, J.J., Glover, T.L., & Fillingim, R.B., (2004). Sensory and affective pain discrimination after inhalation of essential oils. Psychosom Med. Jul-Aug;66(4):599-606.

Ghelardini, C., Galeotti, N., & Mazzanti, G., (2001). Local anesthetic activity of monoterpenes and phenylpropanes of essential oils. Planta Med. Aug; 67(6):564-6.

Sala, A., Recio, M.C., Schinella, G.R., Manez, S., Giner, R.M., & Rios, J.L., (2003). A new dual inhibitor of arachidonate metabolism isolated from Helichrysum italicum. Eur J Pharmacol. Jan 24; 460(2-3):219-26.

Singh, S., (1999). Mechanism of action of anti-inflammatory effect of fixed oil of Ocimum basilicum Linn. Indian J Exp Biol. Mar; 37(3):248-52.

Yip, Y.B, & Tse, S.H., (2004). The effectiveness of relaxation acupoint stimulation and acupressure with aromatic lavender essential oil for nonspecific low back pain in Hong Kong: a randomized controlled trial. Complement Ther Med. Mar; 12(1):28-37.

Nature's aromatherapy featuring Muscle Wellness for muscles:

Ammon, H.P., Safayhi, H., Mack, T., & Sabieraj, J., (1993). Mechanism of anti-inflammatory actions of curcumine and boswellic acids. J Ethnopharmacol. Mar; 38(2-3):113-9.

Arnold, M.D., (1999). Thornbrough LM. Treatment of musculoskeletal pain with traditional Chinese herbal medicine. Phys Med Rehabil Clin N Am. Aug; 10(3):663-71.

Buckle, J., (1999). Use of Aromatherapy as a Complementary Treatment for Chronic Pain. Altern Ther Health Med. Sep; 5(5):42-51.

Darshan, S., & Doreswamy R. (2004). Patented anti-inflammatory plant drug development from traditional medicine. Phytother Res. May; 18(5):343-57.

Ernst, E. Baillieres (2000). Complementary and alternative medicine in rheumatology. Best Pract Res Clin Rheumatol. Dec; 14(4):731-49.

Fellowes, D., Barnes, K., & Wilkinson, S., (2004). Aromatherapy and massage for symptom relief in patients with cancer. Cochrane Database Syst Rev. ;(2):CD002287.

Gedney, J.J., Glover, T.L., & Fillingim, R.B., (2004). Sensory and Effective Pain Discrimination After Inhalation of Essential Oils. Psychosom Med. Jul-Aug;66(4):599-606.

Holdcraft, L.C., Assefi, N., & Buchwald, D., (2003).Complementary and alternative medicine in fibromyalgia and related syndromes.Best Pract Res Clin Rheumatol. Aug; 17(4):667-83.

Lis-Balchin, M., Hart, S., (1997) A preliminary study of the effect of essential oils on skeletal and smooth muscle in vitro. J Ethnopharmacol. Nov; 58(3):183-7.

Lynch, J.R., Schmale, G.A., Schaad, D.C., & Leopold, S.S., (2006). Important demographic variables impact the musculoskeletal knowledge and confidence of academic primary care physicians.J Bone Joint Surg Am. Jul; 88(7):1589-95.

Lynch, J.R., Gardner, G.C., & Parsons, R.R., (2005). Musculoskeletal workload versus musculoskeletal clinical confidence among primary care physicians in rural practice. Am J Orthop. Oct; 34(10):487-91, discussion 491-2.

Peana, A.T., D'Aquila, P.S., Panin F., Serra, G., Pippia, P., & Moretti, M.D., (2002). Anti-inflammatory activity of linalool and linalyl acetate constituents of essential oils. Phytomedicine. Dec; 9(8):721-6.

Weiner, DK, & Ernst E. (2004). Complementary and alternative approaches to the treatment of persistent musculoskeletal pain. Clin J Pain. Jul-Aug; 20(4):244-55.

Yeh, A.C., Franko, O., Day, C.S., (2008). Impact of clinical electives and residency interest on medical students' education in musculoskeletal medicine. J Bone Joint Surg Am. Feb; 90(2):307-15.

Yip, Y.B., & Tse, S.H., (2004). *The Effectiveness of Relaxation Acupoint Stimulation and Acupressure with Aromatic Lavender Essential Oil for Non-Specific Low Back Pain in Hong Kong: a Randomized Controlled Trial.Complement Ther Med. Mar; 12(1):28-37.*

Guided aromatherapy featuring GingerMD for nausea, arthritis, and migraines:

Altman, R.D., & Marcussen, K.C., (2001). *Effects of a ginger extract on knee pain in patients with osteoarthritis. Arthritis Rheum. Nov; 44(11):2531-8.*

Borrelli, F., Capasso, R., Aviello, G., Pittler, M.H., & Izzo, A.A., (2005). *Effectiveness and safety of ginger in the treatment of pregnancy-induced nausea and vomiting. Obstet Gynecol. Apr; 105(4):849-56.*

Chun, K.S., & Surh, Y.J., (2004). *Signal transduction pathways regulating cyclooxygenase-2 expression: potential molecular targets for chemoprevention. Biochem Pharmacol. Sep 15; 68(6):1089-100.*

Ernst, E., & Pittler, M.H., (2000). *Efficacy of ginger for nausea and vomiting: a systematic review of randomized clinical trials. Br J Anaesth. Mar; 84(3):367-71.*

Geiger, J.L., (2005). *The Essential Oil of Ginger, Zingiber officinale, and Anesthesia. The International Journal of Aromatherapy 15, 7-14.*

Grontved, A., Brask, T., Kambskard, J., & Hentzer, E., (1988). *Ginger root against seasickness. A controlled trial on the open sea. Acta Otolaryngol. Jan-Feb; 105(1-2):45-9.*

Hickok JT, Roscoe JA, Morrow GR, & Ryan JL. (2007). *A Phase II/III Randomized, Placebo-Controlled, Double-Blind Clinical Trial of Ginger (Zingiber officinale) for Nausea Caused by Chemotherapy for Cancer: A Currently Accruing URCC CCOP Cancer Control Study. Support Cancer Ther. Sep 1;4(4):247-50.*

Kris-Etherton, P.M., Hecker, K.D., Bonanome, A., Coval, S.M., Binkoski, A.E., Hilpert, K.F., Griel, A.E., & Etherton, T.D., (2002). *Bioactive compounds in foods: their role in the prevention of cardiovascular disease and cancer. Am J Med. Dec 30; 113 Suppl 9B:71S-88S.*

Meyer, K., Schwartz, J., Crater, D., & Keyes, B., (1995). *Zingiber officinale (ginger) used to prevent 8-Mop associated nausea. Dermatol Nurs. Aug; 7(4):242-4.*

Singh, B., Bhat, T.K., & Singh, B., (2003). *Potential therapeutic applications of some antinutritional plant secondary metabolites. J Agric Food Chem. Sep 10; 51(19):5579-97.*

Surh, Y.J., & Kundu, J.K., (2005). *Signal transduction network leading to COX-2 induction: a road map in search of cancer chemopreventives. Arch Pharm Res. Jan; 28(1):1-15.*

Verma, S.K., & Bordia, A.,(2001). *Ginger, fat and fibrinolysis. Indian J Med Sci. Feb; 55(2):83-6.*

Zhao, J., Davis, L.C., & Verpoorte, R., (2005). *Elicitor signal transduction leading to production of plant secondary metabolites. Biotechnol Adv. Jun; 23(4):283-333.*

Chapter 10: Prescription for Success

Ballard, C.G., O'Brien, J.T., Reichelt, K., & Perry, E.K., (2002). *Aromatherapy as a safe and effective treatment for the management of agitation in severe dementia: the results of a double-blind, placebo-controlled trial with Melissa. J Clin Psychiatry. Jul; 63(7):553-8.*

Barja, G., (2004), *Free Radicals and Aging. Trends Neurosci. Oct;27(10):595-600.*

Bastianetto, S., Quirion, R., (2002). *Natural Extracts as Possible Protective Agents of Brain Aging. Neurobiol Aging. Sep-Oct; 23(5):891-97.*

Bonnefoy, M., Drai, J., & Kostka, T., (2002). *Antioxidants to Slow Aging, Facts and Perspectives Presse Med. Jul 27; 31(25):1174-84.*

Campbell, L., Pollard, A., Roeton, C., & Aust, J., (2001). *The Development of Clinical Practice Guidelines For the Use of Aromatherapy in a Cancer Setting. Holist Nurs. Apr; 8(1):14-22.*

Cohen-Mansfield, J., Libin, A., & Marx, M.S., (2007). *Nonpharmacological treatment of agitation: a controlled trial of systematic individualized intervention. J Gerontol A Biol Sci Med Sci. Aug; 62(8):908-16.*

Gold, J.L., Laxer, D.A., Dergal, J.M., Lanctot, K.L., & Rochon, P.A., (2001). *Herbal-Drug Therapy Interactions: A Focus on Dementia.. Curr Opin Clin Nutr Metab Care. Jan; 4(1):29-34.*

Holmes, C., Hopkins, V., Hensford, C., MacLaughlin, V., & Wilkinson, D., Rosenvinge, H., (2002). *Lavender oil as a treatment for agitated behaviour in severe dementia: a placebo controlled study. Int J Geriatr Psychiatry. Apr; 17(4):305-8.*

Jensen, M., Krzywkowski, K., & Ostrowski, K., (1999) *Exercise and Immune Function: Effect of Ageing and Nutrition. Pedersen BK, Bruunsgaard H, Proc Nutr Soc. Aug; 58(3):733-42.*

Kim, J.T., Ren, C.J., Fielding, G.A., Pitti, A., Kasumi, T., Wajda, M., Lebovits, A, Bekker, A., (2007). *Treatment with lavender aromatherapy in the post-anesthesia care unit reduces opioid requirements of morbidly obese patients undergoing laparoscopic adjustable gastric banding. Obes Surg. 2007 Jul; 17(7):920-5.*

Kraus, C.A., Seignourel, P., Balasubramanyam, V., Snow, A.L., Wilson, N.L., Kunik, M.E., Schulz, P.E., & Stanley, M.A., (2008). *Cognitive-behavioral treatment for anxiety in patients with dementia: two case studies. J Psychiatr Pract. May; 14(3):186-92.*

Langreth, R., (2007). *Patient Fix Thyself, Forbes April 9 pg 82-86.*

Lee, S.Y., (2005). *The effect of lavender aromatherapy on cognitive function, emotion, and aggressive behavior of elderly with dementia. Taehan Kanho Hakhoe Chi. Apr; 35(2):303-12.*

Lin, P.W., Chan, W.C., Ng, B.F., & Lam, L.C., (2007). *Efficacy of aromatherapy (Lavandula angustifolia) as an intervention for agitated behaviours in Chinese older persons with dementia: a crossover randomized trial. Int J Geriatr Psychiatry. May; 22(5):405-10.*

Miquel, J., (2002). *Can Antioxidant Diet Supplementation Protect Against Age-Related Mitochondrial Damage? Ann N Y Acad Sci. Apr; 959:508-16.*

Muhlbauer, R.C., Lozano, A., Palacio, S., Reinli, A., & Felix, R., (2003). *Common herbs, essential oils, and monoterpenes potently modulate bone metabolism. Bone. Apr;32(4):372-80.*

O'Keefe, J.H., Gheewala, NM., & O'Keefe, J, O., (2008). *Dietary strategies for improving post-prandial glucose, lipids, inflammation, and cardiovascular health. J Am Coll Cardiol. Jan 22; 51(3):249-55.*

Roberson, L., (2003). *The Importance of Touch for the Patient with Dementia. Home Health Nurse. Jan; 21(1):16-9.*

Snow, L.A., Hovanec, L., & Brandt, J., (2004). *A controlled trial of aromatherapy for agitation in nursing home patients with dementia. J Altern Complement Med. Jun; 10(3):431-7.*

Soden, K., Vincent, K., Craske, S., Lucas, C., & Ashley, S., (2004). *A randomized controlled trial of aromatherapy massage in a hospice setting. Palliat Med. Mar; 18(2):87-92.*

Thurston, R.C., Sowers, M.R., Chang, Y., Sternfeld, B., Gold, E.B., Johnston, J.M., Matthews, K.A., (2008). *Adiposity and reporting of vasomotor symptoms among midlife women: the study of women's health across the nation. Am J Epidemiol. Jan 1; 167(1):78-85.*

Youdim, K., & Deans, S., (1999). *Beneficial Effects of Thyme Oil on Age Related Changes in the Phospholipid C20 and C22 Polyunsaturated Fatty Acid Composition of Various Rat Tissue. Biochim biophys Acta Apr 19; 1438(1):140-6.*

Youdim, K., & Deans, S., (1999). *Dietary Supplementation of Thyme Essential Oil During the Lifespan of the Rat: It's Effect on the Antioxidant Status in Liver, Kidney and Heart Tissues. Mech Ageing Dev Sept 8; 109(3):163-75.*

Notes

Notes

**VENABLE
CAMPILLO
LOGAN &
MEANEY, PC**

A. David Logan, Ph.D.
Registered Patent Attorney.

INTELLECTUAL PROPERTY ATTORNEYS

1938 East Osborne Road
Phoenix, AZ 85016
Phone: 602-631-9100
Fax: 602-631-4529
email: dlogan@vclmlaw.com
www.vclmlaw.com

100% PURE THERAPEUTIC GRADE ESSENTIAL OILS
Quality ~ Purity ~ Expertise

Essential oils, and the therapeutic quality of well being they facilitate, have always been a lifelong passion for Ralf Möller, founder of Aromaland Inc. in Santa Fe, N.M.

"As a European, essential oils were a regular part of my daily life, a regular component of our daily routine for promoting one's health, well being, relaxation and enjoyment," said Möller, a pioneer in the industry of aromatherapy and among the first entrepreneurs to bring high quality essential oils to the U.S.

Intrigued by the healing aspects of essential oils, Möller spent two years in India, working closely with Ayurvedic doctors as part of his initial education in the field. His experience in India inspired him to travel the world as he formed his company, building relationships with farmer/essential oil producers in more than 40 countries. The result became the foundation for Aromaland, one of the leading suppliers of essential oils in the U.S. today.

Aromaland offers only 100 percent pure therapeutic-grade essential oils, and the company's products include over 270 essential oils, essential oil blends and organic essential oils as well as aromatherapy related items. Möller demands the very best from his producers, and each shipment of essential oils is tested thoroughly for purity and quality. Aromaland remains one of the few essential oil companies utilizing in-house testing through a GC/MS (gas chromatograph/mass spectrometer), making the company an industry leader that offers among the best products in the market. "Although I have been sourcing and personally evaluating essential oils for over 30 years, the GC/MS is the only way to truly guarantee, 100 percent pure, therapeutic-grade essential oils," Möller emphasized.

Aromaland offers hundreds of aromatherapy products from around the world. For more information or to buy Aromaland products, visit www.aromaland.com.

- 270+ Essential oils
- GC / MS tested
- Essential oil body care

- Certified organic essential oils
- Wild-crafted essential oils
- Essential oil diffusers

The Essence of Wellbeing™ *...since 1986*

Aromaland Inc.
1326 Rufina Circle
Santa Fe, NM 87507
1-800-933-5267
505 / 438-0402
505 / 438-7223 fax
info@aromaland.com
www.aromaland.com

OTHER BOOKS FROM LIFESUCCESS PUBLISHING

FROM WAGS TO RICHES

For the secrets to attracting success in your life. Just listen to you dog

Kim Kapes
ISBN 978-1-59930-128-0

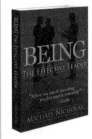

BEING THE EFFECTIVE LEADER

"Before you can do something You first must be something"

Michael Nicholas
ISBN 978-1-59930-093-1

ATTRACTING FREEDOM

Lifestyle, not life sentence

Isha Knill
ISBN 978-1-59930-129-7

THINK PROPERTY AND GROW RICH

Master buying Australian investment properties in changing times like the experts do

Melainie White
ISBN 978-1-59930-167-9

JOURNEY TO JOY

A womans guide to balancing it all

Leanne Hawkes-Sobeck
ISBN 978-1-59930-121-1

THE SCIENCE OF A PERFECT WEIGHT

A new way of thinking, eating and living to achieve your perfect weight

Bob Proctor and Melonie Dodaro
ISBN 978-1-59930172-3

WINGS OF CHANGE

Discover a new formation to success

Jim and Katharina Murdoch
ISBN 978-1-59930-194-5

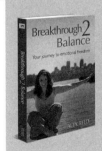

BREAKTHROUGH 2 BALANCE

Your journey to emotional freedom

Alex Reed
ISBN 978-1-59930-127-3-

OTHER BOOKS FROM LIFESUCCESS PUBLISHING

BABY BOOMERS EXPRESS

From long hair to silver hair. Where do we go from here?

Cynthia A. Speir & James A. Speir
ISBN 978-1-59930-103-7

BE DO HAVE

"Before you can do something you first must be something"

Michael Nicholas
ISBN 978-1-59930-213-3

WEALTH MAGNETZ

Your A to Z guide for abundant living

Regina Richardson
ISBN 978-1-59930-197-6

CHANGE YOUR BODY WITH THE WORLDS FITTEST COUPLE

The secret to a great body revealed

Matt Thom & Monica Wright
ISBN 978-1-59930-065-8

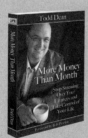

MORE MONEY THAN MONTH

Stop stressing over your finances and take control of your life

Todd Dean
ISBN 978-1-59930-256-0

THE EINSTEIN COMPLEX

Awaken your inner genius live your dreams

Dr. Roger A. Boger
ISBN 978-1-59930-269-0

THE EXIT STRATEGY

How to ensure your success after the military

Benjamin Smith
ISBN 978-1-59930-112-9

THE IMAGE DOCTOR

Introducing the incredibly simple orangecard The ultimate tool for love, health, career and financial success!

Dr. Tory M. Robson
ISBN 978-1-59930-261-4